ADVANCE PRAISE FOR *WORLD CLASS*

"In this timely and forward-looking book, one of the most knowledgeable educators in the world draws on impressive data, keen observations, and considerable wisdom to indicate the paths to effective education for all young people."
– Howard Gardner, Senior Director of Harvard Project Zero and author of *Frames of Mind: The Theory of Multiple Intelligences*

"...a sane and wise vision of how emerging technology can be married to deep human learning to prepare our young people optimally for the challenges they will face in 21st century."
– Sir Anthony Seldon, Vice-Chancellor of the University of Buckingham

"No one knows more about education around the world than Andreas Schleicher. Full stop. For the first time, he's collected 20 years worth of wisdom in one place. *World Class* should be required reading for policy makers, education leaders and anyone who wants to know how our schools can adapt for the modern world – and help all kids learn to think for themselves."
– Amanda Ripley, author of *The Smartest Kids in the World*, a *New York Times* bestseller

"I hope policy makers everywhere will read this book and take its lessons to heart."
– Peter Lampl, founder and Chairman of the Sutton Trust

"*World Class* is the most significant education publication of the decade...Essential reading for anyone seeking to improve educational outcomes for students."
– Sir Michael Barber, former head of the UK Prime Minister's Delivery Unit

"Every visionary leader who is serious about improving student learning should add the data-driven *World Class: How to Build a 21st-Century School System* to the top of his or her reading list."
– Jeb Bush, 43rd Governor of Florida, and founder and Chairman of the Foundation for Excellence in Education

"[Schleicher]...grasps all the key issues, and does so through keeping his ear to the ground and by working out solutions jointly with a variety of leaders at all levels of the system, and in diverse societies."
– Michael Fullan, Global Leadership Director, New Pedagogies for Deep Learning

"In these easy-to-read and concise pages, [Schleicher] shatters the myths that hold many countries back and articulates the path forward for not only building effective education systems but developing the coalitions and collective leadership necessary to make it happen."
– Wendy Kopp, CEO and co-founder, Teach For All

"At a time when many nations are choosing isolation over international engagement, [Schleicher's] book shows the necessity of learning from each other to transform learning for the world's students."
– Bob Wise, President of the Alliance for Excellent Education, and former Governor of West Virginia

"…a no-BS guide to education that is a must read for anyone who cares about our children's future."
− Joel Klein, former Chancellor, New York City Department of Education

"Every person interested in improving education − from government ministers, to teachers and parents − should read this book…"
− David Laws, Executive Chairman of the Education Policy Institute, and former England Schools Minister

"…a unique, global crow's nest view of education… [Schleicher] gives us the broadest perspective informed by science and passion, leaving us with good reason to be optimistic about the future of education."
− Dalton McGuinty, former Premier of Ontario, Canada

"I hope that this book will encourage all who are invested in learning and teaching, from across domains of territory and knowledge, to work and share together to make education relevant and meaningful to future generations facing a changed world."
− Heng Swee Keat, Minister for Finance and former Minister for Education, Singapore

"…a must-read for those who wish to create a future in which economic opportunity can be shared by all."
− Klaus Schwab, Founder and Executive Chairman of the World Economic Forum

"…The road from PISA data to action is a long road, but this book is the best possible guide to get where you want. Emotions infect, so be ready for passion and determination, paved with evidence."
− Olli-Pekka Heinonen, Director General, Finnish National Agency for Education, and former Finnish Minister of Education

"There is no hiding anymore from underachievement in education, as Schleicher convincingly argues, debunking the myths that are the armour of present complacency. A 'must-read' for everyone involved in education policy."
− Jo Ritzen, Professor, Maastricht University, and former Dutch Minister for Education and Science

"[Schleicher and his team have] shown us that innovation is possible, and that it does not depend on invested economic resources, but rather it begins by…[being] willing to discover the abilities of each student."
− Father Luis de Lezama, President of the Colegio Santa María la Blanca, Madrid, Spain

"An important contribution to global, national and local debates on the purpose, shape and design of education systems from someone who has had unparalleled access to decision makers and data for the last two decades. One does not have to agree with every conclusion to find oneself pulled into Schleicher's thoughtful and accessible analysis of complex phenomena and trade-offs."
− David H. Edwards, General Secretary of Education International

"A successful education system lies at the heart of a prosperous and contented society, so Andreas's ideas are crucial to understand."
− Lord Jim O'Neill, Chair Designate of Chatham House and Trustee of SHINE Educational Trust

ANDREAS SCHLEICHER

WORLD CLASS

How to build a 21st-century school system

Please cite this publication as:
Schleicher, A (2018), *World Class: How to build a 21st-century school system*, Strong Performers and Successful Reformers in Education, OECD Publishing, Paris.
http://dx.doi.org/10.1787/4789264300002-en

ISBN (print) 978-92-64-299979
ISBN (PDF) 978-92-64-300002

Series: Strong Performers and Successful Reformers in Education
ISSN (print): 2220-3621
ISSN (on line): 2220-363X

Photo credits:
© iStock/fstop123 (front cover)
© Russell Sach (back cover)
© OECD (inside back flap)

Graphic design © Cho You/Anaïs Diverrez

Corrigenda to OECD publications may be found on line at: www.oecd.org/publishing/corrigenda.
© OECD 2018

To the teachers of the world, who dedicate their lives – often in difficult conditions, and rarely with the appreciation they deserve – to helping the next generation realise their dreams and shape our future.

ACKNOWLEDGEMENTS

For over 20 years at the OECD I have been privileged to accompany education leaders with the design and implementation of education policies and practices. Much of this book builds on the sincerity and openness with which ministers of education, administrators, school leaders, teachers and researchers – far too many to be able to thank individually here – have shared their successes and failures with me, as colleagues, experts and friends. I also feel greatly indebted to my team at the OECD, who have built the tools and methods to compare and analyse education systems internationally, and from whom I continue to learn each day. My particular thanks go to Sean Coughlan, who encouraged me to write this book and who helped me organise my thoughts and prepare the manuscript. Sean also wrote the section that describes high-performing education systems. I am also grateful to Marilyn Achiron, who edited the book and provided advice throughout its preparation. Rose Bolognini, Catherine Candea, Cassandra Davis, Anne-Lise Prigent and Rebecca Tessier gave invaluable support to the production of the book. Last but not least, I thank my wife, Maria Teresa Siniscalco, who accompanied the development of this book through every stage.

TABLE OF CONTENTS

1. Education, through the eyes of a scientist

In 2015, almost one in two students – representing around 12 million 15-year-olds – was not able to complete even basic reading, mathematics or science tasks[1] in the global test known as PISA (the Programme for International Student Assessment) – and these were students living in 70 high- and middle-income countries that participated in the test. Over the past decade, there has been virtually no improvement in the learning outcomes of students in the Western world, even though expenditure on schooling rose by almost 20% during this period. In many countries, the quality of the education a student acquires can best be predicted by the student's or his or her school's postal code.

You might be tempted to drop this book, and any further thought about improving education, right about now. Impossible, you're already thinking, to change anything as big, complex and entrenched in vested interests as education.

But I want to urge you to keep reading. Why? Consider that the learning outcomes among the 10% most disadvantaged Vietnamese and Estonian students now compare favourably with those among the 10% wealthiest families in most of Latin America, and are on a par with those of the average student in Europe and the United States (*FIGURE 1.1*). Consider that in most countries we can find excellence in education in some of the most disadvantaged schools. And consider that many of today's leading education systems have only recently attained these top positions. So it can be done.

And it must be done. Without the right education, people will languish on the margins of society, countries will not be able to benefit from technological advances,

FIGURE 1.1: POVERTY NEED NOT BE DESTINY

Student performance on the PISA 2015 science test, by international decile
on the PISA index of economic, social and cultural status

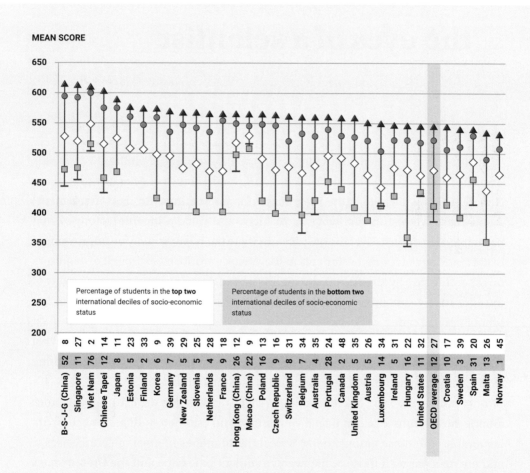

Notes: International deciles refer to the distribution of the PISA index of economic, social and cultural
status across all countries and economies. Only countries and economies with available data are shown.
B-S-J-G (China) refers to Beijing-Shanghai-Jiangsu-Guangdong (China). CABA (Argentina) refers to Ciudad
Autónoma de Buenos Aires (Argentina). FYROM refers to the Former Yugoslav Republic of Macedonia.

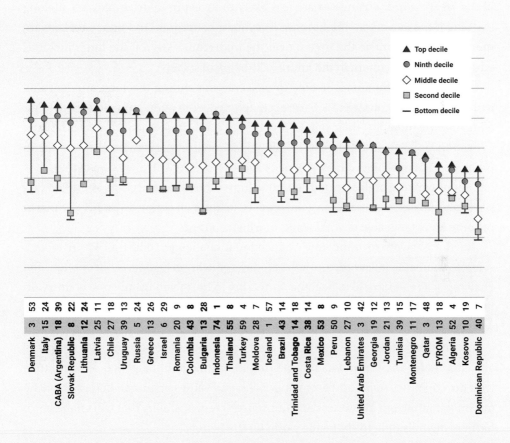

Countries and economies are ranked in descending order of the mean science performance of students in the highest decile of the PISA index of economic, social and cultural status.

Source: OECD, PISA 2015 Database, Table I.6.4a.

StatLink 📊 *http://dx.doi.org/10.1787/888933432757*

and those advances will not translate into social progress. We simply cannot develop fair and inclusive policies and engage all citizens if a lack of education prevents people from fully participating in society.

But change can be an uphill struggle. Young people are less likely to invest their time and energy in better education if that education seems irrelevant to the demands of the "real" world. Businesses are less likely to invest in their employees' lifelong learning if those workers might move away for a better job. And policy makers are more likely to prioritise the urgent over the important – even if the latter includes education, an investment in the future well-being of society.

I have been fortunate to be able to observe outstanding teaching and learning in more than 70 countries. I have accompanied education ministers and other education leaders in their efforts to design and implement forward-looking education policies and practices. While educational improvement is far easier to proclaim than to achieve, there are many successes from which we can learn. This is not about copying prefabricated solutions from other countries; it is about looking seriously and dispassionately at good practice in our own countries and elsewhere to become knowledgeable of what works in which contexts.

But the answers to tomorrow's educational challenges don't all lie in today's school systems, so following the path of today's education leaders is not enough. The challenges ahead have also become far too big to be solved by any one country on its own. This is leading educators, researchers and policy makers from around the world to join forces in the search for better answers.

In a nutshell, the kinds of things that are easy to teach have become easy to digitise and automate. The future is about pairing the artificial intelligence of computers with the cognitive, social and emotional skills, and values of human beings. It will be our imagination, our awareness and our sense of responsibility that will enable us to harness digitalisation to shape the world for the better.

The algorithms behind social media are sorting us into groups of like-minded individuals. They create virtual bubbles that amplify our views and leave us insulated from divergent perspectives; they homogenise opinions while polarising our societies. Tomorrow's schools will need to help students think for themselves and join others, with empathy, in work and citizenship. They will need to help students develop a strong sense of right and wrong, a sensitivity to the claims that others make on us, and a grasp of the limits on individual and collective action. At work, at home and in the community, people will need a deep understanding of how others live, in different cultures and traditions, and how others think, whether as scientists or artists. Whatever tasks machines may be taking over from humans at work, the demands on our knowledge and skills to contribute meaningfully to social and civic life will keep rising.

For those with the right knowledge and skills, digitalisation and globalisation have been liberating and exciting; but for those who are insufficiently prepared, they can mean vulnerable and insecure work, and a life without prospects. Our economies are shifting towards regional hubs of production, linked together by global chains of information and goods, but concentrated where comparative advantage can be built and renewed. This makes the distribution of knowledge and wealth crucial, and that is intimately tied to the distribution of education opportunities.

But while digital technologies can have disruptive implications for our economic and social structure, they don't have predetermined implications. We have agency, and it is the nature of our collective and systemic responses to these disruptions that will determine how we are affected by them.

To transform schooling at scale, we need not just a radical, alternative vision of what's possible, but also smart strategies and effective institutions. Our current schools were invented in the industrial age, when the prevailing norms were standardisation and compliance, and when it was both effective and efficient to educate students in batches and to train teachers once for their entire working lives. The curricula that spelled out what students should learn were designed at the top of the pyramid, then translated into instructional material, teacher education and learning environments, often through multiple layers of government, until they reached and were implemented by individual teachers in the classroom.

This structure, inherited from the industrial model of work, makes change in a fast-moving world far too slow. The changes in our societies have vastly outpaced the structural capacity of our current education systems to respond. Even the best education minister can no longer do justice to the needs of millions of students, hundreds of thousands of teachers and tens of thousands of schools. The challenge is to build on the expertise of our teachers and school leaders and enlist them in the design of superior policies and practices. This is not accomplished just by letting a thousand flowers bloom; it requires a carefully crafted enabling environment that can unleash teachers' and schools' ingenuity and build capacity for change. It requires leaders who tackle institutional structures that too often are built around the interests and habits of educators and administrators rather than learners, leaders who are sincere about social change, imaginative in policy making, and capable of using the trust they earn to deliver effective reforms.

Not less of an art, but more of a science

I entered the world of education with a different perspective from most. I had studied physics and worked for some years in the medical industry. Physicists communicate and collaborate across national and cultural boundaries around accepted principles and an established professional practice. By contrast, educators try to look at every child individually, and often with a fair bit of scepticism towards comparisons that necessarily involve generalisations.

But the biggest difference I discovered between the medical industry and education was the way in which the professions owned their professional practice. People entering the medical profession expect their practice to be transformed by research. Medical doctors would not think of themselves as professionals if they did not carefully study the most effective procedures so far developed to deal with the presenting symptoms, nor would they think of developing their own drugs.

In the medical field, the first thing we do is take the patient's temperature and diagnose what treatment will be most effective. In education, we tend to teach all students in the same way, give them the same treatment, and at times, diagnose at the end of the school year the extent to which that treatment was effective.

At Philips Medical Systems, where I had my first job, my superiors were adamant that I devote sufficient attention to testing and validating every development and piece of equipment, knowing full well that our customers might sue us for any fault they may find with our work. Meanwhile, education policy makers at the time were putting one layer of education reform on top of the previous one, with little experimentation or quality assurance, and little public accountability.

Yet I found the world of education fascinating and understood the power of education to transform lives and societies. I also saw an opportunity to make education reform not necessarily less of an art, but more of a science.

I owe this insight to three distinguished scholars, Torsten Husen, John Keeves and, most important, Neville Postlethwaite, with whom I worked at the University of Hamburg. Neville was not only a distinguished education scholar, he also had an extraordinary capacity to initiate and conduct large-scale research projects, bringing together leading researchers from around the world to advance the field of education.

I met Neville in 1986, when I strayed, out of curiosity, into his seminar on comparative education. From the very first day, I was inspired by the ways in which he would readily share his knowledge, experience and contacts, and how he would not leave a question unanswered, as long as you had sufficiently thought about it in advance.

After a few weeks Neville asked me what I had published so far. I had to admit that I had really nothing to offer. "So", he said, "let's get started on your first paper." He taught me the methodologies of cluster analysis; he provided the data to analyse; he reviewed, corrected and discussed every page; and he convinced a publisher to publish the result. Then he put my name on the final product. Those in academia know that this process usually works the other way around.

Over the following years, as we worked together in Hamburg and in many other places, Neville became like a second father to me. He was someone who derived satisfaction from helping others grow. Even after I left the University of Hamburg to join the Organisation for Economic Co-operation and Development (OECD) in Paris, Neville would read and comment on every paper and article I sent him.

The origins of PISA

It was the idea to apply the rigours of scientific research to education policy that nudged the OECD to create PISA in the late 1990s. I remember my first meeting of senior education officials at the OECD in 1995. There were representatives from 28 countries seated around a table in Paris. Some of them were boasting that they had the world's best school system – perhaps because it was the one they knew best. When I proposed a global test that would allow countries to compare the achievements of their school systems with those of other countries, most said this couldn't be done, shouldn't be done, or wasn't the business of international organisations.

I had 30 seconds to decide whether to cut our losses or give it one more try. In the end, I handed my boss, Thomas J. Alexander, then director of the OECD Education, Employment, Labour and Social Affairs Directorate, a yellow post-it note saying: "Acknowledge that we haven't yet achieved complete consensus on this project, but ask countries if we can try a pilot." The idea of PISA was born – and Tom became its most enthusiastic promoter.

Of course, the OECD had already published numerous comparisons on education outcomes by that time, but they were mainly based on measures of years of schooling, which isn't always a good indicator of what people are actually able to do with the education they have acquired.

Our aim with PISA was not to create another layer of top-down accountability, but to help schools and policy makers shift from looking upward within the bureaucracy towards looking outward to the next teacher, the next school, the next country.

In essence, PISA counts what counts. It collects high-quality data and combines that with information on wider social outcomes; and it makes that information available to educators and policy makers so they can make more informed decisions.

The transformational idea behind PISA lay in testing the skills of students directly, through a metric that was internationally agreed upon; to link that with data from students, teachers, schools and systems to understand performance differences; and then to harness the power of collaboration to act on the data, both by creating shared points of reference and by leveraging peer pressure. Today, PISA is not only a comparison of countries through representative sample-based tests, but thousands of individual schools have voluntarily joined the separate school-based version of PISA to see where they stand globally.

We tried to make PISA different from traditional assessments in other ways too. In our view, education is about promoting passion for learning, stimulating the imagination, and developing independent decision makers who can shape the future. So we did not mainly want to reward students for reproducing material they learned in class. To do well in PISA, students had to be able to extrapolate from what they know, think across the boundaries of subject matter disciplines, and apply their knowledge creatively in novel situations. If all we do is teach our children what we know, they might remember enough to follow in our footsteps; but if we teach them how to learn, they can go anywhere they want.

Some people argued that our tests were unfair, because we confronted students with problems they had not encountered in school. But then life is unfair, because the real test in life is not whether we can remember what we learned at school yesterday, but whether we will be able to solve problems that we can't possibly anticipate today. The modern world no longer rewards us just for what we know, but for what we can do with what we know.

Of course, the downside of a pilot was that we had very little money. In fact, in the first two years, there was no budget allocation for work on PISA. But that turned out to be probably our greatest strength. The way you would normally mount an assessment is that you plan something and then you hire the engineers to build it. That's how you create a test that costs millions of dollars and that is owned by an organisation – but not by the people you need to change education.

We turned that on its head. Soon the idea of PISA attracted the world's best thinkers and mobilised hundreds of educators and scientists from the participating countries to explore what we should expect from students and how we could test that. Today, we would call that crowdsourcing; but whatever you call it, it created the ownership that was critical for success.

There was another way in which building global comparisons from the bottom up turned out to be an advantage. When our first global league tables came out in 2001 and the French didn't see their schools come out well, many observers in that country concluded there must have been something wrong with the test. But Raymond Adams, the principal architect of the methodologies of PISA and co-ordinator of the PISA Project Consortium at the Australian Council for Educational Research, had an answer to this. He used the PISA test questions that had been prepared or rated highly by the French for their cultural and curricular relevance in France and compared the world through the lens of what the French viewed as most important in education.[2] (We also realised we could do this for every country.) When those results came out in remarkably similar ways, the dispute about cross-cultural relevance and the reliability of the testing process died down quickly.

Over the years, PISA established itself as an influential force for education reform. The triennial assessment has helped policy makers lower the cost of political action by backing difficult decisions with evidence. But it has also raised the political cost of inaction by exposing areas where policy and practice were unsatisfactory. Two years after that first meeting around a table in Paris, 28 countries signed on to participate. Today, PISA brings together more than 90 countries, representing 80% of the world economy, in a global conversation about education.

"PISA shock" and the end of complacency

The first results from PISA were published on 4 December 2001 and they immediately sparked heated debate. The education landscape revealed by the test results was very different from what many had thought they knew.

What made the impact even greater was that this was one of the times when an international organisation released the complete information, without whitewashing the results. We had designed a system through which countries would know their own performance scores before agreeing that we would publish those results, but they would not know how their results compared with those of other countries. It meant that when countries decided whether to be included or to withdraw from the publication of results, they did not know how they had performed compared with other education systems.

We also used a process of anonymising the data so that we and our researchers would evaluate and analyse the results without being influenced by how our own or other countries were performing.

But that was just the beginning. With each successive PISA assessment, the results attracted more attention and triggered more discussion. The controversy reached a climax with the release of the results from the 2006 assessment in December 2007, when we examined not just where countries stood at that moment in time, but, with the availability of three data points, how things had changed since the PISA test was first conducted in 2000.

It is easy to explain why one country might not perform as well as another; it is much harder for policy makers to acknowledge that things have not improved, or that improvement has been slower than elsewhere. Inevitably, political pressures ensued. When I briefed our Secretary-General, Angel Gurría, shortly after his arrival at the OECD in 2006, he immediately saw the potential for PISA to transform education policy and he was prepared to fight for its success.

One of the most important insights from PISA was that education systems could be changed and made to improve. It showed there was nothing inevitable or fixed about how schools performed. The results also showed that there is no automatic link between social disadvantage and poor performance in school.

These results challenged anyone who remained complacent. If some countries could implement policies to raise achievement and could close the social divide in school results, then why shouldn't other countries be able to do the same?

In addition, some countries showed that success can become a consistent and predictable education outcome. These were education systems where schools were reliably good. In Finland, for example, the country with the strongest overall results in the first PISA assessment, parents could rely on consistently high performance standards in whatever school they chose to enrol their child.

The impact of PISA was naturally greatest when the results revealed that a country performed comparatively poorly, whether in absolute terms or in relation to a country's expectations. In some countries, PISA raised public awareness to the extent that it created a strong momentum for change. The biggest outcry was heard when test results contradicted the public's perception of the education system. If the public and politicians thought that their schools were among the best in the world, it came as a real jolt when PISA comparisons showed a very different picture.

In my home country, Germany, the education policy debate that followed publication of the PISA 2000 results was intense. Confronted with lower-than-expected results in student performance, policy makers suffered what came to be known as "PISA shock". That shock triggered a sustained public debate about education policy and reform that dominated the news in the country's newspapers and on television for months.

Germans took for granted that learning opportunities were equal across schools, as significant efforts had been devoted to ensuring that schools were adequately and equally resourced. But the PISA 2000 results revealed large disparities in education outcomes, depending on whether the schools were socio-economically advantaged or not. Also, the evidence of consistency across schools in Finland, where performance differences between schools accounted for only 5% of the variation in student performance, left a deep impression in Germany, where performance differences between schools accounted for close to 50% of the variation in student performance. In other words, in Germany, it very much mattered in which particular school you enrolled your child.

Traditionally, the German school system separates children into different tracks at the age of 10, with some expected to pursue an academic path leading to careers as knowledge workers, while the others are routed to vocational pathways and expected to end up in jobs working for the knowledge workers. PISA showed that this selection process largely reinforced the existing social class structure. In other words, the PISA analyses suggested that German students from more privileged socio-economic backgrounds were systematically directed into the more prestigious academic schools, which yield superior education outcomes, while students from less privileged backgrounds were directed into less prestigious vocational schools, which yielded poorer education outcomes.

For many educators and experts in Germany, the disparities that PISA revealed were not entirely surprising. But it was often taken for granted – and deemed beyond the scope of public policy to change – that disadvantaged children do badly in school. What was shocking about the PISA results was that they showed that the impact of socio-economic status on students and school performance varied considerably across countries, and that other countries appeared to reduce that impact much more effectively than Germany did. In effect, PISA showed that improvement was possible, and provided the necessary spur for change.

PISA helped establish a new attitude towards evidence and data in Germany. Remarkably, in a country where the federal government usually has little to say about school education, it was Federal Minister of Education and Research, Edelgard Bulmahn, who showed exceptional leadership in laying out a long-term vision that could transform education in Germany.

Germany virtually doubled federal spending on education in the early 2000s. But beyond money, the debate inspired a wide range of reform efforts in the country, some of which have been transformative. Early childhood care was given a stronger educational dimension, national education standards were established for schools (something that had been hard to imagine in a country where the autonomy of the *Länder* [states] had always been sacrosanct), and greater support was given to disadvantaged students, including students with an immigrant background. Nine years later, in 2009, Germany's PISA results looked much better, showing significant improvements both in quality and equity.

Germany was not the only country that improved its education system in a relatively short time. South Korea's average performance was already high in 2000, yet the Koreans were concerned that only a narrow elite had achieved levels of excellence in the PISA reading assessment. Within less than a decade, South Korea was able to double the share of top-performing students.

A major overhaul of Poland's school system helped reduce the variations in performance between schools, turn around the lowest-performing schools, and raise overall performance by the equivalent of more than half a school year. Portugal was able to consolidate its fragmented school system and improve overall performance, as did Colombia and Peru. Even those who claim that the relative standing of countries in PISA mainly reflects social and cultural factors now had to concede that improvement in education is, indeed, possible.

Estonia and Finland became popular destinations for educators and policy makers in Europe. In these two countries students enter school after the age of six and attend class for fewer hours per year than students in most other countries. But by the time they are 15, students from across the socio-economic spectrum in these countries are among the highest performers in the world. And with virtually no variation in performance among schools, these countries also manage to cultivate both excellence and equity throughout their school systems.

In the early rounds of PISA, most of the high-performing and rapidly improving education systems were found in East Asia. These results challenged conventional wisdom in the West, which had often attributed success in those Asian countries to high pressure on students or to rote learning, sometimes because observers wrongly describe as drill and practice what is instead the consolidation of learning.[3]

To succeed in PISA, rote learning is not enough. When PISA introduced its first assessment of creative problem-solving skills in 2012, many observers predicted these would reverse the league tables, or at least show East Asia scoring at much lower levels of performance. But it was Singapore that came out on top – the country that had transformed itself from a developing country to a modern industrial economy in one generation.

When I presented these results in Singapore in March 2014, Heng Swee Keat, Education Minister at that time, underlined how much importance Singapore attached to nurturing creative and critical thinking, social and emotional skills, and character qualities. While our image of Singapore may still be shaped by limited civil society engagement and political participation, education in Singapore has gone through a silent revolution almost entirely unnoticed in the West. The country is now leading the way in the quality of its educational institutions and in the participation of its educators in designing and implementing innovative education policies.

Japan has been one of the strongest performers in PISA, but the results revealed that while students tended to do very well on tasks that require reproducing subject content, they did much less well on open-ended tasks requiring them to apply their knowledge in novel settings. Conveying that to parents and a general public who are used to multiple-choice university entrance exams was a challenge. The policy response in Japan was to incorporate "PISA-type" open-constructed tasks into the national assessment. That modification seems to have been reflected in a change in instructional practice. Between 2006 and 2009, Japan saw the most rapid improvement on open-ended tasks among OECD countries. I found this improvement most significant because it shows how a change in public policy in response to a weakness can lead to a change in what happens in the classroom.

In the West, we still often underestimate the drive East Asia has to change lives through education. When I spoke at the Asia-Pacific Economic Cooperation Leaders' Meeting in Vladivostok, Russia, in September 2012, I saw how this wasn't just of interest to educators, but how much attention this agenda was getting at the highest levels of government.

In the United States, the first PISA assessments received comparatively little attention. That changed with the release of results from the 2006 assessment. Former Governor of West Virginia, and President of the Alliance for Excellent Education, Bob Wise, had gathered together the National Governors Association, the Council of Chief State School Officers, the Business Roundtable and the Asia Society on 4 December 2007 at the National Press Club to hear the results.

A couple of months later, in February 2008, I spoke about PISA at the National Governors Association's Winter Meeting and saw great interest in international comparisons among state leaders. That same month I sat with the late Senator Edward Kennedy in his Washington office and showed him how Poland had been able to halve the share of poorly performing students within six years. His eyes lit up. My appointment with him, which had been scheduled for 20 minutes, lasted for almost three hours. In May of that year, then US Senate Majority Leader Harry Reid and Senator Kennedy scheduled a special lunch where I discussed the PISA results with some 20 senators.

Interest in PISA was gathering momentum. At a retreat with the US House Committee on Education and the Workforce in August 2009, which I attended as an external expert, there were lively discussions on policy lessons the United States could learn from the world's education leaders. One month later, I accompanied state education leaders to Finland, on a retreat hosted by the Council of Chief State School Officers.[4] No longer were we engaging in abstract discussion; American leaders were travelling to engage with their peers in the highest-performing education systems in the world.

But it was only after the following round of PISA, in 2009, that the federal government paid real attention to the results, with Arne Duncan, US Education Secretary from 2009 through 2015, in the lead. His "Race to the Top" initiative[5] was not merely about stimulating competition among US states, but about inducing states to look outwards to the best-performing education systems internationally. I served on the advisory committee of this initiative for the state of Massachusetts, generally viewed as the education posterchild in the United States. The discussions in this committee were squarely focused on how Massachusetts could close the still-significant gap between its results and those of the highest-performing education systems in the world.

Serving on the validation committee for the Common Core education standards,[6] which sought to design a framework for what students should know at each grade, I saw the impact that comparisons with high-performing education systems around the world were having on the goals for what American students should be learning in the 21st century.

Not surprisingly, PISA's impact around the world has grown thanks to extensive media coverage. (Germany even created a television programme around PISA[7] that became remarkably popular.) This has transformed a specialised debate about education into a public debate about the link between education, society and the economy.

Some governments have used PISA findings as a starting point for a peer review to study policies and practices in comparison with those in other countries that have similar challenges but are getting better results. Such peer reviews, each resulting in a set of specific policy recommendations for improvement, have become the hallmark of our work at the OECD.

PISA has stimulated peer learning not just among policy makers and researchers but also, and perhaps most important, among practitioners, including teachers' organisations and teachers' unions.

Last but not least, PISA has prompted the public to demand better education services. Parents' organisations in many countries have played an active role. In addition to contributing to parliamentary hearings in Germany, Italy, Japan, Mexico, Norway, Sweden, the United Kingdom, the United States and in the European Parliament, I have also had meetings with many organisations and industry leaders, who were not simply seeing education as a factory for the production of future workers for their companies, but who recognised the fundamental role that education plays in shaping the societies in which we live and work.

Raising the cost of political inaction

In 1997, when we embarked on PISA, I received a call from the office of Brazil's president: Brazil was interested in joining PISA. Brazil was the first country that was not a member of the OECD that expressed an interest in joining PISA and, in a way, I was surprised. Then-President Fernando Henrique Cardoso must have been aware that his country would come out at the bottom of the global league tables. But when I discussed that with him later, he told me that the biggest obstacle for improving Brazil's education system at that time was not a lack of resources or capacity, but the fact that students were getting good marks despite low standards. Nobody thought that improvement was needed or possible. President Cardoso felt it was important for people to understand the truth. So Brazil did not just publish a national PISA score, but provided every secondary school with information on the level of progress that would be needed to score at the OECD average level on PISA by 2021.

Since then, Brazil's improvement in PISA has been remarkable. Nine years after it participated in PISA for the first time, Brazil stood out as the country with the largest improvement in reading since the first PISA assessment was conducted in 2000.

Mexico had a similar experience. In the 2007 Mexican survey of parents, 77% of parents reported that the quality of education services provided by their children's school was good or very good even though, as measured by the PISA 2006 assessment, roughly half of Mexico's 15-year-olds were enrolled in schools that scored at or below the lowest level of proficiency established by PISA. There could be many reasons for such a discrepancy between the perceived quality of education and performance in international comparisons. For example, the schools Mexican children attend now might be of higher quality than those their parents had attended.

But the point here is that it isn't easy to justify an investment of public resources when there is no public demand for it. In February 2008, I met Mexico's then-President Felipe Calderón who was considering establishing a PISA-based international performance benchmark for secondary education in Mexico. This performance target would highlight the gap between national performance and international standards. Improvements to narrow this gap, which included incentives for teaching staff and better access to professional development, would be closely monitored.

Many countries followed suit with similar PISA-based performance targets. What this shows is that countries no longer measure the effectiveness of their education systems solely by comparing learning outcomes against past achievements. They now set their goals, and measure their progress towards those goals, against what is achieved in the world's highest-performing education systems.

What's at stake

Education and the well-being of individuals and nations

How a society develops and uses the knowledge and skills of its people is among the chief determinants of its prosperity. The evidence from the Survey of Adult Skills, a product of the OECD Programme for the International Assessment of Adult Competencies (PIAAC), which grew out of PISA, shows that individuals with poor skills are severely limited in their access to better-paying and more-rewarding jobs. Digitalisation is now amplifying this pattern; as new industries rise, others will fall. It is the education available to people that provides a buffer to weather these shocks. When I met Sweden's Prime Minister Stefan Löfven in May 2016, he put his finger on this point by remarking that the only thing that can help people accept that their job may disappear is the confidence that they have the knowledge and skills to find or create a new one.

If there are large sections of the adult population with poor skills, it becomes more difficult to improve productivity and make better use of technology – and that becomes a barrier to raising living standards. But this is about far more than earnings and employment. Our research from the Survey of Adult Skills shows that people with low skills are not just more vulnerable in a changing job market, they are also more likely to feel excluded and see themselves as powerless in political processes (*FIGURE 1.2*).

The Survey of Adult Skills also shows that hand-in-hand with poorer skills goes distrust of others and of institutions. While the roots of the relationship between education, identity and trust are complex, these links matter, because trust is the glue of modern societies. Without trust in people, public institutions and well-regulated markets, public support for innovative policies is difficult to mobilise, particularly when short-term sacrifices are involved and long-term benefits are not immediately evident.

Educators naturally prefer to argue for education on moral grounds, but the link between the quality of education and the performance of an economy is strong. It is not just a hypothesis; it is something that can be measured. Calculations by Eric Hanushek, economist and senior fellow at the Hoover Institution of Stanford University, suggest that OECD countries[8] could lose USD 260 trillion in economic output over the lifetime of the generation born this year because school systems in the industrialised world are not delivering what the best-performing education systems show can be achieved[9] (see Chapter 4 for more details). In other words, deficiencies in our education systems have an effect equivalent to a major economic recession, and this effect is permanent.

Preparing students for their future, not our past

Since Confucius and Socrates, educators have recognised the double purpose of education: to impart the meaning and significance of the past, and to prepare young people for the challenges of the future. When we could still assume that what we learn in school will last for a lifetime, teaching content knowledge and routine cognitive skills was rightly at the centre of education. Today, when we can access content via search engines, and when routine cognitive tasks are being digitised and outsourced, the focus must shift to enabling people to become lifelong learners.

Lifelong learning is about constantly learning, unlearning and relearning when the contexts change. It entails continuous processes of reflection, anticipation and action. Reflective practice is needed to take a critical stance when deciding, choosing and acting, by stepping back from what is known or assumed and by taking different perspectives. Anticipation mobilises cognitive skills, such as analytical or critical thinking, to foresee what may be needed in the future or how actions taken today might have consequences for the future. Both reflective practice and anticipation contribute to the willingness to take responsible actions, in the belief that it is within the power of all of us to shape and change the course of events. This is how agency is built. So modern schools need to help students constantly evolve and grow, and to find and adjust their right place in a changing world.[10]

Schools now need to prepare students for more rapid change than ever before, to learn for jobs that have not yet been created, to tackle societal challenges that we can't yet imagine, and to use technologies that have not yet been invented. And they need to prepare students for an interconnected world in which students understand and appreciate different perspectives and world views, interact successfully and respectfully with others, and take responsible action toward sustainability and collective well-being.

FIGURE 1.2: HIGHLY LITERATE ADULTS ARE MORE LIKELY TO HAVE POSITIVE SOCIAL AND ECONOMIC OUTCOMES

Increased likelihood (odds ratio) of adults scoring at Level 4/5 in literacy reporting high earnings, high levels of trust and political efficacy, good health, participating in volunteer activities and being employed, compared with adults scoring at or below Level 1 in literacy.

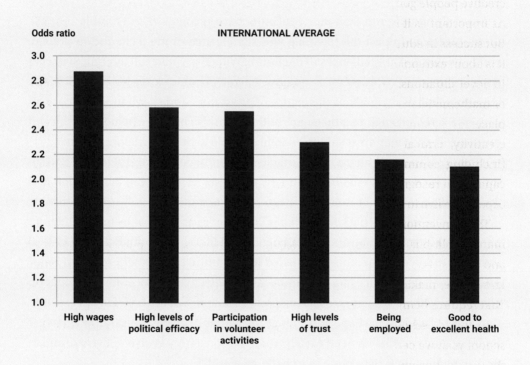

Notes: Odds ratios are adjusted for age, gender, educational attainment, and immigrant and language background. High wages are defined as workers' hourly earnings that are above the country's median.

Source: Survey of Adult Skills (PIAAC) (2012, 2015), Tables A5.13, A5.14.

StatLink 🔍📊 *http://dx.doi.org/10.1787/888932903633*

By strengthening cognitive, emotional and social resilience, education can help people, organisations and systems to persist, perhaps even flourish, amid unforeseeable disruptions. It can provide communities and institutions with the flexibility, intelligence and responsiveness they need to thrive in social and economic change.

Of course, state-of-the-art knowledge will always remain important. Innovative or creative people generally have specialised skills in a field of knowledge or a practice. As important as it is to learn how to learn, we always learn by learning something. But success in education is no longer mainly about reproducing content knowledge; it is about extrapolating from what we know and applying that knowledge creatively in novel situations. Epistemic knowledge – e.g. thinking like a scientist, philosopher or mathematician – is taking precedence over knowing specific formulae, names or places. So schooling today needs to be much more about ways of thinking (involving creativity, critical thinking, problem solving and judgement), ways of working (including communication and collaboration), tools for working (including the capacity to recognise and exploit the potential of new technologies) and about the capacity to live in a multi-faceted world as active and responsible citizens.[11]

The conventional approach in school is often to break problems down into manageable bits and pieces and then to teach students how to solve these bits and pieces. But modern societies create value by synthesising different fields of knowledge, making connections between ideas that previously seemed unrelated. That requires being familiar with and receptive to knowledge in other fields.

In today's schools, students typically learn individually and at the end of the school year, we certify their individual achievements. But the more interdependent the world becomes, the more we need great collaborators and orchestrators. Innovation is now rarely the product of individuals working in isolation, but rather an outcome of how we mobilise, share and integrate knowledge. The well-being of societies depends increasingly on people's capacity to take collective action. Schools therefore need to become better at helping students learn to develop an awareness of the pluralism of modern life. That means teaching and rewarding collaboration as well as individual academic achievement, enabling students both to think for themselves, and to act for and with others.

The reality is that students sit most of the time behind individual desks and there is limited time for collaborative learning. That was made plain – and surprisingly so – in the results from the first PISA assessment of collaborative problem-solving skills in 2015. On average across OECD countries, fewer than one in ten 15-year-old students could complete problem-solving tasks that required them to maintain awareness of group dynamics, take actions to overcome obstacles and resolve disagreements with others, even when the content of these tasks was relatively simple[12] (see Chapter 6 for more details).

More generally, changing skill demands have elevated the role of social and emotional skills. Such skills are involved in achieving goals, living and working with others, and managing emotions. They include character qualities such as perseverance, empathy or perspective taking, mindfulness, ethics, courage and leadership. In fact, developing those kinds of characteristics was what distinguished many of the elite schools that I have visited. But for the majority of students, character formation in school remains a matter of luck, depending on whether it is a priority for their teacher, since there are very few education systems that have made such broader goals an integral part of what they expect from students.

Social and emotional skills, in turn, intersect with diversity in important ways. They can help students live and work in a world in which most people need to appreciate a range of ideas, perspectives and values, and collaborate with people of different cultural origins, often bridging space and time through technology; and a world in which their lives will be affected by issues that transcend national boundaries. Effective communication and appropriate behaviour within diverse teams are also keys to success in many jobs, and will remain so as technology continues to make it easier for people to connect across the globe. Employers increasingly seek to attract learners who easily adapt, and are able to apply and transfer their skills and knowledge to new contexts. Work-readiness in an interconnected world requires young people to understand the complex dynamics of globalisation, and be open to people from different cultural backgrounds.

Engaging with different perspectives and world views requires individuals to examine the origins and implications of others' and their own assumptions. This, in turn, implies a profound respect for and interest in who the other is, their concept of reality and their perspectives. Recognising another's position or belief is not necessarily to accept that position or belief. However, the ability to see through multiple lenses provides opportunities to deepen and question one's own perspectives and to make more mature decisions. Where we are not successful with this, we are building our education systems on sand. The bottom line is that we can try to assert boundaries, but we cannot hold them against the reality of interdependence.

The challenge is that developing these cognitive, social and emotional capabilities requires a very different approach to learning and teaching and a different calibre of teachers. Where teaching is about imparting prefabricated knowledge, countries can afford low teacher quality. And when teacher quality is low, governments tend to tell their teachers exactly what to do and exactly how they want it done, using an industrial organisation of work to get the results they want. Today the challenge is to make teaching a profession of advanced knowledge workers who work with a high level of professional autonomy and within a collaborative culture. They work as competent professionals, ethical educators, collaborative learners, innovative designers, transformational leaders and community builders.

But such people will not work as exchangeable widgets in schools organised as Taylorist workplaces that rely mainly on administrative forms of accountability, and bureaucratic command-and-control systems to direct their work. To attract the people they need, modern school systems need to transform the type of work organisation in their schools to one in which professional norms of control replace bureaucratic and administrative forms of control. The past was about received wisdom; the future is about user-generated wisdom.

The past was also divided – with teachers and content divided by subjects and students separated by expectations of their future career prospects; with schools designed to keep students inside, and the rest of the world outside; with a lack of engagement with families and a reluctance to partner with other schools. The future needs to be integrated – with an emphasis on the inter-relation of subjects and the integration of students. It also needs to be connected, so that learning is closely related to real-world contexts and contemporary issues, and open to the rich resources in the community. Effective learning environments are constantly creating synergies and finding new ways to enhance professional, social and cultural capital with others. They do that with families and communities, with higher education, with businesses, and especially with other schools and learning environments. This is about creating innovative partnerships. Isolation in a world of complex learning systems will seriously limit potential.

Instruction in the past was subject-based; instruction in the future needs to be more project-based, building experiences that help students think across the boundaries of subject-matter disciplines. The past was hierarchical; the future is collaborative, recognising both teachers and students as resources and co-creators.

In the past, different students were taught in similar ways. Now school systems need to embrace diversity with differentiated approaches to learning. The goals of the past were standardisation and compliance, with students educated in age cohorts, following the same standard curriculum, all assessed at the same time. The future is about building instruction from students' passions and capacities, helping students personalise their learning and assessments in ways that foster engagement and talent. It's about encouraging students to be ingenious.

School systems need to better recognise that individuals learn differently, and in different ways at different stages of their lives. They need to create new ways of providing education that take learning to the learner and that are most conducive to students' progress. Learning is not a place, but an activity.

In the past, schools were technological islands, with technology often limited to supporting existing practices, and students outpacing schools in their adoption and consumption of technology. Now schools need to use the potential of technologies to liberate learning from past conventions and connect learners in new and powerful ways, with sources of knowledge, with innovative applications and with one another.

In the past, the policy focus was on providing education; now it needs to be on outcomes, shifting from looking upward in the bureaucracy towards looking outward to the next teacher, the next school and the next education system. In the past, administrations emphasised school management; now the focus needs to be on instructional leadership, with school leaders supporting, evaluating and developing high-quality teachers and designing innovative learning environments. The past was about quality control; the future is about quality assurance.

The challenge is that such system transformation cannot be mandated by government, which leads to surface compliance, nor can it be built solely from the ground up.

Governments cannot innovate in the classroom, but they can help build and communicate the case for change, and articulate a guiding vision for 21st-century learning. Government has a key role as platform and broker, as stimulator and enabler; it can focus resources, set a facilitative policy climate, and use accountability and reporting modifications to encourage new practice.

But education needs to better identify key agents of change, champion them, and find more effective approaches to scaling and disseminating innovations. That is also about finding better ways to recognise, reward and give exposure to success, to do whatever is possible to make it easier for innovators to take risks and encourage the emergence of new ideas. The past was about public versus private; the future is about public with private.

These challenges look daunting, but many education systems are now well on their way towards finding innovative responses to them, not just in isolated, local examples, but also systemically.

Looking outward for inspiration

There is a story about a driver who, on a dark night, finds out that he has lost his car key when getting back to his car. He keeps looking below a streetlight – and when someone asks him if that is where he dropped the key, he says no, but that is the only place he can see anything.

In education too, there is a deep-rooted instinct to look at what is closest to hand and easiest to see. It may not be the best place to look, but it is where there are familiar questions and answers. Often we review progress in education by what is easiest to measure rather than by what is most important. And debates on education are often based only on what's going on within a country's or a region's own schools, rather than on comparisons with what is achieved elsewhere.

While globalisation is having such a profound impact on economies, the workplace and everyday life, education remains very local and often inward-looking. Education systems have a habit of building "walls" that separate teachers, schools or the systems themselves from learning from each another. The way schools are organised and the way information is managed can make it difficult for schools and teachers to share knowledge about their work. While those who run education systems may have access to knowledge about their strengths and weaknesses, those who provide education services at the frontline – school principals and teachers – often do not, or they may not know how to translate that knowledge into more effective practices.

Similar walls separate the education systems of different countries, with few opportunities for countries to look outward to education policies developed and implemented beyond their borders. In other words, there is not much learning from other countries' experiences. This is particularly unfortunate since, in the field of education, there is an ethical component to experimenting with alternative policies and practices, since they will involve the lives and futures of real young people.

That is why international comparisons are so important. They can show what is possible in education, in terms of the quality, equity and efficiency of services achieved by the world's leaders in education. They can help policy makers set meaningful targets based on measurable goals, and they can foster better understanding of how different education systems address similar problems. Perhaps most important, an international perspective provides an opportunity for policy makers and practitioners to have a much clearer view of their own education systems, one that reveals more of the beliefs and structures, strengths and weaknesses that underlie their systems. An education system has to be profoundly understood before it can be changed and improved.

International comparisons also reveal the pace of change in educational development. Take the examples of the United States and South Korea. In the 1960s, the United States had the world's highest rate of young people successfully completing high school.[13] As well as being an economic and military superpower, the United States was an education superpower, benefiting from the "first-mover advantage" of providing universal access to schooling. This investment in universal schooling had helped build its economic success.

But in the 1970s and 1980s, other countries began to catch up. By the 1990s, instead of being in first place in high school graduation rates, the United States was ranked 13th. While the United States remains well ahead of most other nations in the proportion of 55-64 year-olds with both high school and university qualifications,[14] the proportion of graduates among younger age groups has slipped towards the average. The United States didn't go backwards, but it failed to move forward quickly enough, as more and more countries surpassed the United States' average level of education.

By contrast, in the 1960s, South Korea had a standard of living on a level with Afghanistan's today, and it was among the lowest performers in education. Now South Korea has the world's largest proportion of teenagers who successfully complete secondary school.[15] South Korea has transformed itself into a high-tech economy – built on a foundation of education. (One can argue that the high performance of South Korea and other East Asian education systems has come at a cost to students, who often report low levels of satisfaction with life. But according to results from the latest PISA assessment, some high-performing education systems, including Estonia, Finland, the Netherlands and Switzerland, are able to achieve good learning outcomes even as their students report high satisfaction with life – a lesson for East Asia.)

Of course, international assessments have their pitfalls. Designing reliable tests poses major challenges. The criteria for success have to be defined in ways that are both comparable across countries and meaningful at the national level. Tests must be carried out under the same conditions to yield comparable results. Beyond that, policy makers tend to use the results selectively, often in support of existing policies rather than as an instrument to explore alternatives.

Just before the results from the latest PISA assessment were published in December 2016, people from all over the world called me to find out what the major surprises in the global PISA league tables would be. But there are no surprises in international comparisons like PISA. Quality and equity in education are the result of deliberate, carefully designed and systematically implemented policies and practices. In the face of evidence from PISA of the rapid improvements that some school systems have made, even those who claim that education can only be improved on a geological timescale, or that the relative standing of countries mainly reflects social and cultural factors, must concede that it is possible to improve education systems. The most amazing lesson from PISA is that, despite their many differences, high-performing schools and education systems share certain features that transcend cultural, national and linguistic borders. That's why it is worthwhile studying education from a global perspective.

It is time that we ask ourselves: What can we learn from the world's most advanced school systems? How can their experiences help students, teachers and school leaders in other countries? How can politicians and policy makers draw upon lessons from countries facing similar challenges and make better-informed decisions? Even when there are international examples to follow, why has it often proved difficult to learn from them and stop repeating the same mistakes? Such questions have never been more urgent to ask – and answer.

2. Debunking some myths

International tests such as PISA hold up a mirror to show countries how they are performing compared with other school systems. They also reveal the many false assumptions that can stand in the way of improving education.

The poor will always do badly in school; deprivation is destiny

Even as teachers in classrooms around the world struggle to make up for the disadvantage into which some of their students were born, some believe that deprivation is destiny. But PISA results show that this is a false premise – and that there is nothing inevitable about how well or badly different social groups are likely to do in school, or in life.

There are two sides to this story. On the one hand, in all countries that participate in PISA, learning outcomes are associated with the social background of students and schools – a major challenge for teachers and schools.[1] But on the other hand, the strength of the relationship between social background and the quality of learning outcomes varies substantially across education systems – proof that poor results are not inevitable for disadvantaged students. In the 2012 PISA test, the 10% most disadvantaged 15-year-olds in Shanghai showed better mathematics results than the 10% most privileged students in the United States and many other countries.[2] Similarly, in the 2015 PISA assessment, the 10% most disadvantaged students in Estonia and Viet Nam performed as well as the average student in OECD countries (see *FIGURE 1.1*).

So if the poorest students in Estonia, Shanghai and Viet Nam can perform as well as the average student in Western countries, why shouldn't the poorest children in these other countries do as well as their counterparts in Estonia, Shanghai and Viet Nam?

Children from similar social backgrounds can show large differences in performance, depending on the school they go to or the country in which they live. Countries where disadvantaged students succeed are able to moderate social inequalities. Some of them are able to attract the most talented teachers to the most challenging classrooms and the most capable school leaders to the most disadvantaged schools, and provide their educators with whatever support they need to succeed. They apply high standards and challenge all students to meet them. They use methods of instruction that allow students from all backgrounds to learn in the ways that are most suitable and effective for them.

All countries have some excellent students, but few have enabled most students to excel. Achieving greater equity in education is not only a social-justice imperative, it is also a way to use resources more efficiently, and to ensure that all people can contribute to their societies. In the end, how we educate the most vulnerable children reflects who we are as a society.

Some American critics contend that the value of international comparisons of education is limited because the United States has a uniquely large share of disadvantaged students. But the United States has actually many socio-economic advantages over other countries. It is wealthier, and spends more money on education, than most countries; older Americans have higher levels of education than their counterparts in most other countries which, in turn, is a big advantage for their children; and the share of socio-economically disadvantaged students is just around the OECD average.

What past PISA comparisons have shown was that, in the United States, socio-economic disadvantage had a particularly strong impact on student performance. In other words, in the United States, the learning outcomes of two students from different socio-economic backgrounds varied much more than was typically observed in OECD countries.

A PISA primer

The heart of PISA is an internationally agreed set of tests in mathematics, reading, science and a number of innovative domains that is conducted every three years among representative samples of 15-year-old students in the participating countries. The age of 15 was chosen as the point of comparison because it represents the last point at which schooling is still largely universal.

PISA is closely aligned with the OECD Programme for the International Assessment of Adult Competencies (PIAAC), which measures literacy, numeracy, and information and communication technology (ICT) skills among 16-65 year-olds. While PISA looks backwards to establish how effectively school systems have established the foundations for success in life, PIAAC looks forward to how initial skills feed into further learning and important economic, employment and social outcomes.

PISA assesses both subject content knowledge and students' ability to apply that knowledge creatively, including in unfamiliar contexts.

The basic survey design has remained constant since it was first used, in 2000, to allow for comparability from one PISA assessment to the next. This enables countries to relate policy changes to improvements in education outcomes over time.

Considerable efforts are devoted to achieving cultural and linguistic breadth and balance in assessment materials. Stringent quality-assurance mechanisms are applied in the test design, translation, sampling and data collection.

PISA is a collaborative effort. Leading experts in participating countries decide on the scope and nature of the PISA assessments, and the background information collected. Governments oversee these decisions based on shared, policy-driven interests.

But this is where the story becomes interesting: PISA results from the United States also show how the vicious cycle of disparities in schooling outcomes, leading to more unequal life chances and reduced social mobility can be broken.

Between 2006 and 2015 the association between social background and student performance in the United States weakened more than in any other PISA-participating country. Think about it this way: in 2006, fewer than one in five of the most disadvantaged American 15-year-olds was able to achieve excellent performance in science; in 2015, nearly one in three was able to do so. So the share of students who could potentially realise the American dream of social mobility rose by 12 percentage points within a decade. Even if the achievement gap between advantaged and disadvantaged students in the United States persists, these data show how much improvement is possible – and how quickly it can be achieved (*FIGURE 2.1*).

Immigrants lower the overall performance of school systems

In recent years, many thousands of migrants and asylum-seekers – including an unprecedented number of children – have braved rough seas and barbed-wire barricades to find safety and a better life in Europe. Are our schools prepared to help immigrant students integrate into their new communities? And will they succeed in preparing all students for a world in which people are willing and able to collaborate with others from different cultural backgrounds? Many believe it is simply impossible to do so.

But consider the following: results from PISA show no relationship between the share of students with an immigrant background in a country and the overall performance of students in that country (*FIGURE 2.2*). Even students with the same migration history and background show very different performance levels across countries. The education immigrants had acquired before migrating matters, but where immigrant students settle seems to matter much more.

For example, children of Arab-speaking immigrants who had settled in the Netherlands scored 77 points – or the equivalent of two school years – higher in science than students from the same countries who had settled in Qatar, even after accounting for socio-economic differences between the students. They also scored 56 points higher than their peers who had settled in Denmark.

Students born in China who move elsewhere do better than their native peers in virtually every destination country; but here, too, the destination country matters. In Australia, first-generation Chinese immigrants scored 502 points, similarly to their Australian peers, but second-generation Chinese immigrants scored 592 score points, well over two school years ahead of their Australian peers. In other words, and to the extent that social background adequately captures cohort effects, these immigrant students were able to benefit more from the Australian school system than Australian students without an immigrant background, even after accounting for the students' socio-economic status.

Across OECD countries, the performance gap between immigrant students and students without an immigrant background narrowed between 2006 and 2015. This change was particularly striking in Belgium, Italy, Portugal, Spain and Switzerland.[3]

For instance, immigrant students in Portugal improved their science performance by 64 score points during the period – the equivalent of roughly two school years – while students without an immigrant background improved by 25 points. Immigrant students in Italy improved their scores in science by 31 points and immigrant students in Spain improved by 23 points, while in both countries the performance of students without an immigrant background remained stable. In none of the countries can demographic changes in the immigrant population account for these improvements. In both Italy and Spain, for example, the proportion of immigrant students with educated parents was about 30 percentage points lower in 2015 than in 2006.

These improvements show that there is considerable scope for policy and practice to help students with an immigrant background realise their potential.

FIGURE 2.1: DISADVANTAGED STUDENTS CAN BEAT THE ODDS AGAINST THEM AND BE AMONG THE WORLD'S TOP PERFORMERS

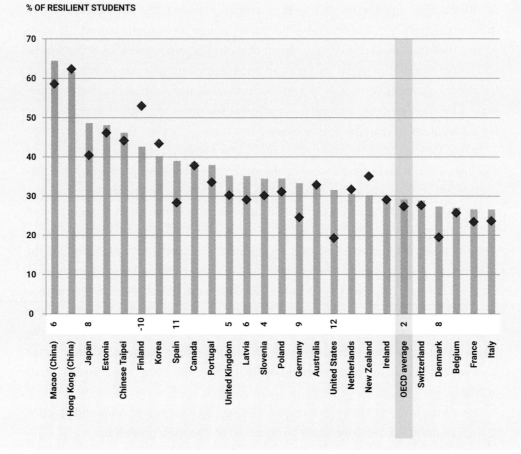

Notes: A student is considered resilient if he or she is in the bottom quarter of the PISA index of economic, social and cultural status but performs in the top quarter of students among all countries, after accounting for socio-economic status.

The percentage-point difference between 2006 and 2015 in the share of resilient students is shown next to the country/economy name. Only statistically significant differences are shown.

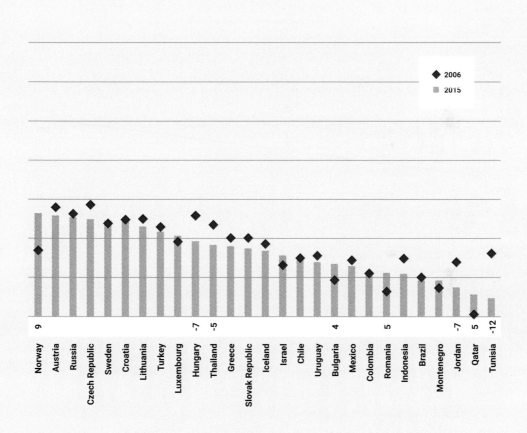

Countries and economies are ranked in descending order of the percentage of resilient students in 2015.

Source: OECD, PISA 2015 Database, Table I.6.7.

StatLink ᴹˢ⁼ *http://dx.doi.org/10.1787/888933432860*

FIGURE 2.2: THE POPULATION OF IMMIGRANT STUDENTS IS UNRELATED TO A COUNTRY'S AVERAGE PERFORMANCE

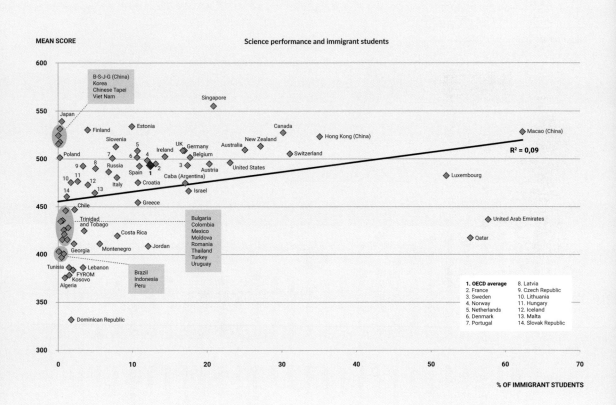

MEAN SCORE   Science performance and disadvantaged immigrant students

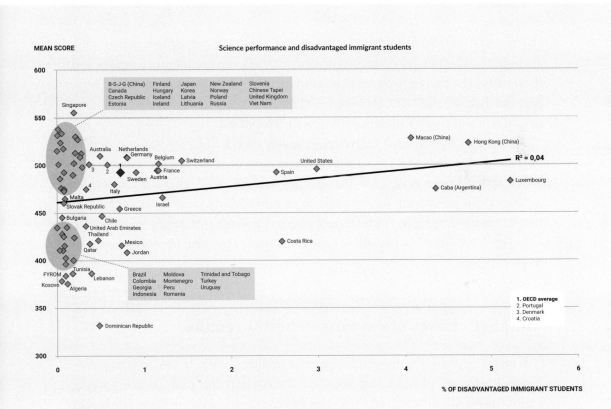

Notes: B-S-J-G (China) refers to Beijing-Shanghai-Jiangsu-Guangdong (China). CABA (Argentina) refers to Ciudad Autónoma de Buenos Aires (Argentina). FYROM refers to the Former Yugoslav Republic of Macedonia.

Source: OECD, PISA 2015 Database, Table I.7.3.

StatLink ⏱️ http://dx.doi.org/10.1787/888933432897

Success in education is all about spending more money

Countries need to invest in education if their citizens are to lead productive lives; but putting more money into education does not automatically result in better education.

For countries that currently invest less than USD 50 000 per student between the ages of 6 and 15, PISA shows a strong relationship between spending per student and the quality of learning outcomes. However, for countries that spend above that level, and that includes most OECD countries, there is no relationship between spending per student and average student performance (*FIGURE 2.3*).

Fifteen-year-old students in Hungary, which spends USD 47 000 per student between the ages of 6 and 15, perform at the same level as students in Luxembourg, which spends more than USD 187 000 per student, even after accounting for differences in purchasing power parities. In other words, despite spending four times as much as Hungary, Luxembourg does not gain any advantage.

In short, success is not just about how much money is spent, but about how that money is spent.

Smaller classes always mean better results

It might be politically popular to argue for smaller classes, but there is no cross-national evidence to show that reducing class size is the best avenue towards improving results. Instead, reducing class size can mean diverting funds that would have been better spent elsewhere – such as higher pay for better teachers.

In fact, the highest-performing education systems in PISA tend to prioritise the quality of teachers over the size of classes; whenever they have to choose between smaller classes and investing in their teachers, they go for the latter.

It may be that reducing class size opens up opportunities for new and more effective instructional practice, and that, all else being equal, smaller classes lead to better outcomes. But that is often the wrong way to look at it, because countries can spend their money only once. Reducing class size means that less money is available

FIGURE 2.3: AFTER A CERTAIN THRESHOLD, THERE IS NO RELATIONSHIP BETWEEN SPENDING PER STUDENT AND AVERAGE PERFORMANCE

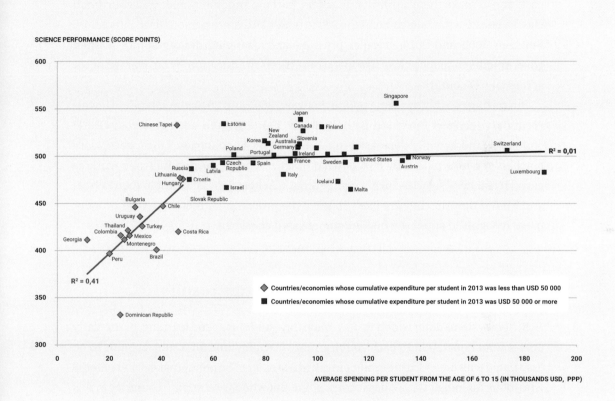

Notes: Only countries and economies with available data are shown. A significant relationship ($p < 0.10$) is shown by the black line. A non-significant relationship ($p > 0.10$) is shown by the grey line. Spending figures are adjusted for differences in purchasing power parities.

Source: OECD, PISA 2015 Database, Tables I.2.3 and II.6.58.

StatLink ᐦᑌ᎙᎑ http://dx.doi.org/10.1787/888933436215

to raise teachers' salaries, provide teachers with opportunities to do things other than teaching, or increase student learning time.

Despite the lack of evidence proving the benefits of smaller classes, many countries continue to make them a priority. Teachers, parents and policy makers favour small classes because they see them as the key to better and more personalised education. Between 2005 and 2014, popular pressure and changing demographics pushed governments to reduce class size in lower secondary education by an average of 6% across OECD countries.[4]

But during roughly the same period, between 2005 and 2015, the salaries of lower-secondary teachers increased by only 6% in real terms, on average across OECD countries, and actually decreased in a third of OECD countries. Lower-secondary teachers are now paid only 88% of what other tertiary-educated full-time workers earn.[5] If teachers' salaries are not competitive, teachers will not invest in themselves; and even if they do, they are likely to leave the profession if their expertise is better used, recognised and more highly compensated elsewhere.

More time spent learning yields better results

School systems differ widely in how much time students spend learning, particularly after school hours. Within each country, more learning time for a subject tends to be associated with better learning outcomes in that subject.[6] So policy makers and parents who lobby for longer school days have a point. But when we compare countries in this regard, the relationship is turned on its head: countries with longer classroom hours and learning time often do worse in PISA (*FIGURE 2.4A*). How can that be?

It's actually quite straightforward. Learning outcomes are always the product of the quantity and quality of learning opportunities. When keeping the quality of instruction constant, adding more time will yield better results. But when countries improve the quality of instruction, they tend to achieve better results without increasing student learning time.

For instance, in Japan and South Korea, students score similarly in science; however, in Japan, students spend about 41 hours per week learning (28 hours at

FIGURE 2.4A: COUNTRIES WITH LONGER LEARNING TIME ARE NOT NECESSARILY AMONG THE BEST PERFORMERS

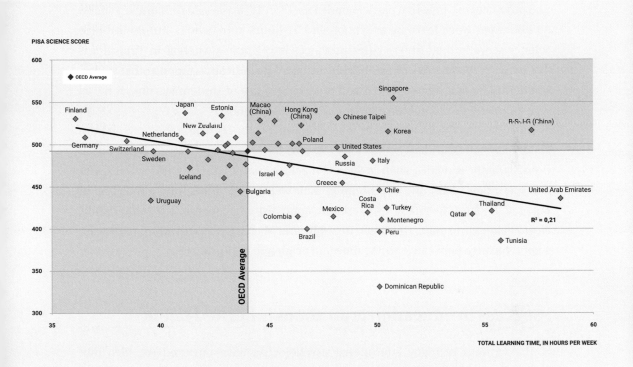

Notes: B-S-J-G (China) refers to Beijing-Shanghai-Jiangsu-Guangdong (China). Total learning time includes time spent in school, on homework, in additional instruction and on private study.

Source: OECD, PISA 2015 Database, Figures I.2.13 and II.6.23.

StatLink ᵐˢᴸ http://dx.doi.org/10.1787/888933436411

school and 14 hours after school), all subjects combined, whereas in South Korea they spend 50 hours per week (30 hours at school and 20 hours after school). In Tunisia and in Beijing, Shanghai, Jiangsu and Guangdong, the four municipalities and provinces of China that participated in the PISA 2015 assessment, students spend 30 hours per week learning at school, and 27 hours after school, but the average science score in the Chinese cities/provinces is 531 points whereas in Tunisia it is 367 points (*FIGURE 2.4B*). These differences might be indicative, among other things, of the quality of a school system and the effective use of student learning time, as well as whether students can learn informally after school.

Most parents would like to see their children in schools where they can acquire solid academic knowledge and skills but also have enough time to participate in non-academic activities, such as theatre, music or sports, which develop their social and emotional skills, and contribute to their well-being. It is always a question of balance. Finland, Germany, Switzerland, Japan, Estonia, Sweden, the Netherlands, New Zealand, Australia, the Czech Republic and Macao (China) all seem to provide a good balance between learning time and academic performance.

Success in education is all about inherited talent

The writings of many educational psychologists have nurtured the idea that student achievement is mainly a product of inherited intelligence, not hard work. PISA doesn't only test what 15-year-olds know, it also asks students what they believe is behind success or failure in such tests. In many countries, students were quick to blame everyone but themselves. In 2012, more than three in four students in France, an average performer on the PISA test, said that the course material was simply too hard; two in three said that the teacher did not pique students' interest in the material; and one in two said that their teacher did not explain the concepts well or that they, the students, were just unlucky.[7]

The results were very different for Singapore. Students there believed they would succeed if they tried hard; they trusted their teachers to help them succeed. The fact that students in some countries consistently believe that achievement is mainly a product of hard work rather than inherited intelligence suggests how school systems and the wider society can make a difference in students' attitudes towards school and achievement.

One of the most consequential findings from PISA is that, in most of the countries where students expect to have to work hard to achieve, virtually all students consistently meet high performance standards (see Chapter 3).

A comparison between school marks and students' performance in PISA also shows that, after accounting for students' reading proficiency, study habits and attitudes towards school and learning, socio-economically advantaged students tend to receive higher marks on their schoolwork from their teachers than their more disadvantaged peers do.[8] This practice could have far-reaching – and long-lasting – consequences for two reasons: students often base their expectations of further education and careers on the marks they receive in school; and school systems use marks to guide their selection of students for academically oriented programmes and, later, for entry into university.

In short, it is unlikely that school systems will achieve performance parity with the best-performing countries until they accept that, with enough effort and support, all children can learn and achieve at high levels.

Some countries do better in education because of their culture

Some argue that comparing the education systems of countries with widely different cultures is pointless because education policies and practices are based on different underlying norms and traditions. As such, they are applicable only in similar cultural contexts or, if they are adopted by countries with different cultural norms, they would produce different results.

Culture can, indeed, influence student achievement. Countries with cultures based on the Confucian tradition, for example, are known to value education and student achievement in school highly. Many observers believe that this cultural characteristic confers a large advantage on these countries.

FIGURE 2.4B: STUDENT PERFORMANCE DEPENDS ON BOTH THE QUANTITY AND QUALITY OF LEARNING TIME

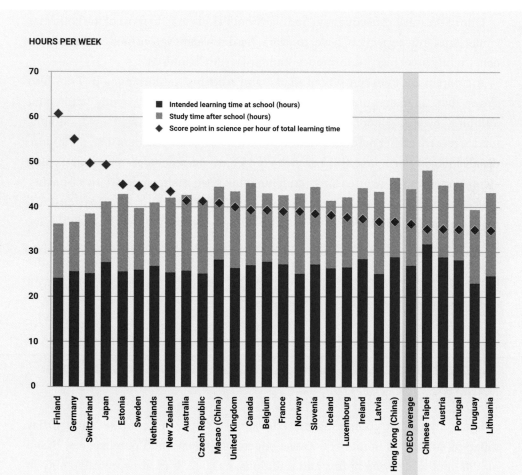

HOURS PER WEEK

- ■ Intended learning time at school (hours)
- ■ Study time after school (hours)
- ◆ Score point in science per hour of total learning time

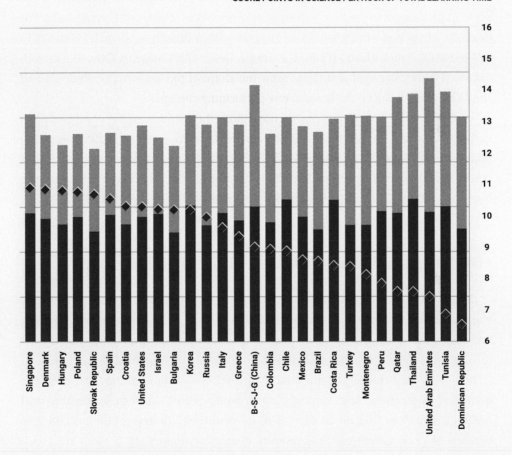

SCORE POINTS IN SCIENCE PER HOUR OF TOTAL LEARNING TIME

Notes: The diamonds show the mathematics score per hour of total learning time. Total learning time includes the hours of intended learning time in school for all subjects as well as hours spent learning in addition to the required school schedule, including homework, additional instruction and private study. B-S-J-G (China) refers to Beijing-Shanghai-Jiangsu-Guangdong (China).

Source: OECD, PISA 2015 Database, Figure II.6.23.

StatLink ⌐⌐⌐⌐ *http://dx.doi.org/10.1787/888933436411*

But not all countries that share that tradition perform at high levels in PISA. A Confucian heritage might be an asset, but it is no guarantee of success. Other top-performing countries in PISA, such as Canada and Finland, show that valuing education is not unique to Confucian cultures.

The strongest argument against culture as the determining factor in success is the rapid improvement in student performance observed in so many different places. For example, mean performance in science improved significantly between 2006 and 2015 in Colombia, Israel, Macao (China), Portugal, Qatar and Romania. Over this period, Macao (China), Portugal and Qatar grew the share of top-performing students and simultaneously reduced the share of low-performing students.

These countries and economies did not change their culture, or the composition of their populations, nor did they change their teachers; they changed their education policies and practices. Given these results, those who claim that the relative standing of countries in PISA mainly reflects social and cultural factors must concede that culture is not just inherited, it can also be created – through thoughtful policy and practice.

Only top graduates should become teachers

One of the claims I have heard most frequently from people trying to explain poor learning outcomes in their country is that their young people who go into teaching are not from among the country's best and brightest. High-performing countries, they say, are able to recruit their teachers from among the top third of graduates.

It sounds plausible, since the quality of a school system will never exceed the quality of its teachers. And, certainly, top school systems select their teaching staff carefully. But does that mean that, in those countries, the top graduates chose to become teachers rather than, say, lawyers, doctors or engineers?

It is hard to know for certain because it is difficult to obtain comparative evidence on the knowledge and skills of teachers. But the Survey of Adult Skills tested the literacy and numeracy skills of adults – including teachers. Using these data, it is possible to compare the skills of teachers with those of other college and university graduates.[9]

The results show that, among the countries with comparable data, there is no single country where teachers are among the top third of adults with a college degree (based on average proficiency in numeracy and literacy); and there is no country where they are among the bottom third of college graduates (*FIGURE 2.5A*). In fact, in most countries, teachers' skills are similar to those of the average person with a college degree. There are just a few exceptions. In Finland and Japan, for example, the average teacher has better numeracy skills than the average college graduate, while in the Czech Republic, Denmark, Estonia, the Slovak Republic and Sweden, the reverse is true.

But there is another way to look at this. While in every country teachers tend to score similarly to college graduates on the Survey of Adult Skills, the knowledge and skills of graduates differ substantially across countries – and these differences are reflected among teachers too. Teachers in Japan and Finland come out on top in terms of their numeracy skills, followed by their Flemish (Belgium), German, Norwegian and Dutch counterparts. Teachers in Italy, the Russian Federation, Spain, Poland, Estonia and the United States come out at the bottom in numeracy skills.

One study[10] found that there is a positive relationship between teachers' and students' skills (*FIGURE 2.5B*). However, in some countries, such as Estonia and South Korea, teachers' proficiency in numeracy is average, but their students are top performers in the PISA mathematics test. In addition, in most high-performing countries, students score above what would be expected based solely on the average knowledge and skills of the teachers in those countries. This suggests that other factors, in addition to teachers' skills, are related to students' high performance.

All in all, unless countries have the luxury of hiring teachers from Finland or Japan, they need to think harder about making teaching a well-respected profession and a more attractive career choice – both intellectually and financially. They need to invest more in teacher development and competitive employment conditions. If not, they will be caught in a downward spiral – from lower standards of entry into the teaching profession, leading to lower self-confidence among teachers, resulting in more prescriptive teaching and thus less personalisation in instruction, which could drive the most talented teachers out of the profession entirely. And that, in turn, will result in a lower-quality teaching force.

FIGURE 2.5A: TEACHERS ARE NEITHER MORE NOR LESS SKILLED THAN THE AVERAGE COLLEGE GRADUATE

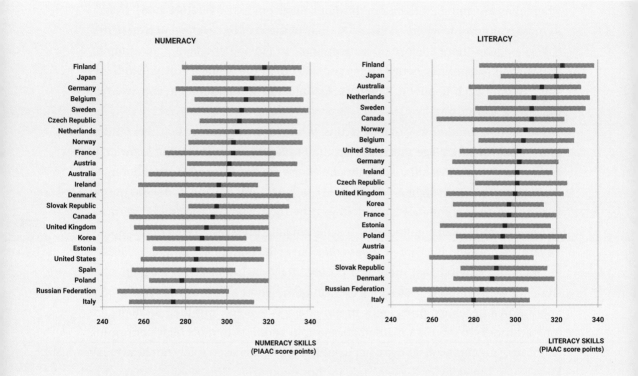

Notes: The dark segment indicates median cognitive skills of teachers in a country. The horizontal bars show the interval of cognitive skill levels of all college graduates (including teachers) between the 25th and 75th percentile. Countries are ranked by the median teacher skills in numeracy and literacy, respectively.

Source: Adapted from Hanushek, Piopiunik and Wiederhold (2014), The Value of Smarter Teachers: International Evidence on Teacher Cognitive Skills and Student Performance.

FIGURE 2.5B: STUDENT PERFORMANCE IS RELATED TO, BUT NOT NECESSARILY DEPENDENT ON, TEACHERS' SKILLS

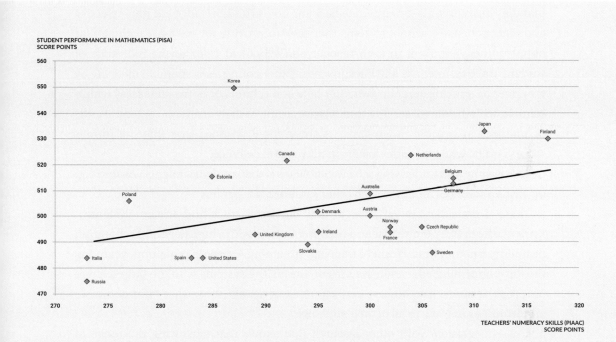

Source: Adapted from Hanushek, Piopiunik and Wiederhold (2014), The Value of Smarter Teachers: International Evidence on Teacher Cognitive Skills and Student Performance.

Selecting students by ability is the way to raise standards

For centuries educators have wondered how they should design school systems so that they best serve all students' needs. Some countries have adopted non-selective and comprehensive school systems that seek to provide all students with similar opportunities, leaving it to each teacher and school to cater to the full range of student abilities, interests and backgrounds. Other countries respond to diversity by grouping or tracking students, whether between schools or between classes within schools, with the aim of serving students according to their academic potential and/ or interests in specific programmes. Conventional wisdom says that the former serves equity, while the latter fosters quality and excellence.

The assumption underlying selection policies is that students' talents will develop best when students reinforce each other's interest in learning.

There is considerable variation in how countries track and stream students.[11] Evidence from PISA shows that none of the countries with a high degree of separation by ability, whether in the form of tracking, streaming, or grade repetition, is among the top-performing education systems or among the systems with the largest share of top performers. The highest-performing systems are those that offer equitable opportunities to learn to all of their students.

This is consistent with other research that shows that narrowing the range of student abilities in classes or schools through tracking does not result in better learning outcomes.[12] The pattern is different for within-class ability grouping or subject-specific ability grouping, which has shown to be effective when appropriate adjustments are made to the curriculum and instruction.

It used to be sufficient for only some students to succeed in school, because our societies and economies needed a relatively small cohort of well-educated people. With the social and economic cost of poor performance in school rising every day, it has become not just socially unjust but also highly inefficient to organise school systems on the basis of exclusion. Equity and inclusion are imperative in modern education systems and their societies.

Now that I've debunked some of the myths about what influences learning outcomes, it is time to analyse what makes high-performing education systems different.

3. What makes high-performing school systems different

What we know about successful school systems

Policy makers' hunger for immediate answers is always frustrated by the snail's pace at which the development of data, evidence and research advances. And sometimes I think policy makers forget that data are not the plural of anecdote.

The data collected by PISA alone leave many questions unanswered. The results offer a snapshot of education systems at a certain moment in time; but they do not – they cannot – show how the school systems got to that point, or the institutions and organisations that might have helped or hindered progress. In addition, the data do not really say anything about cause and effect. Correlations are often deceptive: if the birds sing when the sun rises, and they do so day after day, year after year, and in many different places around the world, it doesn't mean the sun rises because the birds sing.

In a nutshell, knowing what successful systems are doing does not yet tell us how to improve less-successful systems. That is one of the main limitations of international surveys, and that is where other forms of analysis need to kick in. That is also why PISA does not presume to tell countries what they should do. PISA's strength lies in telling countries what everybody else is doing.

And yet, policy makers need to make inferences if they are going to draw lessons from international test results.

Education policy makers can benefit from international comparisons in the same way that business leaders learn to steer their companies towards success: by taking inspiration from others, and then adapting lessons learned to their own situation. For policy makers in education, this can be achieved through various forms of benchmarking: analysing observed differences in the quality, equity and efficiency of education between one country and another, and considering how they are related to certain features of those countries' education systems.

One of the key architects of this approach is Marc Tucker, who has headed the National Center on Education and the Economy in the United States since 1988.[1] In 2009, he and I convened a group of leading thinkers to analyse what the United States might learn from high-performing and rapidly improving education systems as measured by PISA. The research entailed an enquiry of historians, policy makers, economists, education experts, ordinary citizens, journalists, industrialists and educators. Tucker's initiative became the basis of a whole range of sought-after studies that complement the OECD's thematic and country policy reviews in interesting ways.

Any examination of an individual country's trajectory towards high performance must take into account that country's unique history, values, strengths and challenges. But Tucker's benchmarking studies have revealed a surprising range of features common to all high-performing education systems.

- The first thing we learned is that the leaders in high-performing education systems have convinced their citizens that it is worth investing in the future through education, rather than spending for immediate rewards, and that it is better to compete on the quality of labour rather than on the price of labour.

- Valuing education highly is just part of the equation. Another part is the belief that every student can learn. In some countries, students are segregated into different tracks at early ages, reflecting the notion that only some children can achieve world-class standards. But PISA shows that such selection is related to large social disparities. By contrast, in countries as different as Estonia, Canada, Finland and Japan, parents and teachers are committed to the belief that all students can meet high standards. These beliefs are often manifested in student and teacher behaviour. These systems have advanced from sorting human talent to developing human talent.

- In many education systems, different students are taught in similar ways. Top school systems tend to address the diversity of student needs with differentiated pedagogical practice – without compromising on standards. They realise that ordinary students can have extraordinary talents; and they personalise the education experience so that all students can meet high standards. Moreover, teachers in these systems invest not just in their students' academic success but also in their well-being.

- Nowhere does the quality of a school system exceed the quality of its teachers. Top school systems select and educate their teaching staff carefully. They improve the performance of teachers who are struggling and they structure teachers' pay to reflect professional standards. They provide an environment in which teachers work together to frame good practice, and they encourage teachers to grow in their careers.

- Top-performing school systems set ambitious goals, are clear about what students should be able to do, and enable teachers to figure out what they need to teach their students. They have moved on from administrative control and accountability to professional forms of work organisation. They encourage their teachers to be innovative, to improve their own performance and that of their colleagues, and to pursue professional development that leads to better practice. In top school systems, the emphasis is not on looking upward within the administration of the school system. Instead it's about looking outward to the next teacher or the next school, creating a culture of collaboration and strong networks of innovation.

- The best-performing school systems provide high-quality education across the entire system so that every student benefits from excellent teaching. To achieve this, these countries attract the strongest principals to the toughest schools and the most talented teachers to the most challenging classrooms.

■ Last but not least, high-performing systems tend to align policies and practices across the entire system. They ensure that the policies are coherent over sustained periods of time, and they see that they are consistently implemented.

It is worth looking at each of these features in greater detail.[2]

Making education a priority

Many nations claim that education is a top priority. There are some simple questions one can ask to find out whether countries live by that claim. For example: What is the status of the teaching profession; and how do countries pay teachers compared to how they pay others with the same level of education? Would you want your child to be a teacher? How much do the media report on schools and schooling? When it comes down to it, which matters more: a community's standing in the sports leagues or its standing in the academic league tables?

In many of the highest-performing countries in PISA, teachers are typically paid better, education credentials are valued more, and a larger share of spending on education is devoted to what happens in the classroom than is the case in many European countries and in the United States. In these latter countries, parents might not encourage their children to become school teachers if they think they have a chance of becoming attorneys, engineers or doctors.

The value placed on education is likely to influence the decisions students make about what they want to study later on; it will also influence whether the most capable students consider a career in teaching. And, of course, the status accorded to education will have an effect on whether the public values the views of professional educators or fails to take them seriously.

It is perhaps no surprise, then, that the 2013 OECD Teaching and Learning International Survey (TALIS) found wide differences across countries in whether teachers feel that their profession is valued by society. In Malaysia, Singapore, Korea, the United Arab Emirates and Finland, the majority of teachers reported that they feel their profession is valued by society; in France and the Slovak Republic, fewer than 1 in 20 reported so (**FIGURE 3.1**).

FIGURE 3.1: IN SOME COUNTRIES, MOST TEACHERS FEEL THEIR WORK IS NOT VALUED BY SOCIETY

Percentage of lower secondary teachers who "agree" or "strongly agree" with the following statement: I think that the teaching profession is valued in society.

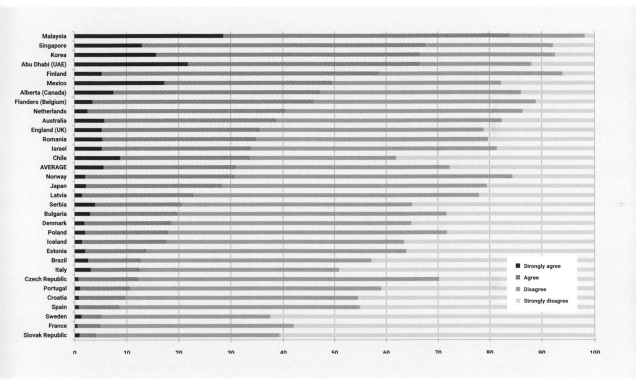

Note: Countries are ranked in descending order, based on the percentage of teachers who "strongly agree" or "agree" that they think that the teaching profession is valued in society.

Source: OECD, TALIS 2013 Database, Tables 7.2 and 7.2.Web.

StatLink ⨇ᵐˢᴸ *http://dx.doi.org/10.1787/888933042219*

Believing that all students can learn and achieve at high levels

Valuing education may be a prerequisite for building a world-class education system; but placing a high value on education will get a country only so far if the teachers, parents and other citizens of that country believe that only a minority of the nation's children can or need to meet high academic standards.

Until recently, people in Germany widely assumed that the children of working-class adults would themselves get working-class jobs and would not profit from the curriculum offered by the more academically oriented *gymnasia*. The education system in many parts of the country still divides 10-year-old students between those who go on to academic schools, geared towards entry into university and the preparation of knowledge workers, and those who go to vocational programmes that prepare them to work for the knowledge workers.

PISA results show that these attitudes are mirrored in students' perceptions of their own future education. While only one in four 15-year-olds in PISA said that they expect to go on to university or earn an advanced vocational qualification (fewer than those who actually will), in Japan and South Korea, nine out of ten students said they expected to do so.[3]

By contrast, in the East Asian countries that perform well in PISA, and also in other high-performing countries, including Canada, Estonia and Finland, parents, teachers and the public at large tend to share the belief that all students are capable of high achievement. The aspiration of the Ministry of Education in Singapore is that every student is an engaged learner, every teacher a caring educator, every parent a supporting partner, every principal an inspiring leader in education, and every school a good school. All of this tends to be mirrored in students' beliefs. Analyses of the Trends in Mathematics and Science Study show that students in many East Asian countries tend to believe in effort rather than inherent talent as the route to success.[4] This is supported by other research suggesting that East Asians are more likely to attribute successes and failures to effort as compared to students in the Western world. In fact, Asian students are often explicitly taught that effort and hard work are the keys to success.[5] Asian teachers are not only helping students succeed, but also helping them believe that it is their own ability and effort that are the sources of their success.

In other countries, when students struggle, teachers respond by lowering standards. In doing so, they imply that low achievement is the consequence of a lack of inherent ability. Unlike effort, talent is seen as something that students have no control over, so students may be more likely to give up trying harder. According to some research, teachers give more praise, more help and coaching, and lengthier answers to questions to those students whom they perceive have greater ability.[6]

When teachers don't believe that pupils can develop and extend themselves through hard work, they may feel guilty pressing students who they perceive to be less capable of achieving at higher levels. This is concerning because research shows that when a teacher gives a student an easier task and then praises that student excessively for completing it, the student may interpret the teacher's behaviour as reflecting a belief that the student is less able.

All of this is important, because of all the judgements people make about themselves, the most influential is how capable they think they are of completing a task successfully.[7] More generally, research shows that the belief that we are responsible for the results of our behaviour influences motivation,[8] such that people are more likely to invest effort if they believe it will lead to the results they are trying to achieve.

All of this may explain why mastery learning is so much more common and successful in East Asia than in the West, where the concept was first defined and researched. Mastery learning builds on the understanding that learning is sequential, and that mastery of earlier tasks is the foundation on which mastery of subsequent tasks is built. According to American psychologist John Carroll,[9] student learning outcomes reflect the amount of time and instruction a student needs to learn, and whether the opportunity to learn and quality of instruction are sufficient to meet students' needs. For teachers, that means that they do not vary the learning goals, which hold for the entire class, but that they do whatever is needed to ensure that each student has the opportunity to learn the material in ways that are appropriate to him or her. Some students will require additional instruction time, others will not; some students will require different learning environments than others. Behind this thinking is the deep belief that all students can learn and succeed, and that the task of teachers is to design the learning environments, whether inside or outside the classroom, that help students realise their potential. Because all students succeed at completing each successive task, the result is less variation and a weaker impact of socio-economic background on learning outcomes – precisely the results that set many East Asian education systems apart in PISA.

FIGURE 3.2 offers another perspective on this. PISA asked students to report on the level of support they receive from their teachers. Their responses were closely related to the age at which students were selected into different school tracks. Countries where students reported the least support from teachers were often those where students were divided by academic ability at a young age: Austria, Belgium, Croatia, the Czech Republic, Germany, Hungary, Luxembourg, the Netherlands, the Slovak Republic, Slovenia and Switzerland. Even if different response styles mean that country comparisons need to be interpreted with caution, these results are not entirely surprising. Sorting students into different types of schools creates more homogeneous classes, where teaching becomes more straightforward, and teachers may feel they do not need to pay as much attention – "show interest", "give extra help" or "work with students" – to individual students.

Singapore, the top-ranked country in PISA 2015, had a system of streaming in its elementary schools that it later modified as the country raised its standards. Singapore now uses a wide range of strategies to make sure that struggling students are identified and diagnosed early, and are given whatever help is needed to get them back on track. Even though the results from the PISA 2015 assessment show that Singapore still has a way to go to reach the levels of equity in education achieved by Canada and Finland, the government's economic and education policies have increased social mobility, creating a shared sense of mission and instilling a value for education that is nearly universal.

Finland's special teachers fulfil a similar role, working closely with classroom teachers to identify students in need of extra help, and then working individually or in small groups with struggling students to help them keep up with their classmates. It is not left solely to the regular classroom teacher to identify a problem and alert the special teacher; every comprehensive school has a "pupils' multiprofessional

FIGURE 3.2: THE LATER CHILDREN ARE TRACKED, THE MORE THEY FEEL SUPPORTED BY THEIR TEACHERS

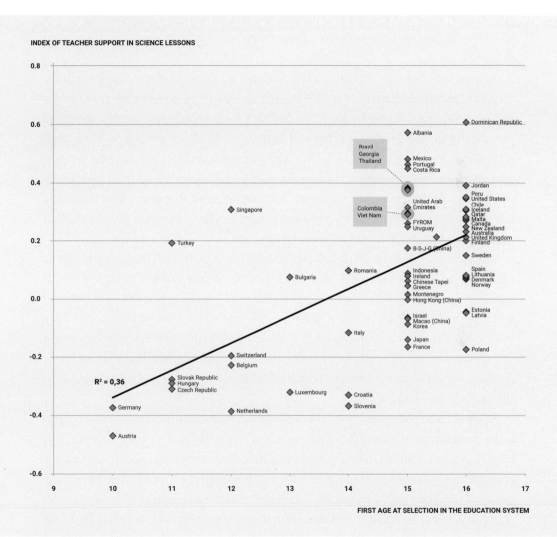

Notes: FYROM refers to the Former Yugoslav Republic of Macedonia. B-S-J-G (China) refers to Beijing-Shanghai-Jiangsu-Guangdong (China).

Source: OECD, PISA 2015 Database, Tables II.3.23 and II.4.27.

StatLink ᨏᨏ᥍ http://dx.doi.org/10.1787/888933435743

care group" that meets at least twice a month for two hours. The group consists of the principal, the special teacher, the school nurse, the school psychologist, a social worker, and the teachers whose students are being discussed. The parents of any child being discussed are contacted prior to the meeting and are sometimes asked to attend.

To prevent dropout, the education ministry in Ontario, Canada, created the "Student Success Initiative" in high schools.[10] The ministry gave the districts money to hire a Student Success leader to co-ordinate local efforts, and funded meetings among the district leaders during which they could share strategies. Each high school was given the resources to hire a province-funded Student Success teacher and was required to create a Student Success team to identify struggling students and design appropriate interventions. The outcomes of this and other initiatives have changed Ontario's system profoundly: within a few years, the province's high school graduation rate increased from 68% to 79%.

In many countries, it has taken time to move from a belief that only a few students can succeed to embracing the idea that all students can achieve at high levels. It takes a concerted, multifaceted programme of policy making and capacity building to attain that goal. But one of the patterns observed among the highest-performing countries is the gradual move from a system in which students were streamed into different types of secondary schools, with curricula demanding various levels of cognitive skills, to a system in which all students go to secondary schools with similarly demanding curricula.

Among OECD countries, Finland was the first to take this route in the 1970s; Poland is the most recent, with its school reform in the 2000s. These countries "levelled-up", requiring all students to meet the standards that they previously expected only their elite students to meet. Students who start to fall behind are identified quickly, their problem is promptly and accurately diagnosed, and the appropriate course of action is quickly taken. Inevitably, this means that some students are targeted for more resources than others; but it is the students with the greatest needs who benefit from the most resources.

It takes strong leadership, and thoughtful and sustained communication to bring parents along in this effort, particularly those benefiting from the more selective tracks. I learned that lesson in my home city, Hamburg, in 2010. In October 2009, policy makers from across the political spectrum agreed on a school reform that would reduce the degree of stratification in the school system and moderate its impact.[11] The politicians had understood that this would be the most effective way to provide better and more equitable learning opportunities. But proponents of the initiative had not worked hard enough to convince parents of its merits, and a citizens' group lobbying against the reform, mainly involving families whose children were in the elite track, soon emerged. These families were worried about losing out in a more comprehensive school system. The reform was eventually overturned in a referendum in July 2010.

But the bottom line remains: no education system has managed to achieve sustained high performance and equitable opportunities to learn without developing a system built on the premise that it is possible for all students to achieve at high levels – and that it is necessary for them to do so. I cannot overstate the importance of clearly articulating the expectation that all students should be taught and held to the same standards. PISA shows that this is possible in all types of cultural settings, and that progress towards that end can be made rapidly.

Setting and defining high expectations

Establishing standards can shape high-performing education systems by creating rigorous, focused and coherent content; reducing overlap in the curriculum across grades; reducing variation in how curricula are delivered in different schools; and perhaps most important, reducing inequity between socio-economic groups.

Most countries have incorporated standards into their curricula and often also into their external examinations, which, in secondary school, are commonly used as gateways for students to enter the workforce or the next stage of education, or both. Across OECD countries, students in school systems that require standards-based external examinations score more than 16 points higher, on average, than those in school systems that do not use such examinations.[12] But getting the design of exams wrong can hold education systems back, narrowing the scope of what is valued and what is taught, or encouraging shortcuts, cramming or cheating.

It is noteworthy that most of the high-performing education systems in PISA focus on the acquisition of complex, higher-order thinking skills and, in many of those, on the application of those skills to real-world problems. In these countries, we find teachers continually probing for understanding and prompting for further thinking, by asking students questions such as: Who is correct? How do you know? Can you explain why he or she is correct?

The re-organisation of traditional subjects into "learning domains" in Shanghai provides an example of such efforts. Finland has gone furthest in this respect, with an instructional system that is now largely cross-curricular, requiring both students and teachers to think and work across the boundaries of school subjects.[13]

For that reason, examinations in some high-performing countries do not rely mainly on multiple-choice, computer-scored tests. Instead, they also use essay-type responses, oral examinations, and sometimes factor into the final grade pieces of work that could not be produced in a timed examination.

At the same time, some countries are making greater efforts to improve rigour and comparability. I served on the advisory board that created a common school-leavers' exam in Nordrhein Westfalen, Germany's largest state, and could see how policy makers and experts struggled to move from entirely school-based written exams to more standardised forms of assessment, without sacrificing relevance and authenticity.

The goals of validity and comparability, and relevance and reliability, may seem difficult to reconcile at first, but there has been considerable progress in many countries towards building high-quality exam systems that capitalise on the merits while mitigating the risks of high-stakes exams.

One of the countries that have surprised me most in how they were able to change their examination culture is the Russian Federation. For a long time Russians had lost trust in exam scores and degrees because of fraud and misconduct in examinations. But for well over a decade, Russia has worked persistently on addressing these issues. Its unified state exam now offers an advanced and transparent way of assessing student learning outcomes.

For a start, Russia has not fallen into the trap of sacrificing validity for efficiency or relevance for reliability that is so common to many exam systems. There are no bubble sheets and few multiple-choice questions. Instead, tasks are open-ended and often involve essays, focusing on the acquisition of advanced knowledge, complex higher-order thinking skills and, increasingly, the application of those skills to real-world problems.

But the biggest accomplishment of Russia's unified state exam has been in re-establishing trust in education and examinations. Trust cannot be legislated; nor does it just happen. Trust is at least as much a consequence of the design of an exam system as it is a pre-condition for conducting an exam.

So how did Russia do it? For a start, it invested in state-of-the art test security that is now available across the country. The exam papers are packaged and printed at the point of delivery, in the classroom, under the eyes of the students and the examiners – and in the lens of a 360-degree camera that monitors and records the entire exam process.

At the end, the exam papers are scanned, digitised and anonymised, once again as students watch. Where more complex responses to essays cannot be scored by machines, they are marked centrally by independent and specially trained experts, with extensive checks for raters' reliability. Of course, there is always some judgement involved in scoring essays. So how can students trust that they were graded fairly? They can see for themselves. The fully marked exam papers are posted on line and all students can review their results. Students can contest the marks if they are not happy, something which a small percentage of them do each year. Schools, too, can see and track their exam scores. So if Russian students, teachers, school leaders and employers are now much more confident in schooling and examinations, this has not happened by chance.

Exams as a step towards qualifications

After exams, newspapers in some countries publish exam questions and the ministry releases examples of answers that earned top grades. In this way, students, parents and teachers all learn what is considered to be high-quality work, and students can compare their own work against a clear example of work that meets the standard.

Often these examinations are linked to national qualifications systems. In countries with systems of this sort, one cannot go on to the next phase of education or begin a career in a particular field without showing that one is qualified to do so. In these systems, everyone knows what is required to get a given qualification, in terms of both the content studied and the level of performance that has to be demonstrated to earn it.

In Sweden, and a number of other northern European countries, the qualifications systems are modular and are established such that it is never too late to earn a given qualification. In such systems, it cannot be said that one has failed the exams, but only that one has not yet succeeded on them. Perhaps it is not a coincidence that Sweden is also the OECD country where adult learners have the most discretion over what they learn, how they learn, where they learn and when they learn – and that is reflected in the highest participation rates in both formal and non-formal adult learning programmes among OECD countries.[14] Sweden's adults are also among the world's most proficient in literacy and numeracy.[15]

In such systems, where it is never too late to earn a qualification, examinations are always available and standards are never lowered or waived. Students know that they have to take tough courses and study hard in order to earn the qualification. A student does not get to go on to the next stage simply because he or she has put in the requisite time. This is a system with high stakes for students, but usually low or no stakes for the teachers in these systems.

Because the examinations are typically externally graded, the teacher, student and parents feel that they are all on the same side, working towards the same end. Rarely do parents go to the school administration to try to change the student's grade, pitting the teacher, who wants to preserve some standard, against parents, who want the best possible future for their child. Parents and students know that neither the teacher nor the administration can change the grade, and therefore the only way to improve the outcome is for the student to learn.

It is true that high-stakes examinations can lead to a focus on test preparation at the expense of real learning, the development of large private-tutoring industries that tend to favour the wealthy, and incentives for cheating. These dangers are real, but they can be mitigated.

Parents and educators sometimes also argue that testing can make students anxious without improving their learning. In particular, standardised tests that could determine a student's future – entry into a certain education programme or into university, for example – may trigger anxiety and undermine self-confidence. However, analyses of PISA data show that the frequency of tests, as reported by school principals, is not related to the level of test anxiety reported by students.[16] In fact, on average across OECD countries, students who attend schools where they have to sit standardised or teacher-developed tests at least once a month reported similar levels of test anxiety as students who attend schools where assessments are conducted less frequently.[17] The relationship between student performance and the frequency with which schools or countries assess students is also weak.

By contrast, the data show that students' experience in school has a stronger relationship with their likelihood of feeling anxious than the frequency with which they are assessed. For example, PISA shows that students reported less anxiety when their teachers provide more support or adapt the lessons to their needs. Students reported greater anxiety when they feel that their teachers treat them unfairly, such as by grading them harder than other students, or when they have the impression that their teachers think they are less smart than they are.

Exams as a factor in designing curricula

Education standards and examinations are where the system of instruction begins, not where it ends. The key is how those standards and examinations translate into the curriculum, instructional material and ultimately instructional practice. I have often been surprised at how little attention and resources countries devote to developing their curriculum and instructional material and aligning them with education goals, standards, teacher development and examinations.

It is not uncommon to find a few academics and government officials in a country who determine what millions of students will learn. They will often defend the scope and integrity of their discipline rather than consider what students need to know and be able to do to be successful in tomorrow's world. When studying national mathematics curricula for the development of the PISA 2003 assessment, I often asked myself why curricula devoted as much attention to teaching things like trigonometry and calculus. The answer cannot be found in the internal structure of the mathematics discipline, in the most meaningful learning progressions for students, or in the way mathematics is used in the world today. The answer lies in how mathematics was used generations ago by people measuring the size of their fields or performing advanced calculations that have long since been digitised.

Since student learning time is limited and we seem unable to give up teaching things that may no longer be relevant, young people are held prisoners of the past, and schools lose the opportunity to develop valuable knowledge, skills and character qualities that are important for students' success in the world.

In the late 1990s, Japan responded to this situation by removing almost a third of the material in the national curriculum with the aim of creating space for greater depth and interdisciplinary learning. Teachers tended to agree with the goals of this *yutori kyoiku* reform[18] but were insufficiently supported by the government and local school authorities to work towards those objectives in their classrooms.

Moreover, secondary teachers, in particular, were reluctant to diverge from practices that had proven effective in the past and that were valued by the Japanese examination system. When results from PISA showed a decline in mathematics performance in 2003, parents lost confidence that the reformed curriculum would prepare their children for the challenges that lay ahead. They looked increasingly to private tutoring to fill what they perceived as a gap in their children's education. Much of the public was unaware that between 2006 and 2009 Japan had improved faster than any other country in students' abilities to solve the kinds of unstructured, open-ended tasks found in PISA. These were tasks that tapped the kind of creative and critical thinking skills that the *yutori* reform had sought to strengthen. But pressure mounted to reverse the reform, and over the past few years curriculum content became more dominant again.

Other countries have responded to new demands on what students should learn by layering more and more content on top of their curriculum, with the result that teachers are ploughing through a large amount of subject-matter content but with little depth. Adding new material provides an easy way to show that education systems are responding to emerging demands, while it is tough to remove material from instructional systems.

Parents often expect their children to learn what they had learned, and they may equate a reduction in content with lowered standards. The work of teachers will become more demanding when the curriculum is less detailed and less prescriptive, and therefore requires greater investment in deepening student understanding.

I learned this first-hand through PISA. In the wake of the financial crisis of 2008, policy makers sought to strengthen financial education in school and requested that these skills be tested in PISA too. The assumption was that more financial education would translate into better student performance in financial literacy. But when the first results were published in 2014,[19] they showed no relationship between students' financial literacy and the amount of financial education they were exposed to. The top performer in the PISA assessment of financial literacy was Shanghai, whose schools did not provide much financial education. Shanghai's secret to success on the PISA assessment of financial literacy was that its schools cultivate deep conceptual understanding and complex reasoning in mathematics. Because students in Shanghai could think like mathematicians, and understand the meaning of concepts such as probability, change and risk, they had no difficulties transferring and applying their knowledge to unfamiliar financial contexts.

This all highlights how important it is to assemble the best minds in the country – leading experts in the field, but also those who understand how students learn, and those who have a good understanding of the demand for and use of knowledge and skills in the real world – in order to determine and regularly re-examine what topics should be taught in what sequence through the grades.

So it really matters how standards feed into well-thought-out curriculum frameworks that can guide the work of teachers and textbook publishers. Rigorous examinations should focus on complex thinking skills that assess the extent to which students have met the standards across the core curriculum; and a system of gateways, based on those examinations, should be constructed as part of a well-developed qualifications system.

It is also crucially important that education systems are built around what learning science tells us about how students learn and progress, rather than simply around academic disciplines. For example, in establishing its curriculum, Singapore was explicit about learning progressions. As students advance from primary, through secondary and on to post-secondary education, they are expected to advance from distinguishing right from wrong, through understanding moral integrity, towards having the moral courage to stand up for what is right. Similarly, teachers are expected to help their students progress from knowing their strengths and weaknesses, through believing in their abilities and being able to adapt to change, to becoming resilient in the face of adversity. Students are expected to advance from co-operating and sharing with others, through being able to work in teams and show empathy to others, to being able to collaborate across cultures and be socially responsible. They are expected to progress from having a lively curiosity in primary school, through being creative and having an enquiring mind in secondary school, to being innovative and enterprising in tertiary education. Teachers are expected to guide students from being able to think for themselves and express themselves confidently, through being able to appreciate diverse views and communicate effectively, towards being able to think critically and communicate persuasively. Not least, students are expected to progress from taking pride in their work, through taking responsibility for their own learning, towards pursuing excellence.

It is surprising that it has taken until this decade for countries to advance towards taking a more intentional and systematic approach to curriculum design. This move has largely been inspired by the work of people like Charles Fadel and his Center for Curriculum Redesign at Harvard University.[20] That shift was also mirrored in the OECD Education 2030 project on curriculum design, which we launched in 2016. After years of countries refusing to discuss curricula from an international perspective (countries tend to perceive curricula as the domain of domestic policy only), they put the OECD at the helm of developing an innovative global framework for curriculum design. They recognised that the gap between what society expects from education and what our current educational institutions deliver has been getting wider, and that it required a concerted international effort to narrow that gap.

Recruiting and retaining high-quality teachers

We demand a lot from our teachers. We expect them to have a deep and broad understanding of what they teach and whom they teach, because what teachers know and care about makes such a difference to student learning. That entails professional knowledge (e.g. knowledge about a discipline, knowledge about the curriculum of that discipline, and knowledge about how students learn in that discipline), and knowledge about professional practice so they can create the kind of learning environment that leads to good learning outcomes. It also involves enquiry and research skills that allow them to be lifelong learners and grow in their profession. Students are unlikely to become lifelong learners if they don't see their teachers as such.

But we expect much more from our teachers than what appears in their job description. We also expect them to be passionate, compassionate and thoughtful; to encourage students' engagement and responsibility; to respond to students from different backgrounds with different needs, and promote tolerance and social cohesion; to provide continual assessments of students and feedback; to ensure that students feel valued and included; and to encourage collaborative learning. And we expect teachers themselves to collaborate and work in teams, and with other schools and parents, to set common goals, and plan and monitor the attainment of those goals.

There are aspects that make the job of teachers much more challenging and different from that of other professionals. As the head of Singapore's prestigious National Institute of Education, Oon Seng Tan, describes,[21] teachers need to be experts at multitasking as they respond to many different learner needs all at the same time. They also do their job in a classroom dynamic that is always unpredictable and that leaves teachers no second to think about how to react. Whatever a teacher does, even with just a single student, will be witnessed by all classmates and can frame the way in which the teacher is perceived in the school from that day forward.

Most people remember at least one of their teachers who took a real interest in their life and aspirations, who helped them understand who they are and discover their passions; and who taught them how to love learning.

For me, it is a given that the quality of an education system can never exceed the quality of its teachers. So attracting, developing and retaining the best teachers is the greatest challenge education systems have to face. To meet that challenge, governments can look to corporations to see how they build their teams. Companies know that they have to pay attention to how the pool from which they recruit and select their staff is established; the kind of initial education their recruits get before they present themselves for employment; how to mentor new recruits and induct them into their service; what kind of continuing education their employees get; how their compensation is structured; how they reward their best performers and how they improve the performance of those who are struggling; and how they provide opportunities for the best performers to acquire more status and responsibility.

Attracting high-quality teachers

One of the first things I learned when studying how high-performing education systems recruit teachers is that they make the teaching profession exclusive and teaching inclusive.

When any industry or organisation recruits professionals, they will do whatever is possible to create a pool of potential employees that comes from the highest-performing segment of the population. Most firms and industries rely heavily on schools and universities and the exam system to do that sorting for them. That is what the top Japanese ministries are doing when they decide to recruit from Tokyo University and what the top Wall Street firms are doing when they recruit mainly from among Harvard, Yale and Stanford graduates. They target these institutions because they believe they are good at recognising the most talented young people, not because of any specific knowledge or skills their graduates can offer. Because no industry can afford to source all of its professionals from the highest-performing segment of graduates, they also structure their operations so that they can put the best of the best in key positions and use others who might not be quite as good in supporting positions. More often than not, they use career structures that permit them to make the most of their most advanced professionals.

So what shapes the pool from which industry selects its professionals? Generally it is a combination of the social status associated with the job, the contributions a candidate feels he or she can make while in the job, and the extent to which the work is financially and intellectually rewarding.

The status of the teaching profession in a country has a profound impact on who aspires to enter the profession. Teaching is a highly selective occupation in Finland, with highly skilled, well-educated teachers spread throughout the country. Few occupations in the country have a higher reputation. In the traditionally Confucian cultures, teachers have long had higher social status than most of their counterparts in the West. In some East Asian countries, teachers' pay is fixed by law to make sure that teachers are among the highest paid of all civil servants.

In England, Tony Blair's Labour administration faced one of the worst shortages of teachers in British history when it took office. Five years later, there were eight applicants for every opening. To some extent this had to do with raising initial pay, and with significant changes in teachers' work environment. But a sophisticated and powerful recruitment and advertising programme also played an important part in the turnaround.[22]

Singapore is notable for its sophisticated approach to improving the quality of the pool from which it selects candidates for teacher education. The government carefully selects its teacher candidates and offers them a monthly stipend, during initial teacher education, that is competitive with the monthly salary for fresh graduates in other fields. In exchange, these teachers-in-training must commit to teaching for at least three years. Singapore also keeps a close watch on starting salaries and adjusts the salaries for new teachers. In effect, the country wants its most qualified candidates to regard teaching as just as financially attractive as other professions. PISA data show that schools in Singapore have comparatively limited leeway in making hiring decisions. But the principal of the school to which student-teachers are attached will sit on the recruitment panel and weigh in on those decisions, well aware that wrong hiring decisions can result in 40 years of poor teaching. So it's not all just about your school, but about the success of the system.

While it is relatively easy to make teaching more financially attractive, it tends to be much harder to make teaching more intellectually attractive. But it is the latter that is key to drawing highly talented individuals into the profession, particularly as many people who go into teaching do so to make a difference to their society. It is hard because it depends on how the work of teachers is organised, the opportunities teachers have for professional growth, and how their work is regarded in the profession and by society at large (*FIGURE 3.1*). Given this, it is remarkable that the teaching profession does not have more ways of recognising and rewarding excellence internationally. In 2016, the film industry presented its 88th Academy Awards, but it was the first year that a Global Teacher Prize[23] was awarded.

But as discussed in Chapter 2, the Survey of Adult Skills shows that there is no country where teachers are drawn from the top third of the highest-achieving college graduates (see *FIGURE 2.5A*). In fact, teachers tend to come out remarkably similarly to the average employee with a college or university degree. Even more interesting is that some of the countries where the skills of teachers do not compare favourably either internationally or with regard to the average college graduate (Poland is one such country) have seen the most rapid progress. That shows that recruiting top-performing graduates is only one component of improving education; the investments countries make in teachers' continued professional development are at least as important.

Educating high-quality teachers

What makes an effective teacher? Education researchers Thomas L. Good and Alyson Lavigne[24] summarise some of the telling characteristics: these teachers believe their students are capable of learning and they themselves are capable of teaching; they spend the bulk of their classroom time on instruction; they organise their classrooms and maximise student learning time; they use rapid curriculum pacing based on taking small steps; they use active teaching methods; and they teach students until the students achieve mastery.

But how do we educate such teachers? I'll use an analogy from nature: frogs release a very large number of eggs in the hope that some of their tadpoles will survive and ultimately metamorphose into the next generation of frogs; ducks lay a few eggs, protect and warm them until they hatch, then defend their ducklings with their life. In a way, these different philosophies of reproduction are mirrored in the approaches towards teacher education in different countries. In some countries, teacher education is open to everyone, but it often becomes an option of last resort, and one with a high dropout rate. In other countries, teacher education is highly selective. In these countries, resources are focused on helping those who are admitted become successful teachers.

Many top-performing education systems have moved from recruiting teachers into a large number of specialised, low-status colleges of teacher education, with relatively low entrance standards, towards a relatively smaller number of university-based teacher-education colleges with relatively high entrance standards and relatively high status in the university. By raising the bar to enter the teaching profession, these countries discourage young people with poor qualifications from becoming teachers. They understand that capable young people who could go into other high-status occupations are not likely to enter a profession that society perceives as easy to get into and therefore attractive to people who could not get into more demanding professions.

Finland has made teacher education one of the most prestigious academic programmes. Each year there are typically more than nine applicants for every place in Finnish teacher education; those who aren't selected can still become attorneys or doctors. Applicants are assessed on the basis of their high school record and their score on the matriculation exam. But the more rigorous selection comes afterwards. Once applicants make it beyond the initial screening of their academic credentials, they are observed in teaching-like activity and interviewed. Only candidates with a clear aptitude for teaching in addition to strong academic performance are admitted.

A combination of raising the bar for entry and granting teachers greater autonomy and control over their classrooms and working conditions has helped lift the status of the profession. Teaching is now one of the most desirable careers among young Finns. Finnish teachers have earned the trust of parents and the wider society, not least by showing that they can help virtually all students become successful learners.

Top-performing education systems also work to move their initial teacher-education programmes towards a model based less on preparing academics and more on preparing professionals in classroom settings, in which teachers get into schools earlier, spend more time there, and get more and better support in the process. These programmes put more emphasis on helping teachers develop skills in diagnosing struggling students early and accurately, and adapting instruction correspondingly. They want prospective teachers to be confident in drawing from a wide repertoire of innovative pedagogies that are experiential, participatory, image-rich and enquiry-based.

In some countries the initial preparation of teachers includes instruction in research skills. Teachers are expected to use those skills as lifelong learners to question the established wisdom of their times and contribute to improved professional practice.

Research is an integral part of what it means to be a professional teacher. In Finland every teacher finishes his or her initial education with a research master's-degree thesis. Because Finland is at the frontier of curriculum design to support creativity and innovation, teachers' work has many of the attractions of the professions that involve research, development and design.

One of the biggest challenges for the future is that we become better at recognising teachers for what they know and can do, rather than how they became a teacher. I have been following the Teach For All movement for some time with great interest. The aspiration of the organisations within the Teach For All network is to enlist promising future leaders from across academic disciplines and careers to teach at least two years in high-needs schools and become lifelong promoters of quality and equity in education.

Soon after becoming a member of its governing board, I went to the Teach First annual conference in London in 2012 to give a talk on "How to transform 10 000 classrooms". I heard many stories of people who had left successful careers to join the teaching force in order to make a significant impact on the lives of disadvantaged children. Still more impressive were the stories told by the young participants who had designed and were delivering intensive teacher-education courses for 400 teachers per year in Nigeria – a country with an essentially non-existent teacher-education infrastructure. A participant from China shared how she was collaborating with local governments to build urgently needed teaching capacity in remote rural areas.

Wendy Kopp, who founded Teach For America more than two decades ago, recounted the evolution of Teach For All, which she co-founded in 2007. What began as a small group of social entrepreneurs from a handful of countries with a shared commitment to equity in education is now a global network of 47 independent partner organisations that are working to develop collective leadership for educating the most vulnerable children. Teach For All's most mature partner, Teach For America, today has an alumni community of more than 50 000 current and former teachers, over 80% of whom continue to work in education or with under-resourced communities. Its more than 6 500 current participants reach nearly 400 000 students across the United States, while its alumni are working to effect lasting change as teachers, school principals, school district leaders, policy makers and social entrepreneurs.

Teach For All's second longest-standing partner, Teach First, currently fields more than 2 500 teachers in the United Kingdom, reaching over 165 000 students. Nearly 70% of Teach First's 7 000 alumni remain working in education, and the organisation has been credited as one of the key players in transforming London's public schools. Across the Teach For All network, organisations are being born and growing in every region of the world. More than 5 000 teachers and 6 000 alumni work outside of the United States and the United Kingdom.

Critics of these organisations maintain that there is just no alternative to the traditional route of undergraduate studies, teacher education and then a career in the classroom, and there is some truth to that. But those critics may simply underestimate the potential for creativity in the field of education that this combination of talent, passion and experience represents.

The fact that these programmes are now so attractive that they can recruit the most promising candidates, even where the general status of the teaching profession is in decline, speaks for itself. These organisations combine good academic outcomes and a support system in which teachers work together to create good practice. They also offer intelligent pathways for teachers to grow in their careers, whether as teachers, or leaders at the school or system level, or even in other areas, such as policy making and social enterprise. What strikes me most is the vision of social transformation behind all this work – from teacher leadership to community organisation. Clearly, Teach for All does not provide an alternative for traditional teacher education; but many of its teachers have become much-needed game-changers and innovators in the teaching profession.

Updating teachers' skills

If we want schools to support more effective learning for students we need to think harder about how to offer more powerful learning opportunities for teachers. But how do good teachers become excellent teachers in a way that is consistent and can be repeated across schools?

Teacher development tends to focus on initial teacher education: the knowledge and skills that teachers acquire before starting work as a teacher. Similarly, most of the resources for teachers' development tend to be allocated to pre-service education. But given the rapid changes in education and the long careers of many teachers, teachers' development must be viewed in terms of lifelong learning, with initial teacher education the foundation for ongoing learning, not the summit of professional development. Think about the challenges teachers face as a result of technological innovations and new media, or those European teachers face as a result of the recent influx of migrants. No initial teacher-education programme could have predicted these challenges decades ago when today's teachers were educated.

Ontario's former premier, Dalton McGuinty, explained to me in 2010 how, rather than wait for a new generation of teachers, he invested in the existing schools and teachers, enlisting their commitment to reform and supporting their improvement. This involved extensive capacity-building in schools, and quarterly meetings between system leaders and teachers' unions, superintendents' organisations, and school leaders' associations to discuss how the reform strategies were developing.

Other countries have also made significant investments in teacher professional development. Teachers in Singapore are entitled to 100 hours of professional development per year to stay up-to-date in their field and to improve their practice. Teacher networks and professional learning communities encourage peer-to-peer learning. The Academy of Singapore Teachers was opened in September 2010 to further encourage teachers to continuously share best practices. The usual complaint that teacher education does not provide sufficient opportunity for recruits to experience real students in real classrooms in their initial education isn't unknown in Singapore. It is difficult, disruptive and expensive to get an annual cohort of 2 000 teacher recruits into classrooms.

So what can be done? Do you follow the example of the United States and some parts of Europe where teacher education is shaped by myriad decisions made by local authorities who have no idea how their choices are affecting the overall national quality of the teaching profession? Or do you follow the elite universities that offer teacher-education places to a small, select group, while national standards are sinking all around them? Singapore has been experimenting with very different approaches. On top of school teaching-practice attachments of between 10 to 22 weeks, its National Institute for Education uses digital technology to bring classrooms into pre-service education, with real-time access to a selection of the country's classrooms. The Institute also carries out an impressive range of classroom-based research to help teachers personalise learning experiences, deal with increasing diversity in their classrooms and differences in learning styles, and keep up with innovations in curricula, pedagogy and digital resources.

In Shanghai, each teacher is expected to engage in 240 hours of professional development within five years. Shanghai is no exception in China. I hold a guest professorship at Beijing Normal University, China's premier teacher education institution. Every time I give a lecture there, I am deeply impressed by teachers' professionalism and dedication to continued improvement, and how keenly they are interested in the teaching practices used in other countries.

Effective professional development needs to be continuous and include education, practice and feedback, and provide adequate time for follow-up. Successful programmes involve teachers in learning activities that are similar to those they will use with their students.

But the key is often not just a large amount of class-taking by serving teachers; it is the underlying career structures and how they inter-relate with the time teachers work together in a form of social organisation that both requires and provides new knowledge and skills that make the difference. Successful programmes encourage the development of teachers' learning communities through which teachers can share their expertise and experiences. There is growing interest in ways to build cumulative knowledge across the profession, for example by strengthening connections between research and practice, and encouraging schools to develop as learning organisations.

David Hung, at Singapore's National Institute for Education, found changing teachers' beliefs to be the most important point of leverage for change in education.[25] He describes the challenge as a shift in instruction from knowledge transmission to knowledge co-creation, from receiving abstractions in textbooks to learning by experimenting, from summative evaluation to formative monitoring. This often requires transforming a fear of failure into a willingness to try. Teachers with a very high or very low sense of self-efficacy may be less likely to use the new skills they have learned, while those with moderate confidence in their own ability might be the most likely to do so. Self-efficacy, in turn, is related to the ways in which work is organised: the more teachers observe other classrooms, engage in collaborative professional development, and teach jointly, the more they perceive themselves as being effective teachers (**FIGURE 3.3**).[26]

And yet, surprisingly little is known about the ways in which teachers continue to learn throughout their careers. That was motivation for me to give teachers a voice through the first OECD Teaching and Learning International Survey (TALIS). When first results from this survey came out in 2009,[27] they showed how teachers reported far less participation in the kinds of professional development activities that are usually considered to be the most effective. The subsequent TALIS survey in 2013 [28] also showed that, across countries, teachers frequently co-ordinate and engage in informal exchanges, while the kinds of professional development activities that are most closely related to teachers' efficacy, such as classroom observations and lesson study, or team teaching, still occurs much more rarely (**FIGURES 3.3** and **3.4**).

The evidence from TALIS suggests that professional development activities that have an impact on teachers' instructional practices are those that take place in schools and allow teachers to work in collaborative groups. Teachers who work with a high degree of professional autonomy and in a collaborative culture – characterised by high levels of both co-operation and instructional leadership – reported both that they participate more in in-school professional development activities and that those activities have a greater impact on their teaching.[29]

Turning this into practice is not easy. There is often a tension between bottom-up, teacher-led collaboration and guided, systemic improvement processes. In many schools teachers appreciate opportunities to work together, but they don't maximise this time. On the other hand, attempting to overly steer the direction of professional collaboration is poorly received by teachers.

Indeed, building a collaborative culture in schools is easier said than done. Andy Hargreaves, Thomas More Brennan Chair in the Lynch School of Education at Boston College, has often drawn attention to the difficulties of building collaborative cultures in schools, and of extending these beyond a few enthusiastic well-led schools and school districts.[30] He argues that the approach adopted by some school systems amounts to "contrived collegiality", that is, collaboration imposed from above that, by crowding the collegial agenda with requirements about what is to be done and with whom, inhibits bottom-up professional initiative and true collaboration.

But policy can do a lot to encourage genuine collaboration by establishing leadership-development strategies that create and sustain learning communities; building indicators of professional collaboration into school-inspection and accreditation processes; linking evidence of commitment to professional learning communities to performance-related pay and measures of teacher competence; and by providing seed money for self-learning in and among schools. Structures and processes that encourage teachers to co-operate, including providing time and opportunities for collective apprenticeships, are needed to foster collective teacher efficacy. Such activities can include teacher-initiated research projects, teacher net works, observation of colleagues, and mentoring or coaching. By supporting the conditions and activities most associated with effective teacher professional development, policy makers can increase the likelihood that students are positively affected too.

In Finland, teachers are encouraged to contribute to research on effective teaching practices throughout their career. The Chinese teacher-education system also emphasises the importance of research, and improvement to the system relies on research conducted by teachers. I have always been impressed by the amount of teacher-led research conducted in China, and by how easy it is for teachers to obtain government grants for such work. The criterion for success is that teachers can show that they can replicate their findings in other schools with other teachers. Zhang Mingxuan, former director of an experimental school in Shanghai and later president of Shanghai's premier teacher-education university, explained to me how schools are given research grants to pilot new programmes or policies and to test their scalability in other schools. The most experienced teachers in those schools are then enlisted as co-researchers to evaluate the effectiveness of the new practices.

But elsewhere in Asia too, countries make the most of their top-performing teachers. The education authorities often identify the best teachers and relieve them of some of their teaching duties so that they can give lectures to their peers, provide demonstrations, and coach other teachers in their district, their province, or even across the country. At the school level, the best teachers typically lead the process of lesson development. Experienced teachers are also called upon to coach novice teachers and to play a key role in analysing why certain students are having difficulties learning.

FIGURE 3.3: INFORMAL EXCHANGE IS MORE COMMON AMONG TEACHERS THAN DEEP PROFESSIONAL COLLABORATION

Percentage of lower secondary teachers who reported doing the following activities at least once per month

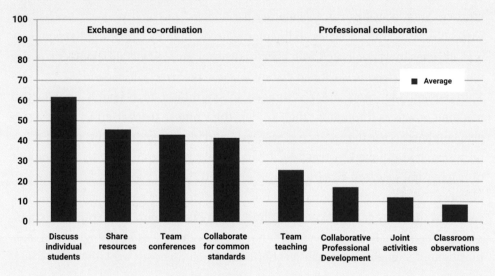

Source: OECD, TALIS 2013 Database, Table 6.15.

FIGURE 3.4: FEELING EFFECTIVE AS A TEACHER IS LINKED TO COLLABORATING WITH COLLEAGUES

INDEX OF TEACHER SELF-EFFICACY (INTERNATIONAL AVERAGE)

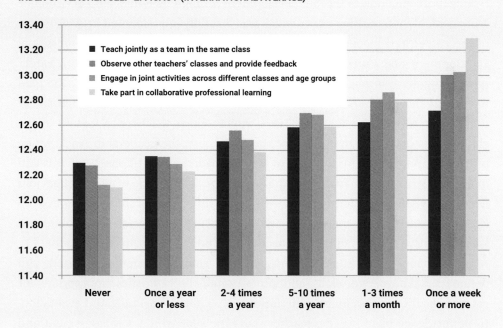

Notes: Teacher self-efficacy by intensity of type of teacher professional collaboration. The more frequently teachers engage in the different types of collaboration, the higher their self-perceived effectiveness.

Source: OECD, TALIS 2013 Database, Table 7.10.

StatLink  *http://dx.doi.org/10.1787/888933042295*

These policies and practices influence the quality of the teaching force itself. For example, the Japanese tradition of lesson study means that Japanese teachers work together to improve the quality of the lessons they teach. Teachers whose practice is inferior to that of teacher leaders can see what good practice is. Because the structure of the profession provides opportunities for teachers to move up a ladder of increasing prestige and responsibility, it also pays for a good teacher to become even better.

Singapore encourages teacher development through its Enhanced Performance Management System. The system, which was first fully implemented in 2005, is part of the career and recognition system under the "Education Service Professional Development and Career Plan". This structure has three components: a career path, recognition through monetary rewards, and an evaluation system. The plan recognises that teachers have different aspirations and provides for three career tracks for teachers: the Teaching Track, which allows teachers to remain in the classroom and advance to the level of Master Teacher; the Leadership Track, which provides opportunities for teachers to assume leadership positions in schools and in the ministry's headquarters; and the Senior Specialist Track, where teachers join the ministry's headquarters to become part of a "strong core of specialists with deep knowledge and skills in specific areas in education that will break new ground and keep Singapore at the leading edge", according to the government of Singapore.

The Enhanced Performance Management System is competency-based, and defines the knowledge, skills and professional characteristics appropriate for each track. The process involves performance planning, coaching and evaluation. In performance planning, the teacher starts the year with a self-assessment and develops goals for teaching, instructional innovations and improvements at the school, and for professional and personal development. The teacher meets with his or her reporting officer, who is usually the head of a department, for a discussion about setting targets and performance benchmarks. Performance coaching takes place throughout the year, particularly during the formal mid-year review, when the reporting officer meets with the teacher to discuss progress and needs.

In the performance evaluation held at the end of the year, the reporting officer conducts the appraisal interview and reviews actual performance against planned performance. The grade given for performance influences the annual performance bonus received for the year's work. During the performance-evaluation phase, decisions regarding promotions to the next level are made based on "current estimated potential". The decision about a teacher's potential is made in consultation with senior staff who have worked with the teacher. It is based on observations, discussions with the teacher, portfolio evidence and the teacher's contribution to the school and community.

This, too, is an area where international exchanges can greatly enrich policy and practice. In 2014, England's then Under Secretary of State for Education and Childcare, Liz Truss, a former mathematics teacher, was inspired by Shanghai's high performance in the PISA mathematics assessment. She went to visit Shanghai and was impressed by the mathematics teaching that she observed and the teacher-to-teacher and school-to-school programmes in the province. She worked with the Chinese to create an exchange programme for teachers between China and England.[31] As part of the government's "maths hubs", a national network of mathematics centres of excellence, the initiative was designed to spread best teaching practice and raise standards in mathematics.

The initiative was met with some scepticism at first. I saw that first-hand when the BBC interviewed me and a leader of the National Union of Teachers when the programme was launched. The union representative raised the usual question of whether what works in one country and culture could be transposed to another context. I countered that the Chinese had spent a thousand years refining methods for teaching mathematics, and asked whether there was nothing that England could learn from their experience. He seemed unconvinced.

Shortly afterwards, the programme took off. Some 50 English-speaking mathematics teachers from China were deployed to more than 30 maths hubs in England. They showed the teaching methods they use, including teaching to the top and helping struggling students one-on-one. They gave daily mathematics lessons, homework and feedback. The Chinese teachers were also running masterclasses for local schools and provided subject-specific, on-the-job teacher education. In turn, leading English mathematics teachers from each of the maths hubs went to work in schools in China. The programme attracted considerable attention in both countries, showing how much teachers can and want to learn from other cultures if they are given the opportunities to do so, and if we dare to pull down ideological walls.[32]

Seeing teachers as independent and responsible professionals

The concept of "professionalism" historically referred to the level of autonomy and internal regulation exercised by members of an occupation. In 18th- and 19th-century Europe, the distinction between occupations and professions lay in the level to which a profession required special knowledge, a formal code of conduct and a state-issued mandate to carry out particular services. Over time, the classic definition of the professions was expanded, and university professors and upper secondary teachers were recognised as experts in education.

In the 20th century, the professionalism of teaching was countered by the growing standardisation of curricula and, with it, the emergence of an industrial work organisation. The expansion of education opportunities around the world during the past 100 years led not only to an increase in the number of teachers but also to more structured and scripted curricula and lesson plans.

At the turn of the 21st century, however, there was renewed focus on teacher professionalism as key to education reform. As improving teacher quality became viewed as the key to student achievement, teacher professionalism gained prominence. Indeed, a strong and coherent body of professional knowledge that is owned by the teaching profession, and to which teachers feel responsible and accountable, together with teachers' continuous professional development, are now widely seen as essential for improving teachers' performance and effectiveness. Teacher professionalism varies significantly across countries (**FIGURE 3.5**), and this variation often reflects cultural and historical differences, as well as disparities in national and local policy priorities.

In some countries, educators consider teaching to be entirely in the purview of the individual teacher in the sanctuary of his or her classroom; but that often leads to a profession without an accepted practice. The challenge is moving from a system where every teacher chooses his or her own approach towards one where teachers choose from practices agreed by the profession as effective. We should not take freedom as an argument to be idiosyncratic. What seems most important in this context is that professionalism and professional autonomy do not mean that

FIGURE 3.5: TEACHER PROFESSIONALISM, AND ITS COMPONENTS, VARY CONSIDERABLY AROUND THE WORLD

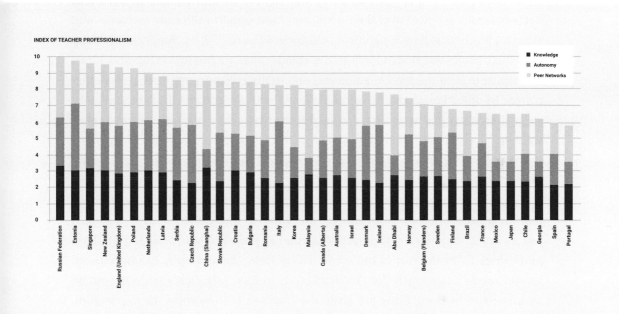

Notes: Knowledge is defined as expertise that is necessary for teaching; the index includes: formal teacher education, and whether the teacher has incentives for professional development (e.g. can participate in activities during professional hours) and participates in professional development. Autonomy is defined as teachers' decision-making power over aspects related to their work; the index includes decision making over: teaching content, course offerings, discipline practices, assessment and materials. Peer networks are defined as opportunities for the exchange of information and support needed to maintain high standards of teaching; the index includes: participation in induction, mentoring programmes and/or network of teachers, receiving feedback from direct observations.

Source: OECD (2016), Supporting Teacher Professionalism: Insights from TALIS 2013.

teachers do what they think or feel is right in a given situation, but rather that they do what they know is right based on their deep understanding of professional practice.

As data from TALIS show, when rated on their professional knowledge base, their decision-making power over their work, and their opportunities for exchange and support, teachers still have significant challenges ahead of them. Rarely do teachers own their professional standards to the extent other professionals do, and rarely do they work with the level of autonomy and in the collaborative work culture that people in other knowledge-based professions take for granted. But the data also show that when teachers teach a class jointly, when they regularly observe other teachers' classes, and when they take part in collaborative professional learning, they are more satisfied with their careers and feel more effective in their teaching (*FIGURE 3.4*).

It is instructive to turn to the high-performing education systems to see what teacher professionalism looks like on the ground. Interestingly, there is almost just as much variation in approaches to teacher professionalism among the high performers as in the rest of the world. Hong Kong, for example, has introduced greater teacher autonomy than its neighbours in East Asia. School administrators and teachers in Hong Kong are given the freedom to customise the curriculum, materials and teaching methods. This breadth and depth of autonomy has fostered high professional self-esteem among teachers and internal motivation for continuous professional development. The government does not intervene in school management even for low-performing schools; it relies instead on the decision-making power of the school administration and teachers.

By contrast, in Shanghai the municipal government designs the policies, manages the schools and works to improve instruction. Teachers in Shanghai are comprehensively and rigorously educated in pre-service programmes and subsequent regular professional-development activities. They are expected to adhere to the standards and curricular approaches defined by the government, and generally have a narrower space for interpreting curricular objectives.

High-quality teachers and school leaders form the cornerstone of Singapore's education system and are considered a major reason for its high performance. Singapore has developed a comprehensive system for selecting, educating, compensating and developing teachers and principals, thereby creating strong capacity on the frontlines of education. Much professional development is school-based, led by staff developers who identify teaching-based problems or introduce new practices. This gives teachers greater autonomy over professional development and facilitates a teacher-led culture of professional excellence. Australia, Canada, Finland and the Netherlands pursue similar strategies and are also known for the latitude they give to their teachers to customise their teaching.

These differences in the degree of autonomy that teachers are granted suggest that the impact of that autonomy depends on the context. In countries in which teacher education and selection procedures produce a well-prepared and independent teaching workforce, autonomy will allow creativity and innovation to flourish; in other cases, autonomy may simply amplify poor judgement and wrong decisions.

The cases of Finland and Ontario provide examples of how formerly centralised systems have shifted emphasis towards improving the act of teaching; towards giving careful attention to implementation, along with opportunities for teachers to practice new ideas and learn from their colleagues; towards developing an integrated strategy and set of expectations for both teachers and students; and towards securing support from teachers for reform.

Other countries, too, have rebalanced their systems to provide more discretion to school heads and school faculties – a factor that, when combined with a culture of collaboration and accountability, seems to be closely related to school performance.[33]

In some countries, great discretion is given to the faculty, as a whole, and its individual members; in others, more discretion is given to schools that are doing well and less to those that might be struggling. In some countries, the school head is little more than the lead teacher; in others, the authorities continue to look to the school head to set the direction and manage the faculty. But common to all is the degree to which these countries are moving away from bureaucratic management of schools to forms of work organisation that are more likely to be found in professional partnerships.

In many cases, these countries concluded that top-down initiatives were insufficient to achieve deep and lasting changes in practice, because reforms were focused on things that were too distant from the instructional core of teaching and learning; because reforms assumed that teachers would know how to do things they actually didn't know how to do; because too many conflicting reforms asked teachers to do too many things simultaneously; or because teachers and schools did not buy into the reform strategy. Therefore, public policy was focused on creating strong social institutions that connect deeply with society, as opposed to assuming that government can directly interact with schools, teachers and other stakeholders.

At one end of the spectrum, the Estonian and Finnish systems of accountability are entirely built from the bottom up. Teacher candidates are selected, in part, based on their capacity to convey their belief in the core mission of public education. The preparation they receive is designed to build a sense of individual responsibility for the learning and well-being of all the students in their care. The next level of accountability rests with the school. Again, the level of trust that the larger community extends to its schools seems to engender a strong sense of collective responsibility for the success of every student. While every comprehensive school in Finland reports to a municipal authority, authorities vary widely in the quality and degree of oversight that they provide. They are responsible for hiring the principal, typically on a six- or seven-year contract, but the day-to-day responsibility for managing the schools is left to the teachers and other education professionals, as is the responsibility for assuring students' progress.

Making the most of teachers' time

One of the most striking findings in the PISA 2015 assessment is the weak link between the ratio of students to staff in the education system and the size of classes in schools (**FIGURE 3.6**). It seems intuitive that having more teachers per student will translate into smaller classes, but that is far from evident in the data. For 15-year-old students, Brazil and Japan both have an average class size of around 37 students, but Brazil has one teacher for every 29 students while Japan has one teacher for every 11 students. Conversely, in the United States and Viet Nam, there are around 15 students per teacher, but classes in Viet Nam are almost twice as large as those in the United States.

What might look like a statistical fluke has a lot to do with education policy. While teachers in Brazil and the United States have little time for things other than

FIGURE 3.6: SIMILAR STUDENT-TEACHER RATIOS CAN BE FOUND IN CLASSES OF VERY DIFFERENT SIZES

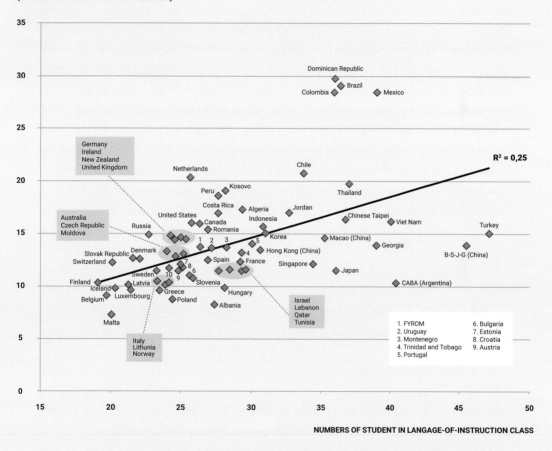

Notes: FYROM refers to the Former Yugoslav Republic of Macedonia. CABA (Argentina) refers to Ciudad Autónoma de Buenos Aires (Argentina). B-S-J-G (China) refers to Beijing-Shanghai-Jiangsu-Guangdong (China).

Source: OECD, PISA 2015 Database, Table II.6.26.

StatLink ᘓᘙ㎐ http://dx.doi.org/10.1787/888933436320

teaching, their peers in Japan and Viet Nam have a fraction of their teaching load and can devote plenty of time to other things besides teaching, such as working with individual students, with parents and, most important, with other teachers.

One might still think that large classes leave teachers little room for dedicating sufficient time to the needs of individual students; but the level of teacher support that students reported in PISA does not seem to correlate with class size.[34] Indeed, I have observed many classes in Japan where there was little lecturing by teachers, but where teachers developed a class discussion that focused on conceptual understanding and the underlying concepts involved in problem solving, in a way that reached both the quickest and the slowest students in the class. In this way, Japanese teachers maximise their contact time with each student in the class. Students are not whiling away their time when the teacher is dealing with a small group in the classroom. In fact, a Japanese teacher in Fukushima once complained to me that classes were becoming too small to show a wide enough range of student solutions to a given problem – the basis for conducting a good lesson.

The Finnish education system pursues similar goals but with different strategies. Finnish schools devote about a third of instruction time to learning outside the classroom, thus giving teachers ample opportunity to tackle underperformance and nurture talent. In Finland, special-needs education is not synonymous with teaching students with learning difficulties. Rather, virtually every student will become a special-needs student at some point in his or her education, simply because the school has recognised that it can do more for him or her outside classroom instruction.

Inside the classroom, there is a considerable emphasis on self-regulated learning and self-assessment by students. By the time students enrol in upper secondary school, they are expected to be able to design their own programme in which, without a grade structure, each student proceeds at his or her own pace.

In Shanghai, the enquiry-based curriculum component asks students to identify research topics based on their experiences, with support and guidance from teachers. The aim is to develop students' capacity to learn to learn, think creatively and critically, participate in society and promote social welfare. In fact, one significant change implemented in Shanghai through the slogan "return class time to students" was the increase in student activities in class relative to teachers' lecturing.[35] This has resulted in a fundamental change in the perception of what makes a good class, which was once typified by well designed presentations by teachers. Training videos showing examples of good teaching used to concentrate on teachers' activities; now, model classes are filmed with multiple cameras, one recording student activities. Teachers are evaluated according to the time given to student participation and how well student activities are organised.

In places as different as Finland, Japan and Shanghai, teachers' work is reviewed by the other teachers in the school. No teacher's classroom is a private domain.

A lesson in creative learning time from Hiroshima

As school principal Kadoshima drove by an office tower on our way to his school in Hiroshima, he explained to me that this had been the place where his grandmother and two uncles had been burned alive like most other residents 69 years earlier. All that had been left, he said, was a shadow on the floor.

But on this day in 2014, a group of students was out on Hiroshima Nagisa High School's playing field. What looked like casual play was actually part of a carefully planned and sequenced curriculum designed to help students develop their five senses, their own identity, and their ability to work with others.

In classroom after classroom I observed lots of lively interaction both among students and between students and their teachers. I found Rudyard Brettargh from Australia and Olen Peterson from the United States co-teaching an English class, showing students that there is not just one, but many ways to speak a language.

Many of the school's pedagogical approaches involved experiences in addition to intellectual engagement. In one classroom I met a group of students cooking *okonomiyaki*, Hiroshima's most popular local dish. Each student was preparing the dish his or her own way – and learning from the mistakes they made as they went along.

Principal Kadoshima showed me pictures from the many field trips his students had taken to other countries, or to businesses and other places in Japan. During these trips, students learned about the global economic, social and political forces that were shaping their lives. One picture showed a group of exhausted students lying on a bridge at dawn. They had walked 44 kilometres through the night, Kadoshima explained. The aim of that exercise was to strengthen their resilience, with the understanding that living in the world means trying, failing, adapting, learning and evolving.

Aligning incentives for teachers, students and parents

To understand why people do the things they do, ask yourself what sort of incentives they have to act that way. Examining whether the incentives that operate on students, parents and teachers in some countries are more likely to result in higher performance than the incentives that operate in other countries can provide important insights into why some countries rank higher on the education league tables than others.

In countries with high-stakes examination systems, systems in which students cannot progress to the next stage of their life – be it work or further education – unless they show that they are qualified to do so, students know what they have to do to realise their dreams, and they put in the required work. In other words, examination systems provide strong incentives for students to study hard. And as the PISA outcomes from countries like Estonia, Finland, the Netherlands and Switzerland show, studying hard and doing well in school does not automatically detract from a strong sense of belonging at school and a high degree of student well-being.

What kinds of incentives do teachers have to work hard? In repetitive, inflexible, industrial work environments, management rewards those whose output exceeds expectations. In those environments, workers compete against one another. Those who resent the co-worker who outperforms them are eventually likely to treat that co-worker as an outcast. But in professional work environments, the success of the whole group depends on maximising the output of each worker, so workers tend to collaborate.

In schools, the environment is also shaped by the influence of parents. In many countries in both Europe and Asia, certain teachers are designated as classroom teachers. These teachers follow students through a number of grades. They assume a certain responsibility for the students in their class and form a close relationship not only with students but also with parents. In both Asia and Europe, it is typical that information between teachers and parents is shared through social networks. Not only is this a good way to get parents involved but, perhaps even more important, it is a way to provide accountability to parents in a form that seems appropriate to teachers.

Parents in these systems tend to feel a strong bond with their children's classroom teachers. In a series of focus groups conducted in Denmark by the National Center on Education and the Economy, parents were asked what happens when their child is assigned a less-competent classroom teacher. Is that a problem? Parents said that the advantages of the classroom-teacher system far outweigh any disadvantages.

There is another, more subtle, advantage of this system. A teacher who teaches a given student for only one year might feel that, while they will do the best they can with the students to whom they have been assigned, there is little they can do in one year to correct the problems students have inherited from teachers in earlier grades, and little they can do to protect students from teachers in succeeding grades who might be less competent.

But in the classroom-teacher system, the teacher in the earlier grade is the teacher in question, as is the teacher who comes later. In this system, there is no way for the classroom teacher to evade personal responsibility for what happens to the student. As a matter of professional pride, and as a result of being close to the student for years and developing a sense of personal responsibility for the student, it is natural for the teacher to reach out to the student's parents. It is also common for these teachers to co-ordinate the education of their students with those students' specialist teachers, and counsel and guide their students as they grow up.

Focusing on students' well-being

PISA is best known for its data on learning outcomes, but in 2015 we also studied students' satisfaction with life, their relationships with peers, teachers and parents, and how they spend their time outside of school.[36] The results show that students differ greatly, both between and within countries, in how satisfied they are with their lives, their motivation to achieve, how anxious they feel about their schoolwork, their expectations for the future, and their perceptions of being bullied at school or treated unfairly by their teachers. Students in some of the countries that top the PISA league tables in science and mathematics reported comparatively low satisfaction with life; but Estonia, Finland, the Netherlands and Switzerland seem able to combine good learning outcomes with high student satisfaction with life. It is tempting to regard low levels of life satisfaction among students in East Asia or elsewhere as the consequence of long study hours, but the data show no relationship between the time students spend studying, whether in or outside of school, and their satisfaction with life. And while educators often argue that anxiety is the natural response to testing overload, the frequency of tests is also unrelated to students' level of schoolwork-related anxiety.

But there are other factors that affect students' well-being, and many of them are related to teachers, parents and schools.

For a start, PISA finds that one major threat to students' sense of belonging at school is their perception of having negative relationships with their teachers. Happier students tended to report positive relations with their teachers, and students in "happy" schools (schools where students' life satisfaction is above the average in the country) reported receiving much more support from their teachers than students in "unhappy" schools reported.

On average across countries, students who reported that their teacher is willing to provide help and is interested in their learning were also about 1.3 times more likely than students who reported the contrary to feel that they belong at school. Conversely, students who reported some unfair treatment by their teachers were 1.7 times more likely to report feeling isolated at school. This is important. Teenagers forge strong social ties; they value acceptance, care and support from others. Adolescents who feel that they are part of a school community are more likely to perform better academically and be more motivated in school.

There are also big differences between countries on these measures. On average, three out of four students reported that they feel they belong at school; in some of the highest-performing education systems, including Estonia, Finland, Japan, the Netherlands, Singapore, South Korea, Chinese Taipei and Viet Nam, the proportion is even larger. But in France, only around two in five students so reported.

Of course, most teachers care about having positive relationships with their students; but some teachers might be insufficiently prepared to deal with difficult students and classroom environments. Effective classroom management consists of far more than establishing and imposing rules, rewards and incentives to control behaviour; it requires the ability to create a learning environment that facilitates and supports students' active engagement in learning, encourages co-operation, and promotes behaviour that benefits other people. A stronger focus on classroom and relationship management in professional-development programmes may give teachers the tools they need to connect better with their students. Teachers should also be given the time to share information about students' strengths and weaknesses with their colleagues, so that, together, they can find the best approach to make students feel part of the school community.

While it is not the frequency of testing that affects students' well-being, students' perception of tests as threatening has a clear influence on how anxious students feel about tests. On average across OECD countries, 59% of students reported that they often worry that taking a test will be difficult, and 66% reported that they worry about poor grades. Some 55% of students reported that they are very anxious when they are tested, even if they are well prepared.

Again, results from PISA suggest that there is a lot teachers can do about this. Even after accounting for students' performance, gender and socio-economic status, students who reported that their teacher adapts the lesson to the class's needs and knowledge were less likely to report feeling anxious when they are well prepared for a test, or to report that they get very tense when they study. Students were also less likely to report anxiety if their teacher (in this case, their science teacher) provides individual help when they are struggling.

By contrast, negative teacher-student relations seem to undermine students' confidence and lead to greater anxiety. On average across countries, students were about 62% more likely to report that they get very tense when they study, and about 31% more likely to report that they feel anxious before a test if they perceive that their teacher thinks they are less smart than they really are. Such anxiety might be students' reaction to, and interpretation of, the mistakes they make – or are afraid to make. Students might internalise mistakes as evidence that they are not smart enough.

So teachers need to know how to help students develop a good understanding of their strengths and weaknesses, and an awareness of what they can do to overcome or mitigate their weaknesses. For example, more frequent assessments that start with easier goals and gradually increase in difficulty can help build students' sense of control, as can opportunities for students to demonstrate their skills in low-stakes tests before taking an assessment that counts. Interestingly, in all countries, girls reported greater schoolwork-related anxiety than boys, and anxiety about schoolwork, homework and tests is negatively related to performance. The fear of making mistakes on a test often undermines the performance of top-performing girls who "choke under pressure".

Parents have a vital role to play too. Students whose parents reported "spending time just talking to my child", "eating the main meal with my child around a table" or "discussing how well my child is doing at school" daily or nearly every day were between 22% and 39% more likely to report high levels of life satisfaction. "Spending time just talking" is the parental activity most frequently and most strongly associated with students' satisfaction with life. And it seems to matter for performance too. Students whose parents reported "spending time just talking" were the equivalent of two-thirds of a school-year ahead in science performance. Even after accounting for socio-economic status, these students were still one-third of a school year ahead. The results are similar when considering parents who reported that they eat meals with their children. This relationship is far stronger than the impact on students' performance of most of the school resources and school factors measured by PISA.

Parents can also help children manage test anxiety by encouraging them to trust in their ability to accomplish various academic tasks. PISA results show that, even after accounting for differences in performance and socio-economic status, girls who perceive that their parents encourage them to be confident in their abilities were 21% less likely to report that they feel tense when they study, on average across OECD countries.

Most parents also want their children to be motivated at school, and motivated students tend to do better. PISA finds that students who are among the most motivated score the equivalent of more than one school year ahead of the least-motivated students, on average. Achievement motivation is also related to life satisfaction in a mutually reinforcing way. Students who are highly satisfied with their life tend to have greater resiliency and are more tenacious in the face of academic challenges. A greater motivation to achieve, paired with realised goals, might give students a sense of purpose in life. That might be why students with greater motivation to achieve reported higher satisfaction with life.

But there can also be downsides to achievement motivation, particularly when this motivation is a response to external pressure. PISA results show that countries where students are highly motivated to achieve also tend to be those where many students feel anxious about tests, even if they are well prepared for them. Both teachers and parents need to find ways to encourage students' motivation to learn and achieve without generating an excessive fear of failure.

All in all, a clear way to promote students' well-being is to encourage all parents to be more aware of their children's interests and concerns, and show interest in their school life, including in the challenges children face at school. Schools can create an environment of co-operation with parents and communities. Teachers can be given better tools to enlist parents' support, and schools can address some critical deficiencies among disadvantaged children, such as the lack of a quiet space for studying. If parents and teachers establish relationships based on trust, schools can rely on parents as valuable partners in the education of their students.

Developing capable education leaders

In September 2003, I had a visit from Johan van Bruggen, who was leading the Standing International Conference of Inspectorates.[37] I was impressed with the importance he attached to effective school and system leadership and the elaborate techniques school inspectorates had developed to observe and characterise effective leadership. He made the point that poor leadership can undercut even the best teacher. Put a great teacher in a poorly managed school and the school will "win" every time. Too often teachers – and their students – are the victims of dysfunctional schools, not their creators.

OECD's comparative review of school leadership identifies four groups of inter-related leadership responsibilities as central to improving learning outcomes:[38]

- Supporting, evaluating and developing teacher quality. This includes recruiting high-quality teachers; providing a strong induction programme for new teachers; making sure teachers have the skills and knowledge needed to teach the curriculum; organising and supporting teachers to work together to improve the quality of teaching and instruction; monitoring and evaluating teacher practice; promoting teacher professional development; and supporting truly collaborative work cultures. If you want to effect real and lasting change, don't ask yourself how many teachers support your ideas, but how many teachers are capable of and engage in co-operation with their colleagues.

- Establishing learning objectives and assessments to help students reach high standards. This involves aligning instruction with central standards, setting school goals for student performance, measuring progress against those goals, and making adjustments in the school programme to improve individual and overall performance. School leaders also need to be able to use data to ensure that the progress of every student is charted. They need to be confident when engaging with those who have different approaches to learning.

- Using resources strategically and aligning them with pedagogy.

- Building partnerships beyond the school to foster greater cohesion among all those concerned with the achievement and well-being of every child. This requires finding innovative ways to enhance partnerships with families and communities, higher education, businesses, and especially with other schools and learning environments.

As our analysis of TALIS results show, there also seems to be a link between teachers' ability to improve their own working practice and their development as leaders.[39] When teachers can take the lead in initiating improvement and innovation in their schools, they feel more competent and confident – and both their professional status and their morale get a boost.

Good leadership is, of course, required at every level of the education system (see Chapter 6). This is becoming increasingly important for many reasons. In many countries, greater devolution is being coupled with more school autonomy, more accountability for school and student results, better use of the knowledge base of education and pedagogical processes, and broader responsibility for supporting the local communities in which schools are located, other schools and other public services.[40]

Michael Fullan, the architect of Ontario's widely known education-reform strategy, describes how the best leaders of education systems engage others and distribute leadership throughout the system.[41] As he notes, these leaders can identify emerging trends and issues that may be important to their teachers and schools. They have an inclusive style that encourages collaboration and provides the space for staff to take risks. They are strategic planners and entrepreneurial, in the sense that they can mobilise the people and money needed for innovation, and they attract talented staff. They build strong linkages across sectors and countries, engaging government leaders, social entrepreneurs, business executives, researchers and civil society leaders as partners in innovation for education and training.

Finding the right level of school autonomy

Many countries have shifted their focus on education towards results. At the same time, they have devolved more responsibility to schools, encouraging them to be more responsive to local needs (*FIGURE 3.7*). Many schools have been granted greater autonomy so that principals, school boards and teachers can assume more responsibility for policies related to resources, the curriculum, assessments, school admissions and discipline.

The data from PISA suggest that, once the state has set clear expectations for students, school autonomy in defining the details of the curriculum and assessments is positively related to the system's overall performance. For example, school systems that provide their schools with greater discretion in student assessments, the courses offered, the course content and the textbooks used, tend to be the school systems that perform at higher levels on PISA, whatever the causal nature of that relationship.[42]

Another argument in favour of autonomy in an education system is that it can create stronger incentives for innovation. Successful schools will be places where people want to work, and where they find that they can realise good ideas. By

FIGURE 3.7: AUTONOMY IN DECISION MAKING IS ASSOCIATED WITH SCHOOL CHARACTERISTICS AND STUDENT PERFORMANCE

Results based on school principals' reports

Notes: The index of school autonomy is calculated as the percentage of tasks for which the principal, teachers or the school governing board has considerable responsibility. Socio-economic status is measured by the PISA index of economic, social and cultural status. FYROM refers to the Former Yugoslav Republic of Macedonia. CABA (Argentina) refers to Ciudad Autónoma de Buenos Aires (Argentina). B-S-J-G (China) refers to Beijing-Shanghai-Jiangsu-Guangdong (China).

Countries and economies are ranked in descending order of the index of school autonomy.

Source: OECD, PISA 2015 Database, Table II.4.5.

StatLink ᐰᔑ⅃ http://dx.doi.org/ 10.1787/888933435854

INDEX OF SCHOOL AUTONOMY (%)

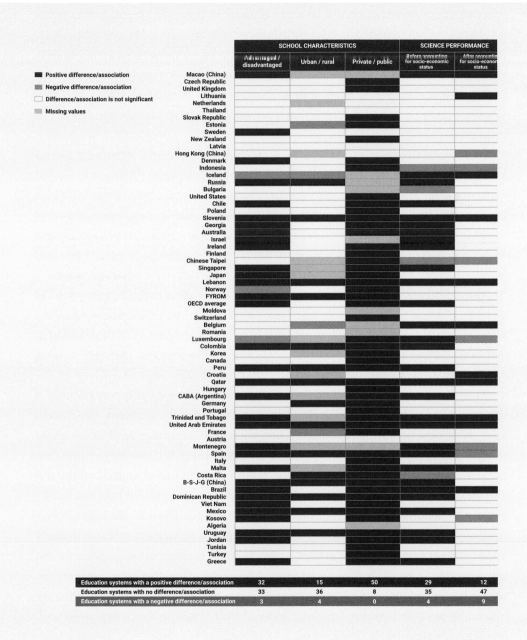

contrast, innovative change can be more difficult in hierarchical and bureaucratic structures that are geared towards rewarding compliance with rules and regulations.

An attempt to measure the innovation in education systems between 2000 and 2011 found that countries with a high degree of school autonomy and decentralisation, such as Denmark and the Netherlands, were at the top of the "composite innovation index", which summarises various measures of innovative change in schools and classroom practices.[43]

A recent OECD study on "Innovative Learning Environments" examined several innovative schools and school networks across OECD countries.[44] While the sample cannot be regarded as representative, the case studies came from a broad range of schools in various education systems. Some were mainstream public schools, others belonged to networks of charter schools of similar environments, still others were private schools, working within or outside public systems. But all flourished because governance and oversight arrangements gave them the freedom to create spaces for experimentation.

The study also underscored the risk of autonomy leading to the "atomisation" of schools. Working with others can spur innovation and sustain the drive to innovate. However, school autonomy will be self-defeating if it is interpreted as functioning in isolation. Instead, autonomy should take the form of freedom and flexibility to work with many partners.

An important yet often underestimated barrier to achieving coherence within a school system is the lack of shared understanding about the problems the system faces. When teachers or parents do not know what problems the government is trying to solve, it is hard to understand the policies that have been designed in response. The tireless efforts of the Ontario government to build a sense of shared understanding and common purpose among stakeholder groups provides an example of how this can be achieved. Ontario's strategy for improving literacy and numeracy skills, for example, was not just about raising reading, writing and mathematics achievement, although it clearly accomplished that goal. It was at least as much about building broad support for the improvement of key skills through an impressive range of initiatives that resulted in a shift in the culture of Ontario schools. Increased awareness of the importance of literacy and numeracy skills led to changes in attitudes and behaviours at the classroom, school, board and ministry levels.[45]

Singapore's "thinking schools – learning nation" reform organised schools into geographic clusters that were given more autonomy, with successful principals appointed as cluster superintendents, to mentor others and promote innovation.[46] Along with greater autonomy came new forms of accountability. The old inspection system was abolished and replaced by a school-excellence model, under which each school sets its own goals and annually assesses its progress towards those goals, including academic performance. Greater autonomy also led to a laser-like focus on identifying and developing highly effective school leaders who can lead school transformation. Schools undergo an external review every six years.

I had always assumed that teachers and schools in the United States, with its tradition of local control, and as the country where I have seen many of the most innovative and inspiring schools, would have more autonomy than teachers and schools in other countries. When I met with American school leaders in July 2009 at the annual conference of the National Association of Secondary School Principals, I was surprised by their reports on how constrained their decision-making ability actually was, at least according to them.

When I studied the PISA results on this, I found that, indeed, American schools tend to get much more direction from the local district office than is the case in many other countries. In that sense, the United States may have traded one form of centralised bureaucracy for another. It is also true that the relatively recent rise of unions in American education, given the American style of union-management relations and the pressure to have contracts mirror those in neighbouring localities, may have produced a more rule-bound environment than is found in systems embracing more professional forms of work organisation. So there, as elsewhere, the devil is in the details.

In fact, some countries provide most of their public schools with a scope for decision making that is similar to that among charter schools in the United States. The academies in England are an example. These are state schools that have been granted autonomy but are still expected to conduct state tests, produce the same public data on their performance, have the same budget resources, be accountable to the public, and admit students as other state schools are expected to do. England's education ministers have viewed academies and their greater independence as the way to tackle underperformance.

But how much is known about the dynamics involved? How would granting greater school autonomy actually lead to better student performance? And if the reform is a one-way street, and academy status means lifetime independence for schools, then some years down the road new policy interventions might not be effective. As schools become more autonomous, how can they avoid becoming more isolated?

The academies show how important it is to combine professional autonomy with a collaborative culture, both among teachers and among schools. The challenge for an academy-style system is to find a way to share knowledge among schools. Knowledge in the field of education is very sticky; it doesn't spread easily. It tends to remain where it is unless there are powerful incentives to share it. That means the leaders of the academies programme and similar initiatives need to think hard about how to shift knowledge around pockets of innovation, and how to attract the most talented teachers to the most challenging classrooms, and get the strongest principals into the toughest academies.

It is certainly not impossible. Schools in Denmark, Finland, Japan, Norway, Shanghai and Sweden have a good history of autonomy, teamwork and co-operation. They build networks and share resources and ideas to create new and innovative practice. But this collaborative culture does not happen by accident; it needs to be carefully crafted by policy and practice. In some Finnish municipalities, for example, school leaders also work as district leaders, with one-third of their time devoted to the district and two-thirds to their own schools. In this way they promote a common vision of schooling between schools and municipalities.

For school leaders to take on this larger system-level role, leadership is shared, with leadership teams assuming some of the school leaders' tasks. The result is that school leaders regularly meet with their peers. They no longer work under a local school administration, they *are* the local school administration. The district office is not filled with administrators, but with people who know what is involved in running a school. Or take Shanghai. If you are a vice principal of a great school in Shanghai and you want to become a principal, you can be – but only after showing that you can turn around one of the system's lowest-performing schools.

A characteristic of the English school system is that all schools are subjected to a stringent inspection regime. It is, in my view, one of the most effective in the world.

To be judged as outstanding in leadership, schools have to show they are helping improve education beyond their own walls.

But more than that might be needed. PISA data show that in school systems where knowledge is shared among teachers, autonomy is a positive advantage; but in school systems without a culture of peer learning and accountability, autonomy might actually adversely affect student performance. There needs to be enough knowledge mobilisation and sharing, and checks and balances to make sure that academies are using their independence effectively – and wisely.

Nonetheless, the reform holds significant promise for improving school systems. If autonomy can be combined with a culture of collaboration, not only will schools benefit, but individual teachers will too.

Moving from administrative to professional accountability

To reconcile school autonomy with overall coherence in the school system, there must be ways to see clearly how schools are providing education and the learning outcomes they are producing. Assessment and accountability allow educators and policy makers to keep their finger on the pulse of progress in education. Most high-performing education systems have an accountability system of some sort. Some systems publish data on the performance of schools, although that is far from common among high-performing education systems. In systems that allow parents to choose the school their child attends, comparative data can influence their decisions. In some systems these data are also used by school administrators to allocate resources, often to provide additional resources to struggling schools.

But approaches to accountability evolve as school systems themselves evolve – as rules become guidelines and good practice, and ultimately, as good practice becomes culture. Often this progression involves a shift in the balance between "administrative accountability" and "professional accountability".

"Administrative accountability" typically uses data to identify good teachers and good schools, and to intervene in underperforming schools. Among the features of administrative accountability are often test-based accountability systems that use data on student performance to make decisions about which teachers and school principals to hire, promote and retain, and to decide on compensation for individual teachers.

By contrast, "professional accountability" refers to systems in which teachers are accountable not so much to administrative authorities but primarily to their fellow teachers and school principals. Professionals in most fields feel themselves accountable to other members of their profession. In the case of education, professional accountability also includes the kind of personal responsibility that teachers feel towards their peers, their students and their students' parents.

Jurisdictions such as Ontario in Canada, Finland, Japan and New Zealand that place greater emphasis on the more professional forms of work organisation tend to pursue more collegial forms of teacher and school-leader accountability. The aim is to ensure that reform is a collaborative endeavour, not something imposed from above. They would argue that people who expect to be treated as professionals and think of themselves that way are more likely to respond to professional and informal modes of accountability, and would resent the use of more administrative forms of accountability that they associate with industrial work environments.

The experience of Ontario shows how partnerships among the government, schools and teachers can be created to identify good practices, consolidate them, and use them more widely. Rather than mandating reform, in Ontario seed money was put into schools to encourage local experimentation and innovation, sending a strong signal that teacher-generated solutions to students' problems with reading and mathematics were likely to be more successful than solutions imposed from above. The dramatic reduction in the number of low-performing schools in the province was not achieved by threatening to close those schools, but by flooding them with technical assistance and support. The underlying assumption was that teachers are professionals who are trying to do the right thing, and that any inadequacies in teachers' performance are much more likely to stem from a lack of knowledge than from a lack of motivation.

At the same time, the Ontario government made no attempt to dismantle or weaken the assessment regime put in place by the previous government. The government consistently communicated the message to schools and to the public that results, as defined by performance on provincial assessments, matter.

In Singapore, administrative and professional accountability are combined Teachers, principals, ministry staff and students all have strong incentives to work hard. The government sets annual goals, provides support to achieve them, and then assesses whether or not they have been achieved. Data on student performance are included, but so, too, are a range of other measures, such as teachers' contributions to the school and community, and judgements by a number of senior practitioners. Reward and recognition systems include honours and salary bonuses. Individual appraisals are conducted within the context of school-excellence plans.

▪ The importance of trust

Some argue that it is not possible to derive any real lessons from Finland because of the trust-based culture of the Finnish school system. That kind of culture does not travel easily, they would argue. But in the relationship between teachers and the wider society, one could also argue that trust is at least as much a consequence of policy decisions as it is a precondition.

Given the respect that teachers have historically enjoyed in Finland, there was a solid base on which to build reforms. Finnish leaders empower their teachers by trusting them, and in doing so they create a virtuous circle of productivity and innovative learning environments. In turn, the high level of policy coherence, meaning that decisions will be followed through across electoral cycles and political administrations, leads to Finnish teachers' trust in their education leaders: they trust their leaders' integrity and count on their capacity to do what they say.

This is not blind trust. In fact, the pressure of professional accountability in Finland is high. The fact that just 5% of the variation in student performance in Finland lies between schools[47] shows that the system is capable of intervening when additional support is needed. While some portray Finland as a paradise with no standardised testing, reports from students in the PISA 2015 assessment prove that image wrong. The frequency with which standardised tests are conducted in Finnish schools is close to the OECD average.[48] The difference is that tests are not used to find faults in the system or document underperformance, but to help students learn better, teachers teach better and schools to work more effectively.

Indeed, trust and accountability might be more closely linked than one might think. Clear accountability might be a necessary feature of a high-trust culture: if people don't have a clear understanding of where the goal posts are and what is being measured, then trust is difficult to build. Trust is also a function of specific competence: you trust your mother; but would you trust her to fly a 747? The significant investment Finnish leaders make in the professional development of their teachers is a critical part of the equation. It is the combination of much more rigorous preparation and the devolution of much greater decision-making authority over things like curriculum and assessment that enables teachers in Finland to exercise the kind of autonomy enjoyed by other professionals in other fields – and to command the trust to do so. The granting of trust from the government, coupled with their status as university graduates from highly selective programmes, empower teachers to pursue their profession in ways that deepen the trust accorded them by parents and others in the community.

Who says she's a great teacher?

It is important to be sure that emphasising professional accountability at the frontline does not conflict with establishing a culture of evaluation throughout the system. There are some countries where mentioning the phrase "teacher evaluation" around educators, teachers' union leaders and policy makers prompts heated arguments.[49] Teachers in the United States and France have gone on strike over the issue; England's teachers' unions and those that represent head teachers have found themselves on opposite sides of debates about whether to link teachers' pay to their performance.

Nearly everyone agrees that school systems need to find a way to encourage promising teachers, reward those who have demonstrated their effectiveness, and remove consistently underperforming teachers from the profession. But what makes a teacher great? And who gets to decide? Students? Parents? Fellow teachers? Principals?

In the 23 countries that participated in TALIS in 2013, 83% of teachers who had been appraised and received feedback considered them to be fair assessments of their work; of those, 79% found that the appraisals were helpful in developing their work as teachers.[50] But agreement on how to measure teachers' skills is harder to come by.

Teacher-appraisal systems in most countries are still a work-in-progress – where they exist at all. Some 13% of teachers in countries that participated in TALIS had never received any feedback or appraisal of their work from any source. This is partly because such systems can be costly to design and maintain – not just in terms of money and time, but also in the political capital and courage it takes to establish them. More often, though, it is because there is no consensus on what criteria should be used to measure teacher performance. Should it be students' test scores? A teacher's ability to engage a classroom full of students? The opinions of students and parents? Who should do the measuring: an inspector from a central education authority, the school principal or fellow teachers? And how should the results of an evaluation or appraisal be used? Should it determine salary? Should it shape the trajectory of a career? Should it be a way of signalling professional-development needs? Should it be used to weed out ineffective practitioners?

However, consensus is beginning to take shape around some of these questions. Student test scores offer important information, but they cannot provide a complete picture of teaching quality. A reliance only on test scores will unduly narrow perspectives. Teacher-appraisal systems need to be part of a holistic approach to the profession, including teacher education and professional development, nurturing school leaders, and engaging teachers in reform and in creating attractive working environments.

Like all government employees and many other professionals in Singapore, teachers are appraised annually, by a board, against 13 different competencies. These are not just about academic performance, but include teachers' contributions to the academic and character development of the students in their charge, their collaboration with parents and community groups, and their impact on their colleagues and the school as a whole. It was intriguing for me to see how teachers did not seem to view this as a top-down accountability system, but rather as an instrument for improvement and career development. Teachers who do outstanding work receive a bonus from the school's bonus pool. After three years of teaching, teachers are assessed annually to see which of three career paths would best suit them – master teacher, specialist in curriculum or research, or school leader. Significantly, the individual appraisal system sits within the school's overall plan for excellence in education.

The buck stops...where?

In most high-performing education systems there is a certain level of authority at which the buck stops – some agency or group of agencies that is responsible for the effectiveness and efficiency of the whole system. Usually this is the national or state ministry of education. Because they are held accountable for the quality and efficiency of education in their country, these over-arching authorities assume responsibility for long-range planning. They commission research and make deliberate use of that research in their decision making. Working in these agencies is widely thought to be a worthy goal for leading educators in these countries. Their wishes are taken seriously because of the respect in which their staff are held.

The various parts of an education system need to be designed to work harmoniously with each other. Systems need to make effective plans and make sure those plans are carried out. They need to have the capacity to do the necessary analyses, deliver support to the field, monitor the degree to which their plans are being implemented, judge the results and change course if needed. If a country or a state or group of states in a federal system lacks this capacity, it might not be able to make comprehensive, coherent plans; and even if it has the capacity to plan, it might not matter very much what its policies are if the country or state lacks the capacity needed to implement them.

The experience of countries with federal oversight for education provides useful insights into how states can collaborate. Canada's Council of Ministers of Education[51] and the German Standing Conference of Education Ministers[52] provide fora through which provincial ministers of education meet frequently to co-ordinate. While their formal powers are limited, these bodies fulfil an important function by enabling good ideas and practices to spread across provincial borders. The power of ideas and the possibilities for dissemination have generated good practice and encouraged jurisdictions to learn from each other.

In Germany, the constitution prohibits the federal government from doing much more than supporting education research; but the government has provided the stimuli and ideas for many of the most significant reforms over the past decade. For example, it was the federal government that developed the original concept of competency-based national school standards, even if it was the states, operating through the council of state ministers, that established and oversaw the national standards and reporting system.

Articulating a consistent message

Trends across education systems today are nothing if not paradoxical. On the one hand, people are concerned about a growing gap between what societies expect from schools and actual learning outcomes. On the other hand, there are mounting complaints among educators about a too-rapid pace of education reform that leaves little time or space for thoughtful implementation. Behind the perceptions that reform is happening both too slowly and too fast is a lack of direction and alignment between policies and the components of reform. School leaders and teachers are rarely involved in designing policies; sometimes they only hear about them when they are announced in the media. Since they do not see the bigger picture, they are less likely to be able to help craft the delivery chain linking intention and implementation of policies that is central to success.

Policy makers, in turn, have few incentives to promote and see to fruition their predecessors' ideas, or they don't see that they won't have to do everything differently in order to do some things better. They are generally more inclined to put their own proposals at the top of an already crowded policy agenda. That, in turn, reinforces short-term-ism and misalignment, as well as distrust among teachers on the frontline who have to change course with every new political administration.

There is a great need for consistency and continuity when a school system is trying to improve. Whether changes to the curriculum or funding, or a different way of supporting teachers, these various parts of the process need to be moving in the same direction – towards a coherent vision.

That is not to say that the process of reform is smooth; it is often fraught with political controversy and sometimes difficult to follow. Quite apart from political and economic challenges, moving from centralised, administrative control towards professional autonomy can be counterproductive if a nation does not yet have teachers and schools with the capacity to implement these policies. Devolving authority to lower levels can be problematic if there is no agreement on what students need to know and be able to do, and if standards are not high enough. Recruiting high-quality teachers will not be sufficient if those who are recruited are so frustrated by an inadequate system of initial teacher education, or so turned off by a top-heavy bureaucracy that they leave the profession entirely.

Speaking with one voice in Singapore

As a visiting professor at Singapore's National Institute of Education, I have had the chance to learn a lot about the country's approach to education reform. The Ministry of Education, the National Institute and individual schools share responsibility and accountability for aligning policies with implementation. Professors from the National Institute are regularly involved in ministry discussions and decisions, so it is easy for the Institute's work to be aligned with ministry policies; school principals learn about major reform proposals directly from the minister rather than through the media. No policy is announced without a plan for building the capacity to implement it. The ministry functions in a culture of continuous improvement, constantly assessing what is and isn't working, using both data and practitioner experience from around the world to inform its policy design and implementation. Teacher-education programmes are designed with the teacher in mind, rather than to suit the interests of academic departments. Teachers typically go into the classroom with a first degree, then a master's programme puts this practical experience into a coherent theoretical setting later on, in mid-career.

One of the most striking things I find in Singapore is that I hear the same clear focus on the same bold outcomes wherever I go – whether in the ministries of education, national development or community development, or in the universities, technical institutes or schools. The system in itself is very porous, in the sense that professionals can and do move between research, policy making, administration and teaching practice, often multiple times in their careers. The close connection among policy, research and practice keeps the vision forward-looking and dynamic. Education is expected to change as conditions change; it is not stuck in the past.

"Milestone" courses, as they're called, bring together top officials from all the ministries to create a shared understanding of national goals. A focus on effective implementation runs throughout the government. "Dream, Design and Deliver" is Singapore's apt characterisation of its approach to public administration.

The government of Singapore understands the critical relationship between people's skills and economic development, so it provides a clear vision of what is needed in education. While the ministry of education designs the policies that will realise this vision, teachers, in turn, are entitled to spend 100 hours per year developing their skills, often in the National Institute of Education; and that institution, in turn, helps design education reform, including related policy.

Spending more vs spending wisely

The first lesson I learned when researching the countries that came out on top of the PISA comparisons is that their leaders seem to have convinced their citizens to make choices that value education more than other things. In these countries, a well-equipped school turns more heads than a shiny new shopping mall. Parents in China will often invest their last *renminbi* in the education of their children, their future and the future of their country. In much of the Western world, governments have started to borrow money from the next generation to finance consumption today. Economic and social progress is running straight into the pile of debt they are amassing.

In 2013, I had an interesting lunch with vice mayor Fu Yonglin of Chengdu, China, one of the key influencers behind the rapid transformation in education that his municipality has seen over the past decade. What struck me most was his take on how China's power and role in the world would ultimately not be determined primarily by what and how many goods China produces, but by what China will be able to contribute to the global knowledge pool and to global culture, through education. In a country where the average graduate takes home a salary that is little more than a maid could earn in one of China's big cities, money is clearly not the only incentive for learning. China's political and social leaders still seem to be able to persuade their citizens to value education, their future, more than consumption today.

It was also interesting how the vice mayor of Chengdu reconciled the need to preserve and build on the past – in his words, "nothing comes from nothing; everything has a history and evolves from there" – with the need to embrace change. He was well aware of the learning curve the Chinese have in front of them, the need for China to play an active role in globalisation, and the importance of education as the gateway to understanding different cultures and fields of knowledge. He was also aware of the need to change the nature of education itself. I asked him why he and other city officials were so interested in our work on the future of education, which, in those days, some OECD countries still viewed with some scepticism. He looked at me and said that today, Chengdu is the world's factory for digital equipment, providing a population of 14 million with jobs and wealth. Within a decade, he said, every single one of those jobs will have been taken over by a robot. The challenge for us, he continued, is not just to create new jobs, but to create new jobs that humans can do better than robots, and to educate humans who can think and work differently than robots.

But, as I discussed in Chapter 2, education systems do not improve simply by throwing money at them. Two countries with similarly high spending levels can produce very different results. In other words, once a minimum threshold of spending is met, it is not how much countries spend on education, but how they spend those resources. If average-performing OECD countries are to move from the middle ranks in performance to the top ranks, either they will have to radically improve the efficiency of their education systems, or they will have to increase the amount spent on them enormously.

Most governments face severe financial constraints, and that situation is not likely to change any time soon. So a great expansion in education spending is unlikely in the foreseeable future. The challenge is thus to wring much more from every dollar spent. The question is how to do that. The experiences of high-performing education systems offer several possible approaches.

For example, Japan puts a large share of its resources into core instructional services by spending much less than most OECD countries on extravagant school buildings, school services, glossy textbooks and expensive sports programmes.[53]

Some of the savings are used to pay teachers relatively well. The rest is returned to taxpayers (in 2014, public and private spending on schools in Japan amounted to 3% of GDP, the fourth lowest percentage among OECD countries after the Czech Republic, the Slovak Republic and Hungary).

Another way to get better results without spending more money is to make basic changes in the way the education system is organised. Up until the decline in the population of school-age children in Japan, student-teacher ratios in the United States and Japan were almost identical. But the Japanese chose to keep classes large – sometimes as much as twice as large as classes in the United States. That choice gave Japanese teachers much more time to prepare their lessons, confer with other teachers about struggling students, and tutor students who were falling behind. The two countries spent the same (in terms of student-teacher ratios), but Japanese policy makers traded larger classes for giving teachers more time to plan and work with small groups of students, while American policy makers opted for smaller classes and less time for teachers to plan and work with small groups of students.

Japan is not alone in this. As already noted, whenever high-performing education systems have to choose between smaller classes and better teachers, they seem to go for the latter. Many Western countries have opted for the former.

Between 2006 and 2015, expenditure per primary, secondary and post-secondary non-tertiary student increased by almost 20% across OECD countries.[54] But over the same period, most OECD countries prioritised smaller classes over better teachers, over more instruction time and individualised support for students, and over more equitable access to education. Popular pressure and changing demographics have pushed governments to reduce class size in lower secondary education by an average of 6% across OECD countries. In other words, spending has been driven by choices that are popular with parents and teachers but not necessarily by what helps students succeed in the long run.

Countries that opt for large classes can afford to pay their teachers better. If classroom teachers are paid well, recruitment into the profession is more competitive and candidates can be educated in higher-status teacher-education institutions. Those teachers stay in teaching longer, need to be replaced less frequently and require much less specialised assistance in the classroom. That means that fewer teacher-education institutions are needed and more money can be spent on those who remain. An apparently low-cost solution (hiring lower-quality teachers and educating them in lower-cost institutions) can turn into a higher-cost solution in the long run, after all costs are taken into account.

Employing lower-cost teachers means that more specialist staff are needed in schools and more managers are needed to supervise and co-ordinate those specialists. In the top-performing countries, although teachers may earn relatively higher pay, fewer administrators are needed and fewer additional specialists are required, making it possible to employ higher-quality teachers and still enjoy lower net costs. This is why it is important to think about the design of the system, as a whole, and the net costs of that system, rather than thinking about individual costs in isolation.

The bottom line is that there is a striking asymmetry in the relationship between skills and money. While improved skills consistently generate more benefit for individuals and nations, more money does not automatically generate improved education.

The evidence of PISA has shown how some countries have re-invented themselves through a systematic process of reform and investment in the education of their populations such that the relative standing of education systems has changed fundamentally. That also means the world is no longer divided between countries that are rich and well-educated and those that are poor and badly educated. Countries can choose to develop a superior education system, and if they succeed it will yield huge rewards. This is a path that leads to better lives and better jobs, which drive societies forward.

But there is a lot more than money required to raise education outcomes. This includes the belief in the success of every child. The fact that students in most East Asian countries consistently believe that achievement is mainly a product of hard work, rather than inherited intelligence as Western children would often say, suggests that education and its social context can make a difference in instilling values that foster success in education.

And nowhere does the quality of a school system exceed the quality of its teachers. High-performing school systems all pay great attention to how they select and train their teachers and education leaders. When deciding where to invest, they prioritise the quality of teachers over the size of classes. They provide intelligent pathways for teachers to grow in their careers.

High-performing countries have also moved on from bureaucratic control and accountability to professional forms of work organisation. They encourage their teachers to make innovations in pedagogy, to improve their own performance and that of their colleagues, and to pursue professional development that leads to stronger education practice.

Snapshots of five top education systems

As should be obvious by now, what makes high-performing countries different is not where they are located or how wealthy they are or what culture they are endowed with. What makes them different is their acute awareness of underperformance and inequities in their education systems and their ability to mobilise the resources, innovation and will to tackle them. Here are a few brief profiles.

Singapore

Singapore scored higher than any other country or economy in PISA 2015. Such a triumph raised interest about how this Asian city-state, with a population of about five million, had developed such a successful education system. Other countries wanted to know what lessons they could learn from Singapore's rapid progress.

One of the most remarkable features of Singapore's achievement is that success was built from an extremely low starting point. Singapore, which gained independence in 1965, was an impoverished country with few natural resources and a population with poor proficiency in literacy. There were few schools and colleges, and the country had an underdeveloped and low-skilled economy. The population was composed of different ethnic groups, speaking different languages and observing different religions.

But in five decades, Singapore went from nowhere to the top of the international rankings, overtaking the major economies in Europe and North America and high-achieving rivals in East Asia. It has made the leap from "third world" to "first" in little more than one lifetime.

So what are the ingredients of this success?

Perhaps the first is intention. Singapore's improvement in education was not an accident, or some kind of natural phenomenon; it was a deliberate decision to use education as a foundation for building an advanced economy. Education was to be the engine of economic growth.

Without natural resources, and with much bigger and more powerful neighbours, Singapore saw an educated population as its most valuable asset. Education was also integral to the nation-building of a young country. It helped construct a shared sense of identity and bring together different ethnic groups and religions.

This emphasis on education went through a series of re-inventions, reflecting and reinforcing the country's economic progress. In the years after independence, Singapore was in a survival phase; the education system was expanded to provide a basic education for workers in an economy that was trying to attract overseas manufacturers.

A unified education system was established, teachers were hired in large numbers, schools were built, textbooks were printed. Within a decade, all children had a primary education. By the 1970s, Singapore offered universal access to lower secondary education.

This was not a particularly high standard of education, and that was addressed by the next phase of industrial development, where Singapore, in the late 1970s, moved from survival to efficiency. This was an attempt to move upwards from a low-pay, low-skills economy towards one with a higher-skilled workforce that would attract international high-tech companies. This economic upgrade was accomplished by overhauling the education system – introducing a new curriculum and different pathways for academic and vocational studies. In the early 1990s, campuses of the Institute for Technical Education were established to raise the status and quality of vocational education, and to provide technical training comparable to that offered in universities.

At the end of the 1990s, the system was further refined to prepare for the knowledge economy, in which Singapore would have to depend on a highly skilled workforce to be able to compete in a globalised economy. This idea of deeper and more effective learning was captured in the "Teach Less, Learn More" campaign, which was promoted by Prime Minister Lee Hsien Loong, along with the continuing campaign for "Thinking Schools, Learning Nation".

Underpinning these developments was a sustained belief in the importance of improving education. It was a systematic approach, maintained over decades and supported by public policy and spending. In 2010, education represented 20% of government expenditure, the biggest item apart from defence. Seen through the prism of this national ambition, education spending has been a key plank of economic investment, feeding into the country's earning capacity.

This alignment of education with the economy and the needs of employers is part of a highly integrated system. There are clear goals for what schools and individuals are expected to achieve, a rigorous exam system and high academic standards. Progress through education is intended to be a meritocratic process in support of social mobility, allowing students to achieve the highest results that their potential will allow.

But even such smoothly running structures need a human face to bring them alive. What has often been highlighted in the success of Singapore's schools is its teachers. Singapore has become a model of the principle of hiring teachers from among the best graduates, and keeping them well-trained and motivated.

Singapore introduced a process for recruiting and educating high-quality staff, with the aim of attracting the brightest and the best into the classroom. In addition, there is a strong emphasis on professional development, so that teachers keep up to date with their skills. With the expectation that these bright, ambitious teachers will want to keep advancing through their careers, teachers are entitled to 100 hours of professional development per year.

This tightly controlled, centralised system, makes a virtue of consistency. All teachers are trained at the same institution, so that every teacher will have emerged from the same "production line", meeting the same standards. Teachers are appointed with the aim of ensuring that all schools have a fair share of the best teachers. They will go into schools with a clear notion of what is expected of them; in return, they can expect high status and public approval.

Singapore's story is that of a small, hungry country looking for a better future. The education system has had to improve and adapt at each stage to make this possible.

Singapore shows how much in education can change in a relatively short period of time. By raising its education standards it has been able to become a beneficiary of globalisation, rather than a victim. Singapore is recognised as one of the world's top-performing school systems; its next challenge will be to stay there.

Estonia

Estonia was one of the top 10 highest performers in mathematics, science and reading in the 2015 PISA assessments.

The small Baltic state has been dubbed the "new Finland" for its success, particularly since it overtook Finland in mathematics and science in PISA 2015. Experts from Finland advised Estonia on education reforms in the 1990s. Indeed, there is one key similarity in the success of both countries' education systems: they both, whether through strategy or cultural inclination, have a strong sense of equity in their education system. This is made manifest in the small differences between the results of affluent students and those of disadvantaged students.

In Estonia, the impact of such socio-economic status is conspicuously weaker than in most other countries. In this respect, Estonia is similar to Canada, Hong Kong and Norway, rather than countries such as Austria, France and Germany, where there was a much stronger link between socio-economic status and students' performance.

What is particularly striking about Estonia's high-ranking performance in PISA 2015 is not the proportion of high achievers, but that so few of the country's students were among the low performers in any of the three core subjects.

Equity is also apparent in access to early childhood education, which feeds into the school system. Compulsory schooling does not begin until children are seven years old, but large proportions of three- and four-year-olds are in state-provided early education. Teacher-pupil ratios in these early education settings are half the OECD average.

At the other end of the age range, a high percentage – one of the highest in the industrialised world – of students in Estonia successfully complete secondary school. This suggests that all students are expected to attain a good level of education, regardless of their family background.

After independence, Estonia decentralised the school system, giving schools greater autonomy, with the freedom to make decisions about the curriculum, budgets, and hiring and dismissing teachers. Families have the right to choose a school for their children and, as a result, schools have to compete to attract students.

The decline in the population of school-age children means that Estonia's school system must make sure that there are schools close enough to where children are living, while at the same time making sure that schools have enough students for them to be viable and to offer a wide enough range of subjects. This is particularly important for secondary schools, when students will want to specialise.

This situation prompts a question of funding: Is it better value to invest in big schools that serve a wide area, or should local schools be protected? As of this writing, Estonia has some of the smallest secondary school classes in the developed world.

The demographic decline has become a big issue for Estonia's university sector too, with the country's universities having to fight to recruit from a shrinking pool of potential applicants; it also faces competition from universities in other countries. Estonia's businesses are worried about having an adequate supply of young graduates.

In addition, Estonia's teaching force is ageing – more so than almost any other OECD country. The need to attract more young graduates into the profession has prompted a significant rise in teachers' salaries, but teaching is still not a competitive career choice.

Education in Estonia, as in other Nordic and Baltic countries, is publicly funded; there is relatively little private funding for education. That said, Estonia does not spend as much on education as Norway, for example; and even though pre-school education is well-staffed, the teachers earn relatively low pay. Estonia's GDP is far below the OECD average, so whatever is driving its success in education, it is not high spending.

To understand Estonia's high achievement in the PISA rankings, the place to look is the share of low achievers. When it comes to top achievers across all three core PISA subjects (science, reading and mathematics), Estonia is a good, but not spectacular, performer. There are several countries ranked below Estonia that are as good or better on this measure. In top-scoring Singapore, for example, 39.1% of students attained this level, compared with 20.4% in Estonia.

Where Estonia really excels as a world leader is in its relatively small proportion of low achievers. Only 4.7% of 15-year-olds in Estonia score below the baseline level of proficiency across all three subjects – a better outcome than observed in high-flyers such as Finland, Hong Kong, Singapore and South Korea, and about half the share of low achievers in Germany and the United States.

Canada

Canada was one of the highest-achieving countries in the 2015 round of PISA tests, ranked third for reading and in the top 10 for mathematics and science. This puts Canada ahead of Finland for reading and mathematics.

The stand-out characteristic of Canada's education system is its emphasis on equity and its ability to elicit excellent results from students of different social backgrounds, including students with an immigrant background. The difference in performance between rich and poor students in Canada is small by international standards. It reflects a state ethos that supports the health and well-being of families.

Canada's schools have a high proportion of children from immigrant families – and their performance is often not any different from that of non-immigrant children. Indeed, Canada's school system is something of a model for integration – especially considering that immigrants enter a country that already hosts French- and English-speaking populations and First Nation indigenous people. What makes the approach in Canada unique is that it integrates content from different cultures into the curriculum, so that students learn early on how to see the world from different perspectives. Teachers also help students develop positive attitudes towards diversity and modify their teaching so that students from different social and ethnic groups can succeed.

Canada's result in the PISA tests is a national score, but the education system is run at the level of provinces and territories, with local ministers running regional school systems. This has raised questions about how Canada's success in PISA can be explained when there isn't any single federal system to analyse. While some successful education systems are highly centralised and controlled, Canada has a system of dispersed responsibility, which still seems to deliver.

Apart from the success of Canada's schools in PISA rankings, the country has an unusually large proportion of tertiary-educated adults. As another indicator of a well-educated society, young people in Canada are more likely than students almost anywhere else in the world to read for pleasure.

So what could be the factors behind Canada's strong academic performance?

As in most high-performing countries in PISA, entry into the teaching profession in Canada is selective – and better-quality (and better-paid) teachers tend to get better student results.

But the feature that might be of greatest interest is Canada's capacity to integrate large numbers of immigrant children into its schools. Canada's results in PISA show that there is nothing inevitable about immigrant children performing worse than the rest of their classmates. It shows that one of the highest-achieving school systems can welcome many immigrant families without suffering any reduction in standards.

Immigration into Canada is now mostly from Asia – from China, India, the Philippines and Pakistan. A large proportion of these immigrants head for the big cities of Montreal, Toronto or Vancouver. But PISA results suggest that within three years of arrival, the children of new immigrants are scoring as high as their non-immigrant schoolmates.

There are a number of reasons why this might be the case.

First, Canada is a large country with a relatively small population, and it has had a long history of wanting to attract immigrants who might contribute to its economy. Many new arrivals are well-educated families seeking professional careers. Their children are soon able to catch up with their classmates, even if they have to learn a second language. In other words, these are immigrants who are already receptive to what schools can offer.

Immigrant children, whether from families with high or low levels of education, also benefit from Canada's support for new arrivals and efforts to make sure that they are able to integrate. There is extra help for language learning and support for children with special needs. The education system is able to find the balance between respecting different cultures and helping establish a common Canadian identity.

The combination of these factors seems to have a beneficial impact. Large numbers of immigrants are welcomed and carefully integrated into a high-achieving system. Immigrant students quickly meet the system's high standards. There is no negative impact from what are, by international standards, high levels of immigration.

But Canada is, admittedly, a curious example: it shows, to a certain extent, that success can be achieved without a single national strategy. Rather, the local approaches, which can be distinctive, move broadly in the same direction.

If that suggests that there is no one-size-fits-all approach to raising standards, it also shows that it is entirely possible to have a much larger proportion of immigrant children in school than found in most developed countries and, at the same time, have student results that would be the envy of most countries.

Finland

Finland has been one of the most consistently successful countries in global education rankings. Its name has become almost synonymous with excellence in education; indeed, many other countries have sent experts to Finland to get a first-hand look at the successful policies and practices that they could apply to their own schools.

In PISA 2015, Finland was ranked 4th in reading, 5th in science and 13th in mathematics. This might be a little down on its top-ranking performances of previous years (the proportion of low achievers in mathematics, science and reading in Finland was larger than that in other top-performing countries and economies, such as Canada, Estonia, Hong Kong, Singapore and Viet Nam, which dragged down mean scores in all three subjects), but Finland remains one of the most reliable of high achievers.

Finland shows that there are many different paths to success. This is a system where students spend less time in school than is observed in many of the highly competitive Asian systems, where there is little homework and where school inspections have been abolished.

But like many other high achievers, the Finnish system is based on the assumption that disadvantaged students can also succeed in school, and that all schools, no matter where they are located, should be of high quality. As in other Nordic and Baltic countries, the impact of socio-economic status on results is much weaker than average.

There is another strong link with the highest achievers, and that is the emphasis on the quality of teaching. Finland has made teaching a sought-after career, with high social status and great demand for places in initial teacher education: only about one in ten applicants is accepted. This is not only a profession for graduates, it is a job for people with master's degrees, appealing to the brightest graduates. Once teachers are deployed to schools, they are expected to keep learning, with professional development compulsory. While not particularly highly paid (per-pupil budgets and teachers' salaries are mid-range, by European standards), teaching is seen as an important and well-respected profession, and teachers are trusted and given great independence.

Anyone looking to Finland for inspiration may find that it reinforces the argument that no education system can be better than the quality of its teachers. But Finland also shows that success in education can take many decades to achieve. Finland's status as an education superpower was built slowly and deliberately through a series of education reforms and in response to changing economic needs. In the late 1960s, there was a decision to move to a comprehensive system, making high-quality education available to all students, not just to the minority selected for grammar schools. Implementation was not complete until the late 1970s. To make the transition successful, and to allay concerns about the changes, there was an accompanying drive to significantly improve the quality of teaching. The education of teachers was moved into the universities and was made much more rigorous.

The economic context in which Finland's education system evolved wasn't always benign. In the early 1990s, unemployment in Finland approached 20%, GDP was falling and public debt was rising. Education offered a means of re-shaping Finland's economy, with a shift towards investing in technology and the growing market in telecommunications. The number of Finns working in research and development grew rapidly, in tandem with the rise of companies such as Nokia, which went from a 19th-century pulp-mill business to becoming one of the biggest names in mobile phones in the early 21st century.

This combination of factors meant that Finland had an economic need for a better-educated workforce – and an education system with open access and high-quality teaching that was able to produce it.

There is also a distinctive flavour to Finland's concept of excellence. The schools are comprehensive in more than the range of their students' abilities. They are places where everyone can have a free hot meal, where there are health and dental services, and where psychological and counselling services are available. Support for children with special needs is seen as an integral part of the school system. Children also often receive individual attention in school.

Shanghai

When students in the Chinese city of Shanghai first sat the PISA test in 2009, they went straight to the top of the rankings in all three subjects – reading, mathematics and science. They repeated this remarkable performance three years later, sparking even more interest in how this regional education system could be so successful.

Shanghai is not representative of China; but with a population of over 24 million, Shanghai is larger than many other countries that participate in PISA.

In 2015, Beijing, Jiangsu and Guangdong also agreed to participate in PISA along with Shanghai – with a combined population of 232 million. Together, this entity ranked among the top 10 performers in mathematics and science.

It was only in the mid-1990s that Shanghai's school system was able to deliver the basics of six years of primary education and three years of secondary education for all students. Before then, the city's education system focused on rebuilding itself after being destroyed, between 1966 and 1976, during China's Cultural Revolution.

Indeed, Shanghai, an international, outward-looking city, was at the forefront of China's education reform, taking advantage of opportunities to develop its own approaches. Under the banner "First-rate city, first-rate education" Shanghai made a priority of raising education standards to realise its economic ambitions.

Looking at the results from 2009, what is striking is how few students scored poorly. There were plenty of students in Shanghai who did very well, but it was the absence of underachievers that propelled Shanghai to the top of international rankings. Of course, there are still many 15-year-olds in Shanghai, including internal migrants, who still do not have full access to upper secondary education. But for those who do, including students from disadvantaged families, the system produces strong results.

This is a system based on the assumption that every student can succeed, or at least can reach an adequate level of academic performance. It is not a "sorting mechanism" system, in which only a minority of winners crosses the finishing line. The system is designed to make sure that almost everyone completes the academic course.

This applies to children of all backgrounds who enrol in school. While the system does not – nor can it – completely eradicate the gap in results between advantaged and disadvantaged students, it assumes that such social factors will not be an excuse for failure. As a consequence, in the 2012 PISA results, children from poor families in Shanghai outperformed middle-class children in the United States.

The school system has been structured to achieve this. The best teachers are directed towards the schools needing the greatest support. Strong schools are expected to support weaker schools, with the aim of raising the overall standard. It is a systemic approach, built on meritocratic principles with the aim of getting the most from students.

Education is also intensely competitive. Students in Shanghai often supplement their learning in school with long hours of homework and private tuition. The expectations for these students are high: about 80% of students continue into tertiary education. But Shanghai's students believe that they are in control of their ability to achieve. They do not think that being good at mathematics is a natural gift; they have been taught that it depends on their own hard work and getting the right support from their teachers. Parents are also ready to support their children and to show that education is a priority for their family.

Another key feature in the Shanghai school system, consistent with other top performers, is the high quality of its teachers. The selection, education and deployment of excellent teachers is how the system can put its policies into practice. Professional development continues throughout a teacher's career, with an emphasis on education research.

4. Why equity in education is so elusive

Perhaps the most impressive outcome of world-class school systems is that they deliver high-quality education across the entire school system so that every student benefits from excellent teaching. Achieving greater equity in education is not only a social-justice imperative, it is also a way to use resources more efficiently, and to increase the supply of knowledge and skills that fuel economic growth and promote social cohesion.

In early 2015, I worked with Eric Hanushek from Stanford University and Ludger Woessmann from the German Institute for Economic Research on a report for UNESCO's Education World Forum. The forum was exploring global targets for education as part of the Sustainable Development Goals.[1]

Hanushek had worked out a methodology that calculates the long-term economic benefits of raising the quality of education, and it showed the potential benefits to both advanced and developing economies. PISA provided a way of measuring the quality of education across different countries. So combining PISA and Hanushek's work was a good way to examine the economic impact of improved education.

The first thing that Hanushek and Woessman's results showed was that the quality of schooling in a country is a reliable predictor of the wealth that countries will produce in the long run.

At the most basic level, making sure that everyone has access to schooling, without touching the quality of the school system, will yield some economic gains, particularly in poorer countries where many children still miss out on school.

But there is a much bigger impact from an increase in the quality of education. If every student can demonstrate that he or she has basic skills, direct and major long-term benefits to the economy accrue. Indeed, Hanushek and Woessman showed that if every 15-year-old student reached at least baseline Level 2 on the PISA proficiency scale by 2030 the benefits for economic growth and sustainable development would be enormous (*FIGURE 4.1*).

Of the countries that Hanushek and Woessmann studied, Ghana in West Africa had the lowest enrolment rate for secondary schools (46%) and also the lowest achievement levels for those 15-year-olds who are in school. If Ghana could educate all of its students to at least the basic level of reading and mathematics skills, it would see a gain over the lifetime of children born today that, in present value terms, is 38 times its current GDP.

For lower-middle income countries, the gains would be 13 times current GDP and would average out to a 28% higher GDP over the next 80 years. And for upper-middle-income countries, whose students generally perform better academically, it would average out to a 16% higher GDP.

What is obvious from this research is that improving education is not only beneficial for poor countries, it is beneficial for wealthy countries too.

The oil-producing countries are a good example. In March 2010, I was speaking to education ministers of the Arab states in Egypt, and wondered how these countries had succeeded in converting their natural resources into purchasing power, but had failed to convert their wealth into new generations of skilled young people who could secure their countries' economic and social well-being over the long run.

Israel's late Prime Minister Golda Meir once quipped that Moses led the Jewish people through the desert for 40 years – just to bring them to the one place in the Middle East where there was no oil. But the people of Israel have made up for their country's lack of "black gold": today, Israel has an innovative economy and its population enjoys a standard of living that is out of reach to most residents in its oil-rich neighbours. More generally, our data show that countries with greater income from natural resources tend to be economically and socially less developed, as exports of national resources tend to bolster the currency, making imports cheap and the development of an industrial base more difficult. As governments in resource-rich countries are under less pressure to tax their citizens, they are also less accountable to them.

Our findings deliver an important message for countries rich in natural resources: the wealth that lies untapped in the undeveloped skills of their people is far greater than the wealth they extract from their natural resources. And while natural resources are exhaustible – the more you use the less you have – knowledge is a growing resource – the more you use the more you have. The scientific discovery that had the largest impact on human development was the discovery of ignorance, and learning as the means to advance knowledge.

PISA data also show a significant negative relationship between the money countries earn from their natural resources and the knowledge and skills of their school population. As New York Times columnist Thomas Friedman put it, PISA and oil don't mix easily.[2] Israel is not alone in outperforming its oil-rich neighbours by a large margin when it comes to learning outcomes at school: most of the highest-performing education systems are poor in natural resources.

The exceptions – Australia, Canada and Norway, which are rich in natural resources but still score well on PISA – have all established deliberate policies of investing the profits made through these resources, not just consuming them.

One interpretation is that in countries with little in the way of natural resources – good examples include Finland, Japan and Singapore – citizens understand that their country must live by its wits – literally, its knowledge and skills – and that these depend on the quality of education provided. So the degree to which a country values education seems to depend at least in part on the country's view of how knowledge and skills fit into the way it fills its national coffers. Placing a high value on education might thus be a prerequisite for building both a top-notch education system and a thriving economy.

As a group, high-income countries that are not part of the OECD would see an economic gain equivalent to almost five times the value of their current GDP – if they equipped all students with at least basic skills. Again, this is just the direct economic benefit; imagine the social impact on large parts of populations that currently lack basic knowledge and skills.

It is only recently that countries in the Arab world have begun to take action. The United Arab Emirates was the first country in the region that began to formally

FIGURE 4.1: IF EVERY CHILD ACQUIRED AT LEAST BASIC SKILLS IN SECONDARY SCHOOL, ECONOMIES WOULD FLOURISH

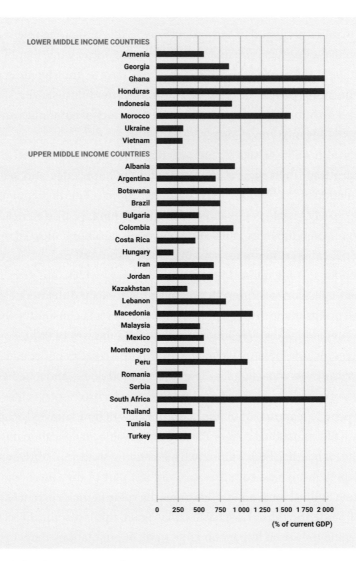

¹Latvia acceeded to the OECD on 1 July 2016.

Notes: Estimated discounted value of future increases in GDP until 2095, given a reform that achieves full participation in secondary school and where every student attains a minimum of 420 points on the PISA test, expressed as a percentage of current GDP. Value is 3 881% for Ghana, 2 016% for Honduras, 2 624% for South Africa.

Source: Hanushek and Woessmann (2015), Universal Basic Skills: What Countries Stand to Gain.

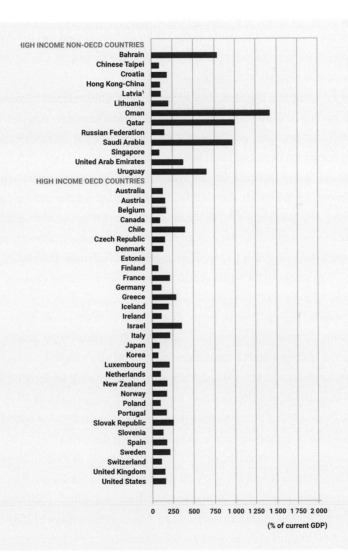

Notes: Estimated discounted value of future increases in GDP until 2095, given a reform that achieves full participation in secondary school and where every student attains a minimum of 420 points on the PISA test, expressed as a percentage of current GDP.

benchmark its performance internationally by setting a PISA-based performance target. When I gave the Ramadan Majlis Lecture in Abu Dhabi in August 2015, the crown prince and his cabinet expressed a deep commitment to improve the education system rapidly and profoundly. The country is now on its way to raising the status of education. The lesson its leaders have drawn is that a high income doesn't compensate for shortcomings in education.

One may be tempted to think that at least the wealthy OECD countries would have all the means to eliminate extreme underperformance in education. But that isn't the case. For example, one in four 15-year-olds in the United States does not successfully complete even the most basic tasks in PISA.

If the United States were to ensure that all of its students had basic skills, the economic gains could reach over USD 27 trillion in additional income for the economy over the working life of these students. So even high-income OECD countries would gain significantly if all of their students left school with at least basic knowledge and skills. For this group of countries, the average future GDP would be 3.5% higher than it would be without this improvement. That is close to what these countries now spend on school education.

In other words, the economic gains that would accrue solely from eliminating extreme underperformance in high-income OECD countries by 2030 would more than pay for the primary and secondary education of all students.

Such improvements in student performance are entirely realistic. For example, Poland was able to reduce the share of underperforming students in PISA by one-third, from 22% to 14%, within less than a decade. Between 2009 and 2012, Shanghai reduced the share of underperforming students from 4.9% to 3.8%.

Of course, more ambitious improvements can result in much larger potential gains. The calculations based on all students having basic skills are lower estimates because they assume that the improvement does not affect students who have already acquired higher knowledge and skills. But evidence from PISA indicates that school reforms that lead to improved performance among low achievers invariably also help higher achievers.

The calculations from Hanushek show that the economic impact of the share of students with basic skills is similar across all levels of development. They also show that the economic impact of expanding the share of top-performing students is significantly larger in countries that have further to go to catch up to the most productive countries. The process of economic convergence seems accelerated in countries with larger shares of high-performing students. This underlines the importance, particularly for middle-income countries, of investing in excellence in education.

Countries that have a large proportion of top-performing students are also more likely to succeed in providing equitable education opportunities to all their students. Investments in excellence and equity in education seem to reinforce each other. When countries develop a student population with strong foundation skills, they will most likely also develop a larger share of high performers.

To be sure, such long-term projections are just that – forecasts; and forecasts are only as solid as the assumptions on which they are based. But Hanushek's analyses rely on just two major assumptions. The first is that a better-educated workforce leads to a larger stream of new ideas that produces technological progress at a faster rate. For some, that assumption might even seem conservative, given that the world is becoming increasingly knowledge-intensive and is rewarding better skills at an ever-higher rate.

For those who remain sceptical, Hanushek provides an alternative scenario in which productivity is frozen, and every new worker will simply expand the pool of existing workers with similar skills and continue to work with the same productivity until the end of their working life. This rather pessimistic scenario, in which people just keep doing what their predecessors have been doing, leads to smaller but still impressive economic rewards after schooling has been improved.

The second assumption is that the improved skills will actually be used in the economy. Here, the Survey of Adult Skills (PIAAC) shows that there are significant differences in how well different countries extract value from their talent pool.[3] So while improved schooling is a necessary condition for economic progress, countries also need to ensure that they add higher value-added jobs that help get more people with better skills working – and for better pay. The projections factor these issues into the analyses by assuming that new skills in a country will be absorbed as effectively as has occurred across countries that had undergone similar transitions in the past.

Towards inclusive social progress

The links between income inequality and economic growth are well established. If income inequality becomes too high, large numbers of people no longer have the means to participate in the economy; they will also be unable to invest in their own skills to climb up the social ladder. Of course, if incomes are too similar, there is less incentive to progress at work, and growth and development might suffer too.

A conventional way to strike a balance between those two undesirables is to redistribute income, for example, through taxes. But instead of dealing with the consequences of income inequality through redistribution of wealth, it seems much smarter to start at the root of the problem and address the sources of income inequality. Then things are not a zero-sum game and more people stand to gain.

A major source of inequality in wages is inequality in skills. Inequality in skills equals inequality in society. Our parents told us that we should study hard to get a good job and a decent salary – and that piece of advice has never been more true than today.

As the OECD's annual publication, *Education at a Glance,* shows, highly educated people have never had better life chances than they enjoy today, while those with poor qualifications have never faced a greater risk of social and economic exclusion.[4] Those people with lower skills are facing a decline in pay, while rising numbers of higher-skilled workers have generally maintained, if not boosted their incomes.

The consequences of inequalities in skills within and across countries go well beyond economic and social concerns. In February 2008, I had an intensive exchange with NATO ambassadors about OECD work on inequality in skills and education. This topic had been put on the agenda because the ambassadors were concerned about the long-term effects these inequalities could have on geopolitical stability. Policy makers are realising that inequalities in education provide a fertile breeding ground for radicalism. In today's interconnected world, a country's future might depend as much on the quality of education outside of its borders, as on the quality of education offered within.

My colleague, Marco Paccagnella, has used data from the Survey of Adult Skills to study the relationship between education and earnings more closely.[5] He found that if all adults were simply to complete an additional year of education (which no doubt would be good for each of them as well as for the overall economic and social well-being of their country), top earners would actually benefit much more than those with lower wages. So wage inequality would rise. Essentially, the data show that the more people earn, the more further improvements in their education boost their earnings. The data also show that the financial returns to university-level education would increase more steeply at the top end of the wage scale, while returns from secondary education would actually decline.

This might be because higher education is where individuals acquire the specialised knowledge and skills that are more highly rewarded in the labour market. Another explanation is that technological advances mainly benefit the most skilled individuals, boosting their earnings most.

In a nutshell, raising overall levels of educational attainment alone could actually widen the wage gap rather than shrink it. In much of Europe and North America, the shift towards knowledge-based economies has led more people to acquire more education, and education has played an ever more important role in social progress. But it has not been a story of growing opportunity and mobility across the board. Rather, it has been a story of opportunity and reward being concentrated increasingly among people who began life with access to wealth and knowledge. School and university choices have become reflections of social and economic class, often reinforcing, rather than mitigating, social inequality.

But Paccagnella's analysis also shows that ensuring that more people acquire essential foundation skills, whatever their skills or formal qualifications, can be an effective way of achieving more equitable increases in earnings. Given that finding, increasing investment in foundation skills – by raising the quality of basic education for everyone – would not only result in higher productivity and greater employability among adults, it would also ensure that the benefits of economic growth are more equally shared across the population.

In this sense, improving education differs from simple tax and redistribution schemes that might change how income is spread throughout a society, but do not add to output. More inclusive growth, made possible through universal attainment of basic skills, has tremendous potential to ensure that the benefits of economic development are shared more equitably among citizens.

Countries where people are more highly skilled, on average, are also those where proficiency in skills is spread more evenly across the population. But the analysis also shows that countries with greater inequality in skills are also those where parents' education has a stronger impact on their children's skills. In other words, where skills are less evenly distributed in the population, young adults are less likely to acquire higher skills than their parents – and thus inequality in both skills and wages becomes more firmly entrenched.

There are several things we can learn from this. Countries where the skills and income of people vary widely also tend to be those where social background has the strongest impact on the acquisition of skills, educational attainment and, ultimately, wages. Investing in high-quality basic education – and in adult education and education programmes for those who need to catch up on foundation skills – is an effective way to improve a country's talent pool, and a way to achieve an economically and socially more inclusive society. In addition, combating increasing wage inequality requires a package of policies that covers education and training, the labour market, and the tax and transfer systems.

The struggle to level the playing field

What wise parents want for their children is what the government should want for all children. Children from wealthier families will find many open doors to a successful life. But children from poor families often have just one chance in life, and that is a good school that gives them an opportunity to develop their potential. Those who miss that boat rarely catch up, as subsequent education opportunities in life tend to reinforce early education outcomes.[6]

There has been much discussion about the extent to which countries' performance on tests like PISA is shaped by the socio-economic context of families, schools and the country itself. Indeed, where there are students with economic, social and cultural advantages, it is likely that they will be better equipped to do well. This is not just about poverty of material resources, but equally important about poverty of aspiration and hope. School systems tend to reproduce social advantage and disadvantage; results from PISA show this. It is particularly disappointing that, in many countries, surprisingly little headway has been made towards giving all children an equal chance to succeed.

However, the fact that the impact of social background on educational success varies greatly across countries shows there is nothing inevitable about disadvantaged students performing worse than more advantaged students. As I mentioned earlier, results from education systems as different as Estonia, Hong Kong, Shanghai and Viet Nam show that the poorest students in one region might score higher than the wealthiest students in another country.

In 2015, Yuan Yuan Pan, a brilliant student from Tsinghua University, worked as an intern with our PISA team.[7] When I had to go to Dujiangyan city in the Sichuan province of China that summer, I sought her advice to plan some school visits. It turned out that she had been born in a small town in that province, with very poor resources. But her teachers recognised her talent and did everything possible to support her. She passed the demanding Chinese entrance exam system as well as the interview for what is arguably China's most prestigious university – a university that consistently tops international league tables in engineering and computer sciences, and attracts over 10 million applicants each year.

Yuan Yuan Pan is not an exception; more recently, the government has taken additional measures to boost the chances of bright students from poor areas to make it into China's prestigious universities. Students from poor and remote areas who pass the university entrance exam are now receiving bonus scores to better their chances of admission. The best of them will receive full scholarships from top-ranked universities.

Providing access to high-quality early childhood education and care is often regarded as the most effective way to level the playing field in education and in life. But, as illustrated in *FIGURE 4.2*, reality hasn't yet caught up with theory. Perhaps not unexpectedly, the figure shows that today's 15-year-olds had widely different exposure to pre-primary education, ranging from one year in Turkey to over four years in Estonia and Sweden, on average. But it is disappointing that in most countries children in privileged schools had benefitted from more years in pre-primary education than had children in disadvantaged schools. This shows how

FIGURE 4.2: FIFTEEN-YEAR-OLDS IN ADVANTAGED SCHOOLS ARE MORE LIKELY TO HAVE ATTENDED PRE-PRIMARY SCHOOL

Number of years in pre-primary education among students attending socio-economically disadvantaged and advantaged schools

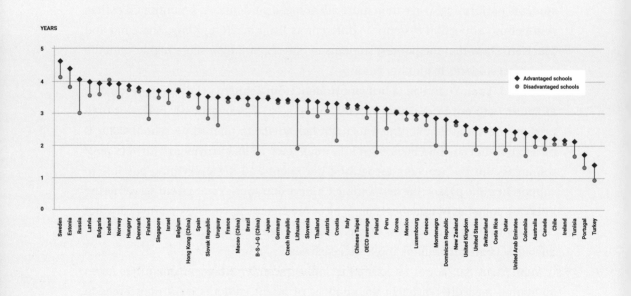

Note: B-S-J-G (China) refers to Beijing-Shanghai-Jiangsu-Guangdong (China).

Source: OECD, PISA 2015 Database, Table II.6.51.

early childhood education and care offered without much of a plan can actually reinforce rather than moderate social inequality.

As I have said many times, excellence in education and equity in education are not mutually exclusive. For example, while students from the most privileged families in France and the Netherlands perform similarly in PISA, the poorest students in the Netherlands do as well as those from middle-income families in France.[8] What strikes me most when studying these data is that the perception of poverty can matter as much as actual poverty rates.

There are some countries where school principals recognise that they are teaching in places of relative poverty or relative advantage. Principals in Brazil, Chile, Malaysia, Mexico and Portugal are right to observe that they have large shares of disadvantaged students in their schools. Similarly, head teachers in the Czech Republic, Denmark, Finland, Iceland, Japan, Norway and South Korea know when they are in charge of schools where there is limited disadvantage.

But actual disadvantage and principals' perceptions of disadvantage aren't always aligned.[9] In the PISA 2012 assessment, 65% of principals in the United States reported that more than 30% of their students are from disadvantaged homes – a proportion far larger than reported in any other country. However, the actual percentage of disadvantaged students recorded by PISA was just 13%, marginally higher than that in Japan and South Korea. But in those two countries, only 6% and 9% of principals, respectively, reported a share of disadvantaged students in their schools comparable to that reported by principals in the United States (*FIGURE 4.3*).

In other words, the actual incidence of child poverty was roughly the same among these three countries, but more than six times as many American principals as principals in Japan and South Korea reported that more than 30% of their students were disadvantaged. Conversely, in Croatia, Serbia and Singapore, more than 20% of students were disadvantaged, while 7% of principals or less reported significant populations of disadvantaged students.

It might be the case that a child considered poor in the United States is regarded as wealthy in another country; but in relative terms, the perceived problem of socio-economic disadvantage in schools is much greater in the United States than the actual backgrounds of students suggests. There is a similar mismatch in France too.

FIGURE 4.3: STUDENTS' ACTUAL DISADVANTAGE, AND PRINCIPALS' PERCEPTION OF DISADVANTAGE, ARE SOMETIMES VERY DIFFERENT

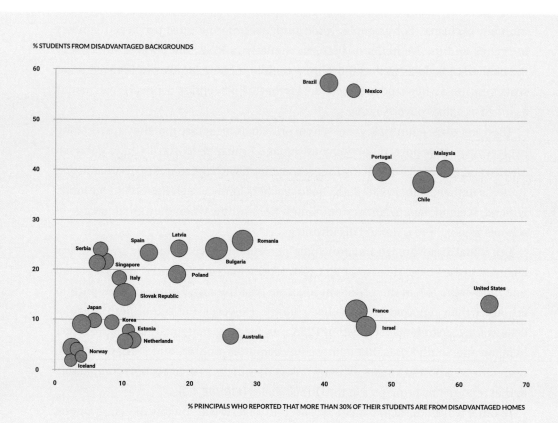

% STUDENTS FROM DISADVANTAGED BACKGROUNDS

% PRINCIPALS WHO REPORTED THAT MORE THAN 30% OF THEIR STUDENTS ARE FROM DISADVANTAGED HOMES

Note: The size of the bubbles represents the strength of the relationship between socio-economic status and student performance in the PISA mathematics test.

Source: http://oecdeducationtoday.blogspot.fr/2014/07/poverty-and-perception-of-poverty-how.html.

Socio-economic disadvantage has an observable impact on learning outcomes – observable, but not inevitable. In fact, that impact reflects the extent to which an education system provides equitable learning opportunities. In Finland, Iceland and Norway, one would expect this impact to be small because these countries have relatively few disadvantaged students in their schools. Achieving equity in school is easy when a society distributes wealth and family education equitably. But the more impressive examples are countries like PISA top-performer Singapore, where socio-economic disadvantage is significant, but its impact on learning outcomes is only moderate.

These countries seem very good at nurturing the extraordinary talents of ordinary students and at ensuring that every student benefits from excellent teaching. By contrast, France has a comparatively small share of disadvantaged students, but school principals there perceive this share to be larger than it really is. Student performance in France is closely related to socio-economic status – more closely, in fact, than in any other country except Chile and the Slovak Republic. Strikingly, the results show that principals' perceptions of disadvantage among their students correlate with inequalities in education opportunities more strongly than actual disadvantage does.

There is another way of looking at this: in Hong Kong, Macao and Viet Nam, more than 60% of students from the bottom quarter of the socio-economic spectrum scored among the top quarter of all the world's students on the PISA 2015 tests; in Estonia, Japan and Singapore, around one in two of the most disadvantaged students did so. By contrast, in Chile, Greece, Iceland, Israel and Mexico, fewer than one in five of the most disadvantged students scored among the top quarter of all students.[10]

So what does all this mean? Socio-economic disadvantage is a challenge to educators everywhere, but in some countries, perceived disadvantage is far greater than real disadvantage, and that perception seems to make a significant difference for student performance. In other countries, real disadvantage is far greater than school principals' perception of it, but their schools and perhaps the broader society seem to be able to help their students overcome that disadvantage.

Similarly, the PISA data show that, for many countries, the problem of underachievement does not just involve poor children in poor neighbourhoods, it is a problem that affects many children in many neighbourhoods. The bottom line is that the country where you go to school seems to have a much greater impact on your learning outcomes than the social background of the family you were born into.

Matching resources with needs

One of the comments that I have heard frequently in discussions about social diversity in the classroom is that schools cannot solve the problems of society. But I always ask myself: what else should we expect from schools than to address the challenges confronting their society? And what could be more important than supporting those teachers and schools working in the most difficult circumstances, and those students with the greatest needs? It seems clear that society increasingly looks to schools to remedy social problems that were, in the past, addressed by others. The task for public policy is to help schools meet those demands.

For a start, many education systems can do better in aligning resources with needs. When it comes to material resources, much progress has been achieved; but attracting the most talented teachers to the most challenging classrooms remains difficult in most countries. It is not as simple as paying teachers who work in disadvantaged schools more; it requires holistic approaches in which teachers feel supported in their professional and personal life when they take on additional challenges, and when they know that additional effort will be valued and publicly recognised.

It is difficult for teachers to allocate scarce additional time and resources to the children with the greatest needs. People who laud the value of diversity in classrooms are often talking about the classes other people's children attend. It is generally difficult to convince socio-economically advantaged parents whose children go to school with other privileged children that everyone is better off when classes are socially diverse. Policy makers, too, find it hard to allocate resources where the challenges are greatest and where those resources can have the biggest impact, often because poor children usually don't have someone lobbying for them.

In too many countries, the postcode tells you all you need to know about what kind of education children are acquiring. If schools are popular, house prices in their catchment areas will rise, further segregating the population. People with fewer assets, and less income and education end up finding housing where education and social opportunities are poorer. The result is that in most countries, differences in education outcomes related to social inequalities are stubbornly persistent, and too much talent remains latent.

But equity is only partly about socio-economic status and the need to spend more resources on the most deprived children. Equally important is the realisation that different individuals learn differently and have different needs. The struggle of the 20th century was about the right to be equal. The struggle in the 21st century will be about the right to be different.

Being open to guidance from students themselves

In 2017, I spent three days with Sir Richard Branson at his home on Necker Island. Sir Richard left school, disillusioned, at age 16 because he felt that school did nothing to develop his creative and entrepreneurial talents. (Nor did his school diagnose his dyslexia.) On his last day at school, his headmaster famously told him he would either end up in prison or become a millionaire. We all know how that worked out: Sir Richard became one of Britain's most successful entrepreneurs (and a billionaire) growing his Virgin Group brand from a record shop in London into a multinational juggernaut that includes health, music, media and travel (including space travel) companies. You could say he was a beneficiary of a world that rewarded his knowledge and skills rather than his academic credentials.

I asked him why his airline company, Virgin Atlantic, thrived at a time when many others went bust. His answer was simple: he approached things differently. When others followed the doctrine of maximising efficiency and tailoring the work organisation to that end, he put his staff first and asked them what they needed to excel. He empowered them to create an environment that would best serve their customers.

He also has a vision for education that puts character and values at its heart. Those aspects seem particularly important in the face of inequity and fragmentation in society, where people need a strong sense of right and wrong, sensitivity to the claims that others make on us, and a grasp of the limits on individual and collective action.

Sir Richard is certainly not alone. School dropouts like Thomas Edison, Albert Einstein, Bill Gates, Steve Jobs and Mark Zuckerberg have all fundamentally transformed their fields. And yet, in economies that still react mainly to qualifications earned at the beginning of a working life rather than to the capabilities acquired throughout life, very few of those who fail at school will become a Sir Richard, let alone have a voice in transforming education.

In those three days with Sir Richard I realised how often the people who make decisions about education are usually those who have been well served by the education system, not those who struggled through it. But it will often be the latter who can help reveal an education system's weaknesses and highlight the urgency of the need for change.

There are many ways in which schools could use the voice and experience of students – both those who succeeded and those who "failed" – to guide improvements to the relevance and organisation of schooling. Portugal's Education Minister Tiago Brandão Rodrigues explained to me in 2016 how the ministry had, as one of its first initiatives, given Portugal's schools an additional euro for every student enrolled, and the students themselves could decide how to spend the money. At first, not all of the money was well spent. In one school, students reportedly voted to buy everyone an ice cream. But as time went by, students in many schools took ownership over resource allocations in their school, well beyond this limited budget, and helped schools better align resources with what really made a difference in the life and learning of students. Marc Prensky, American writer on education, and Russell Quaglia, American researcher on education, have done extensive work on the impact of students' voice and agency. Their insights could have a major impact on efforts to make instruction more relevant to a wider range of learners.[11,12]

How policy can help create a more equitable system

How we treat the most vulnerable students and citizens shows who we are as a society. Providing equitable education opportunities is not a technically complex issue, and the PISA data show that in some countries – and in some schools in many countries – even the most disadvantaged children can be high performers in school. The issue becomes difficult only when it becomes intertwined with politics and vested interests, which can massively distort what is in the best interest of children.

PISA data show that one of the most important factors that can affect a student's performance is the socio-economic background of the other students in the class. The implication is that one of the most important resources to be allocated to schools and classrooms is the students themselves. Germany's failure to join other northern European nations in moving away from a tripartite organisation of secondary schools, based on social class, in the years leading up to and just following the Second World War made it difficult for that country to provide the quality of education to lower-income, and particularly immigrant, students that they needed to have a decent chance in life.

The subsequent decision in some of Germany's states to change from three education streams to two has contributed to the improvement in equity in recent years. Along the same lines, Poland realised a substantial reduction in the share of poorly performing students by converting a secondary school system that was primarily organised by social class into one in which all classes of students are enrolled in comprehensive schools.

Japan's decision, taken in the 19th century, to break with the kind of school and social structure on which Germany's school system is still based made it possible for Japan to create schools in which all Japanese children have a good chance of achieving world-class outcomes. The Meiji government's reform contributed to that country's ability to combine high overall performance with high equity of results.

Sweden calculates the funding that it sends to each school based on a formula intended to make sure that every school has what it takes to implement the country's demanding curriculum. According to this formula, isolated communities above the Arctic Circle get more for the education of their students per capita than Stockholm does. This is because there are fewer students in rural high schools than in the city who will take a certain course – say, physics – so classes will be smaller; but all students, no matter where they live, are entitled to be taught physics because physics is a required course in the curriculum. Along the same lines, Swedish schools with a greater share of immigrant students receive more resources than schools with fewer immigrants.

In 2016, I had the privilege to chair the selection committee for the 2016 Pupil Premium Awards in the England, an initiative that provides schools with additional resources for each disadvantaged student. On the one hand, the pupil premium is not unique. The kind of formula-based funding that Sweden pioneered is now common practice in many countries.[13] On the other hand, the way in which the pupil premium has sparked ideas in some of England's schools is remarkable. England gives schools wide discretion in how to use the pupil premium, and the accompanying accountability requirements are exemplary. Essentially, schools can allocate these resources as they see fit, as long as they can point to and explain the evidence base for their decisions and account for their decisions to the public. That means they can enhance the instructional system, but they can also integrate a wider range of social services into the school environment that are critical for supporting disadvantaged students.

In other countries, similar resource allocations to schools tend to be far more prescriptive and regulated. Creating this kind of ownership for innovative solutions seems to be an important ingredient of empowerment. I was intrigued by the diversity of approaches that schools in England were choosing, and wondered whether government could ever be equally imaginative. Many of the schools went beyond exams and results to prioritise student well-being. Some schools focused on parents, conducting workshops for them to understand current teaching methods or asking parents to come to the school to give presentations to students about their work. Perhaps not surprisingly then, the PISA 2015 assessment showed the United Kingdom as one of the few Western countries where disadvantaged schools reported fewer shortages of material resources than privileged schools. Put another way, the United Kingdom was able to align material resources with socio-economic need (*FIGURE 4.4*).[14]

However, even when countries manage to devote equal if not more resources to schools facing greater socio-economic challenges, few countries succeed in aligning the quality of resources with those challenges (*FIGURE 4.4*). In other words, schools with greater needs sometimes receive more resources, but not necessarily the high-quality resources that could be the most useful.

But some countries have begun to change this. Singapore sends its best teachers to work with the students who are having the greatest difficulty meeting Singapore's high standards. In Japan, officials in the prefectural offices will transfer good teachers to schools with weak faculties to make sure that all students have equally capable instructors.

Sometimes even symbolic action can have a transformative impact. In 2006, Cecilia María Vélez, Minister of Education in Colombia at that time, showed me a former waste-treatment facility that used to poison some of the poorest neighbourhoods of the capital, Bogotá. The facility had been closed and Minister Velez had transformed it into a school and library, now called *El Tintal*. I saw it packed with children and their parents learning to read and studying with the help of teachers, coaches and social workers. I could see how the transformation of this former source of pollution and disease had become a symbol of the new Colombia: a once conflict-ridden country undergoing a profound silent revolution, where education, once the preserve of the wealthy, was finally becoming a public good.

Shanghai manages to attain both high scores in PISA and low variations in student performance across the schools in the province. This has not come about by chance but by determined efforts to convert weaker schools into stronger schools. As Marc Tucker notes,[15] these efforts include systematically upgrading the infrastructure of all schools to similar levels; establishing a system of financial transfer payments to schools serving disadvantaged students; and establishing career structures that incentivise high-performing teachers to teach in disadvantaged schools. It also involves pairing high-performing districts and schools with low-performing districts and schools, so that the authorities in each can exchange and discuss their development plans with each other, and institutes for teachers' professional development can share their curricula, teaching materials and good practices. The government commissions "strong" public schools to take over the administration of "weak" ones by having the "strong" school appoint one of its experienced leaders, such as the deputy principal, to be the principal of the "weak" school, and sending a team of experienced teachers to lead in teaching. The underlying expectation is that the ethos, management style and teaching methods of the high-performing school can be transferred to the poorer-performing school.

There is nothing other than outdated regulations and a lack of imagination that would prevent other education systems from pursuing similar efforts. In fact, there

FIGURE 4.4: DISADVANTAGED SCHOOLS ARE OFTEN ALLOCATED FEWER RESOURCES THAN ADVANTAGED SCHOOLS

INDEX OF DIFFERENCE BETWEEN ADVANTAGED AND DISADVANTAGED SCHOOLS

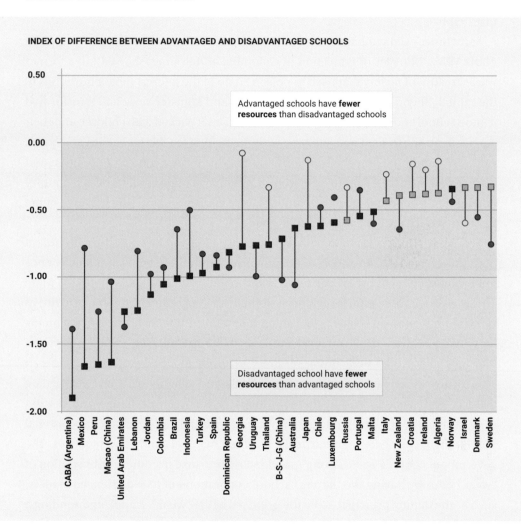

Notes: *The index of shortage of educational material is measured by an index summarising school principals' agreement with four statements about whether the school's capacity to provide instruction is hindered by a lack of and/or inadequate educational materials, including physical infrastructure. The index of shortage of educational staff is measured by an index summarising school principals' agreement with four statements about whether the school's capacity to provide instruction is hindered by a lack of and/or inadequate qualifications of the school staff. Negative differences imply that principals in disadvantaged schools perceive the amount and/or quality of resources in their schools*

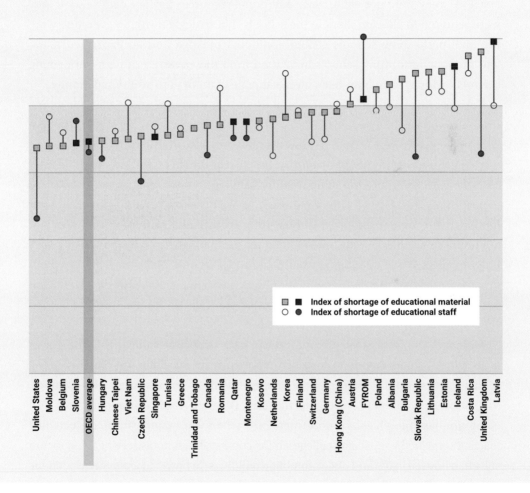

as an obstacle to providing instruction to a greater extent than principals in advantaged schools do. Positive differences mean that the perception of having inadequate resources is more common among principals of schools with a more privileged socio-economic intake. CABA (Argentina) refers to Ciudad Autónoma de Buenos Aires (Argentina). B-S-J-G (China) refers to Beijing-Shanghai-Jiangsu-Guangdong (China). FYROM refers to the Former Yugoslav Republic of Macedonia.

Source: OECD, PISA 2015 Database, Table I.6.13.

StatLink ᴹˢ⌐ http://dx.doi.org/10.1787/888933432823

are similar examples elsewhere. When I visited the state of Ceará, in Brazil, I saw how the highest-performing schools there received a significant reward in additional financial resources that allowed them to hire more specialised teachers and experts. However, they were not using these additional resources in their own school; they were required to allocate them to the schools that struggle most. So everyone won: the high-performing schools gained additional prestige and an expanded team, and the low-performing schools benefitted from the expertise of high-performing schools – which might have been more valuable to them than additional money.

Contrast this with a system of school finance in many US states that, for a long time, allowed wealthy people to form school-tax districts with other wealthy people who, collectively, were able to pay low tax rates and still produce large tax revenues, enabling these wealthy people to hire the best teachers in the state and surround their children with children from other wealthy families, thereby creating overwhelming educational advantages for their children. At the other end of the spectrum, poor families, who could not afford the houses that are available in the communities that are home to wealthy people, often ended up paying high tax rates but raising very little revenue. While adequacy lawsuits in the 1980s and 1990s have made school finance somewhat more equitable, PISA data show that schools in disadvantaged neighbourhoods still report a much greater shortage of human resources than schools in more privileged neighbourhoods.[16]

Moreover, the fact that significant funding gaps exist shows that it is in the power of localities to pass bonds to invest in infrastructure. So while the best-resourced school districts get buildings that are equipped with advanced science laboratories, sophisticated equipment, elaborate theatres, Olympic-sized swimming pools and computer-based graphics labs, not to mention teachers who majored in the subjects they teach at some of the most elite colleges in the country, the schools serving the poor are still often housed in old and often crumbling buildings. In between are many gradations of quality, reflecting the different socio-economic segments of the population.

What Germany accomplished indirectly by having different secondary schools for students from different social classes, the United States achieved directly through its system of local control of school finance. The effect of that system is exactly the same as the effect, in other countries, of having different schools for different socio-economic segments of the population. There are schools for the rich, schools for the middle classes, schools for the working classes and schools for the poor. The difference is that in those few industrialised countries that still practice this sort of streaming, it is practised only at the secondary level, while in the United States this sort of social segregation is evident in elementary or primary school as well as in high school. In this challenging context, it is remarkable that the United States has been able to raise equity in education opportunities at least to the OECD average level.

Canada had a similar system of school financing as that in the United States, but the country has been gradually shifting funding decisions entirely or almost entirely to provincial authorities. Provinces now provide block grants based on numbers of students. There are also grants to fund particular needs, such as special education, or to help districts meet specific challenges, such as transportation in remote districts. There is also "equalisation funding", which is used in the districts that retain some local funding to provide equal support to the poorer districts.

Of course, in the early stages of a country's economic development, the demand for highly educated people is limited, and so are the resources for developing such people. One way to meet that need is to put what money there is into the children who are, by virtue of the education and income of their parents, the most advantaged students in the whole society. That is why segregating schools by social class and concentrating efforts on a small number of students was an efficient strategy for providing education in countries in the first stages of industrialisation. But now, when far larger proportions of highly educated people are demanded in the world's high-wage economies, it is not only socially unjust but highly inefficient to organise an education system this way.

An invitation to the dance in France

Even in education systems where social disparities are considerable, there are many grassroots initiatives that successfully combat inequality.

OECD data show that one of the largest gaps in learning outcomes between children from poor families and those from wealthy families is found in France. In fact, France is one of the few countries that has gone backwards on equity in PISA: differences in opportunity keep growing.

But a show I saw at the *Maison de la Danse* in Lyon in 2015 gave me hope. The performers were all amateurs from one of the poorest neighbourhoods in the city. Some of the actors, aged four to 92, had never before set foot in the place, and even fewer would have attended a classical music concert. And yet all of them danced to Mozart.

Given a history of poor participation in educational and cultural activities in this district of the city, the organisers had recruited 200 volunteer performers in the hopes of ending up with 100. Not only did no one drop out of the project, an additional 100 people showed up spontaneously after news of the project spread across the city. Some of the young performers might have never received a pass grade in school or heard an encouraging word from their teachers, but that night they all received a wild ovation from an audience of well over 1 000 people.

The magic of this initiative was its simple formula, one that could inspire education everywhere. It used artistic expression to transcend ingrained identities and ideas that keep people apart. It united the most inspiring professionals with amateurs to show that those who may have the skills, but not yet the confidence, can still participate. The project demanded rigour in practice and set the highest standards for everyone involved. Choreographers did not insist on their own ideas; they were capable of helping the participants see and develop their own creative approaches. The choreographers and dancers worked together for more than a year until every detail fit perfectly together. The budget for this project was incredibly small compared with the result and its impact.

What impressed me most when speaking with some of the dancers, choreographers, social workers, teachers and school leaders involved was how this project was creating ripples in the wider community. Every participant I spoke with told me how much the work had helped them grow; and the words I heard most frequently were tolerance, identity, respect, fairness, social responsibility, integrity and self-awareness – precisely the kinds of things that school systems are now looking to cultivate in their students.

A parent who admitted that he had been reluctant to send his daughter to this social experiment explained how much his daughter had developed because of it. Other parents said that they had worried that the time their children spent practising the arts would cut into their school work – only to find that their children's academic performance improved over the year. And a primary school teacher described how much her class was inspired, and how much her own teaching was enriched, by working with non teaching professionals.

On my way back to Paris, with the world and all its problems passing by at the pace of a high-speed train, I wondered how the French education system will respond to the mounting challenges it faces, and how open it will be to such innovative experiences. Of course, having certain fundamental knowledge and skills will always remain the cornerstone of success in life, but these are no longer enough. The future will judge French schools on their capacity to help students develop autonomy and prepare them to live and work amid diverse cultures, and to appreciate different ideas, perspectives and values.

Celebrating diversity and partnerships in New Zealand

In 2013, on the other side of the world, I was greeted by a group of ferocious warriors at *Te Kura Kaupapa Māori o Hoani Waititi*, New Zealand's first community school offering Māori medium instruction. They approached slowly, offering the choice between picking a fight or settling for peace. With that choice made, we were warmly received with a traditional *pōwhiri* greeting ceremony at the school's *marae*, a special place for such symbolic meetings. In Māori culture, greeting others is an important opportunity for people to show respect and set the tone for whatever comes after.

That hour-long ceremony included speakers crafting poetic images and an impressive singing performance from the school's entire student population. Principal Rawiri Wright, former leader of the Māori language schooling organisation, asked me later how such artistic and social skills feature in New Zealand' schools standards and in comparisons made by the OECD. He also referred proudly to the latest results on academic performance, which showed his students outperforming schools with much more advantaged students. He saw these results vindicating his stance that the academic performance that we value comes as a by-product of the holistic Māori medium instruction that his school offers.

Wright readily conceded that the school was not without its fair share of social and managerial issues, but it demonstrated how Māori running their own schools can offer their children – who often perform as dismally as minorities in other schools – a viable education that prepares them both to be citizens in the modern world and to be active proponents of their traditional culture. Wright sees helping children understand their cultural heritage as the foundation on which the self-confidence and self-esteem that are so badly needed among the Māori student population is built.

It may seem like something from another era to ask children to remember 700 ancestors, but it also means giving them assurance that they are not alone in facing the challenges of a rapidly changing world. Pita Sharples, Associate Minister for Education with responsibility for some key Māori education priorities, gave a moving account of how he had established this school against all odds but with the deep commitment of the community. This had been after more than a century in which teaching the Māori language and culture had been outlawed.

In very different ways, community engagement and partnership were also the guiding principles of Sylvia Park School in Auckland. Most of us know what it is like to be invited to school for a parents' evening – on the school's terms and according to the school's schedule. We also know who tends to show up at these meetings, and who doesn't – or can't. The Mutukaroa Home School Learning Partnership at Sylvia Park has turned all this on its head.

Arina, an inspiring teacher and counsellor, explained how she did whatever it took to meet each parent at their home or at work, review their child's performance with them individually, and then provide parents with the assistance they needed to assume their responsibilities for the development of their child. The ministry's evaluation found that the Sylvia Park project had lifted the achievement of new entrants from well below the national average to above it in just two years. The ministry was already examining ways to scale-up the initiative, replicating the core elements of the partnership in a way that would work for other schools.

At Newton Central School in Auckland, I met Hoana Pearson, another school principal who defined the world through relationships. For her, there was no bridge too far, no stakeholder too distant, no dispute that could not be resolved through consultation, dialogue and collaboration. No one escaped her warm hug. As we walked from one richly decorated classroom to the next, she greeted every child by name, and picked up pieces of trash to maintain the meticulous order of the premises. Newton Central provides education that reflects a deep commitment to biculturalism and the principles of the Treaty of Waitangi, the agreement struck in the 19th century between Māori leaders and the British.

At Newton Central, socio-economic background and culture were not obstacles to learning; instead, the school capitalised on the diversity of its students. Principal Pearson encouraged her teachers to collaborate and be innovative. She worked with individual teachers to identify any weaknesses in their practice, and that often meant not just creating awareness of what they did, but changing their underlying mindset. She motivated her teachers to have high expectations, a shared sense of purpose, and a collective belief in their common ability to make a difference for every child.

Hoana Pearson made this happen, and New Zealand's liberal and entrepreneurial school system gave her the space to make it happen. Newton Central is an example of how school autonomy works at its best, and it explained why many of New Zealand's schools are among the highest performers in PISA.

The challenge for New Zealand is to get everybody to that level, to spread good practice and make excellence universal. I have heard from some school principals of the difficulties they face in attracting, developing and retaining effective teachers, in managing their resources strategically and in collaborating with other schools. In New Zealand's more privileged schools, the school's trustees provide strong support. They elect talented principals and add the expertise of lawyers, accountants and administrators, essential for running autonomous schools. But schools in disadvantaged neighbourhoods have a hard time finding any trustees; when they do, these trustees are unlikely to provide the governance, oversight and resources needed – and they are even more unlikely to challenge an underperforming principal.

New Zealand's school system does not need to respond to this situation with administrative prescription; improvement can come from the knowledge that is already in the school system. That means that professional autonomy should go hand in hand with a collaborative culture. Teachers need to be independent but not left alone; they can work in multiprofessional teams and be supported by health and social professionals. New Zealand needs its best teachers to help other teachers get on top of changes made to the curriculum or teaching practice; it needs its best school principals to enable other schools to develop and apply effective strategies.

Having successfully introduced a coherent system of education standards – the first of its kind in New Zealand – the government is providing schools and teachers with the tools they need to implement these standards and monitor the progress of individual students. But there is still a long way to go until strategic thinking and planning take place at every level of the system, until every school discusses what the national standards mean for them, until every decision is made at the level of those most able to implement them.

The teachers' unions in New Zealand have contested the setting of standards and public transparency, fearing this will introduce a culture of external accountability and factory-style organisation of the kind that will drive out creative and professional teachers and school leaders. Given the nature of the evaluation tools and their heavy reliance on professional judgement, these concerns seem somewhat misplaced, but they were an undercurrent in many of my conversations. There seem to be too few principals like Hoana Pearson, who cherish autonomy but see their schools as part of a national education system, who embrace national standards as a tool for peer learning and for the continuous improvement of school leaders' and teachers' daily practice.

Getting parents involved

Policies to foster inclusion need to look beyond school walls. Creating an environment of co-operation with parents and communities is at the heart of this. If parents and teachers establish relationships based on trust, schools can rely on parents as valuable partners in the cognitive and socio-emotional education of their students. Indeed, PISA shows that school principals' perceptions of parents' constant pressure to adopt high academic standards and raise student achievement tends to be associated with fewer underperforming students.[17]

I asked a teacher in a rural suburb of Chengdu, China, how she succeeded in bringing parents along on the educational journey of her children, given that few of them had any education themselves. She replied that, like other teachers in her school, she phoned parents about twice a week to discuss the development of their child. She spoke with them not just about classroom issues, but also about more general parental support. When I asked her how she could manage that in addition to her many other responsibilities, she seemed surprised and said she had never thought about this as an additional workload; she felt she would never be able to do her work as a teacher without the help and support of her students' parents. The school system supported her in this endeavour, not least by limiting her classroom teaching time to 15 hours per week.

Reconciling choice and equity

Many countries are struggling to reconcile their aspirations for greater flexibility and more opportunities for parents to choose their child's school with the need to ensure quality, equity and coherence in their school systems.

While enhanced school autonomy seems a common characteristic of high-performing education systems, these education systems differ substantially in how they regulate autonomy. They often pursue very different approaches when it comes to linking school autonomy to school choice, and to reconciling choice with equity. For example, England and Shanghai both emphasise market mechanisms, but while public policy in England mainly operates on the demand side of markets, seeking to improve schooling by enhancing parents' choice, in Shanghai, the main emphasis of public policy lies in creating a level playing field at the supply side: providing schools in the most disadvantaged areas with the best educational resources. While Finland and Hong Kong both emphasise local autonomy, in Finland that autonomy is exercised within a strong public school system, while most schools in Hong Kong are managed by independent school governing boards with relatively loose steering mechanisms.

Some countries have strengthened choice and equity-related mechanisms at the same time. England, for example, has rapidly increased the number of academies,[18] schools funded directly by the Department for Education and independent of local authority control. At the same time, England has established a pupil premium (see above) that provides schools with additional resources based on the socio-economic composition of their student body.[19] Some countries have also made it possible for private schools to be integrated into the public education system as government-dependent schools or as independent schools that receive a certain amount of public funding.

Proponents of school choice defend the right of parents to send their child to the school of their preference – because of quality, pedagogical approaches, religious denomination, affordability or geographic location – regardless of legal restrictions or financial or geographic barriers. The idea is that, given students' diverse needs and interests, a larger number of options in any one school system should lead to better value by reducing the cost of failure and mismatch. More options should stimulate competition and, in doing so, prompt schools to innovate, experiment with new pedagogies, become more efficient and improve the quality of the learning experience. Proponents argue that the increasing social and cultural diversity of modern societies calls for greater diversification in the education landscape, including allowing non-traditional providers and even commercial companies to enter the market.

Critics of school choice argue that, when presented with more options, students from advantaged backgrounds often choose to leave the public system, leading to greater social and cultural segregation in the school system. They are also concerned with over-reliance on theoretical models of rational, price-based economic competition as the basis for the allocation of resources.

At the macro level, such segregation can deprive children of opportunities to learn, play and communicate with children from different social, cultural and ethnic backgrounds; that, in turn, threatens social cohesion. To critics, vouchers and voucher-like systems divert public resources to private and sometimes commercial providers, thereby depriving public schools, which tend to serve large populations of disadvantaged students, of the resources they need to maintain the quality of the education they provide.

A closer look at the evidence shows that the arguments are not so clear-cut. Consider Hong Kong. This is a system that has a market-driven approach in virtually every field of public service, but it has been able to combine high student performance with a high degree of social equity in the distribution of education opportunities.

Education reform in Hong Kong

Schooling in Hong Kong used to be entirely funded by charitable philanthropy; it was only when the economy gathered strength in the 1960s that the government began to subsidise education. With the majority of schools run by charitable entities, the government rarely intervenes directly. Parents have a powerful influence on schools, both through their choice of schools and through local control. Parents sit on school-management committees, parent-teacher associations and on home-school co-operation committees. When I visited Hong Kong in 2012, then-Permanent Secretary for Education Cherry Tse told me that parents have more influence on what happens on the ground than does the Education Bureau. The city's vibrant cyber community has added to the tremendous pressures on schools to maintain a high quality of education.

Most leading newspapers report on policy debates as well as disputes in schools. Ruth Lee, principal at Ying Wa Girls' School, one of Hong Kong's elite schools that I visited at that time, explained how principals and teachers face a daily struggle to balance administrative accountability, client accountability and professional accountability while keeping their focus firmly on nurturing well-rounded children and helping parents see beyond their child's entry into university.

But that does not mean that education isn't a government priority. On the contrary, Hong Kong devotes more of its public budget – 23% – to education than any OECD country. What struck me even more was that the Education Bureau isn't the only body interested in education: education is high on the agenda of virtually every other government agency too. For example, Robin Ip, Deputy Head of Hong Kong's Central Policy Unit at the time, explained to me how important the development and deployment of teaching talent features as a cross-government priority. His unit provides advice on how Hong Kong can maintain its competitive edge in areas such as finance, trade and shipping, nurturing emerging industries (including education), and deepening economic co-operation with mainland China.

Ho Wai Chi, Assistant Director of the Independent Commission Against Corruption, and his team explained how the Commission deploys almost a fifth of its staff to education and community relations throughout the territory, with the aim of moving the agenda from fighting corruption to preventing it, and building a climate of trust in the rule of law and the institutions protecting it. That includes work on a secondary-school curriculum that builds confidence in the rule of law, addresses ethical dilemmas and seeks to change the agency's image from sending people to jail to sustaining society.

2012 was a year of particular importance for Hong Kong's education system, as it was the first year in which a cohort that had gone through the new integrated education system had graduated. The learner-centred reforms over the past years involved significant expansion of education opportunities as well as a shift in emphasis from teaching to learning, from relying on the memorisation of facts to developing learning skills, from serving economic needs to addressing individual needs.

The broader and more flexible curriculum seeks a better balance among intellectual, social, moral, physical and aesthetic facets, with much greater emphasis on the skills important for work, including foundation skills, career-related competencies, thinking skills, people skills, and on developing the values and attitudes that will help students succeed in a multicultural world. The reforms have also included more funding flexibility in support of schools.

Results from PISA suggest that Hong Kong is on the right track. They show high performance and significant improvements in students' more advanced skills and confidence as learners.

But it is also apparent that education in Hong Kong is rife with serious tensions: tension between what is desirable for the long-term and what is needed in the short-term; between the global and local; between the academic, personal, social and economic goals of the curriculum; between competition and co-operation; between specialisation and attention to the whole person; between knowledge transmission and knowledge creation; between the aspirations of a new, innovative curriculum and the narrow focus on exam preparation defended by a powerful private tutoring industry; between uniformity and diversity; and between assessment for selection and assessment for development.

The system is now also more subject to the political economy. Policies are no longer determined by technocrats, but by politicians with an eye on re-election. With teachers and school leaders a large and vocal part of the electorate, maintaining the high-quality examination and assessment regime is already proving to be a struggle.

The Flemish Community of Belgium and the Netherlands are also examples of successful choice-based systems.[20]

School choice in the Flemish Community of Belgium

The Flemish Community of Belgium was a high performer in the PISA 2015 science, reading and mathematics tests; 12% of students there were top performers in science. While some 75% of secondary school students and 62% of primary school students are not enrolled in public schools, most private schools can be considered as "government-dependent": they aim to meet regional attainment targets and are subject to quality-assurance inspections organised by the state. Rare are the private schools that position themselves completely outside the public system, and for-profit private schools are almost non-existent.

Education in the Flemish Community is characterised by the constitutional principle of "freedom of education", which gives any person the right to set up a school and determine its education principles, as long as it fulfils the regulations set by the Flemish government. Schools are not allowed to select students based on the results of admissions tests, performance, religious background or gender. Parents are allowed to choose the school for their child and are guaranteed access to a school within a reasonable distance from their home, with funding allocated to schools on a per-student basis. However, because of insufficient capacity, parents' choice is not always guaranteed and actually can be limited.

While schools managed by public authorities are required to be ideologically neutral, and the authorities must provide a choice of religious and non-denominational lessons, this does not apply to subsidised private schools. The largest share of these schools is run by denominational foundations, predominantly Catholic, but they also include schools, such as Waldorf schools, that use specific pedagogic methods.

Although the Flemish Community relies on an extensive Catholic school sector and other private school providers, schools cannot legally select students; they are obliged to accept all students regardless of religious background. There are no tuition fees in pre-primary, primary and secondary education. While both elementary and secondary schools levy charges, these are strictly regulated.

The Flemish education system is one of the most decentralised among all systems in OECD countries. Both public and private schools enjoy considerable autonomy. They are responsible for recruiting teachers, allocating resources and deciding on spending unrelated to staff. They can also determine course content, within the limits imposed by the publicly defined minimum curriculum targets. Schools can adopt different pedagogical approaches. The result is a comparatively high level of competition among schools in a semi-urban context. However, the between-school variation in PISA performance is one of the largest among OECD countries.

In recent years, school choice has been increasingly regulated in order to mitigate its adverse impact on socio-economic diversity across schools in urban areas. Attempts to ensure equal opportunities in school enrolment were pioneered in 2003 and adjusted in subsequent years. Drawing on lessons learned, a 2011 decree gives priority to certain places in oversubscribed schools to both disadvantaged and advantaged students, in proportion to the socio-economic composition of the neighbourhood in which the school is located. Implementation of this policy is decentralised to so-called "local negotiation platforms", which helps build stakeholder buy-in to the rules.

The Flemish Community of Belgium benefits from many of the advantages of school choice, such as a wide variety of pedagogies, which offers real choice for parents, and a strong drive towards quality, through competition between schools. It also suffers from some of the disadvantages of school choice, such as a relatively high level of socio-economic segregation among schools and a strong relationship between family background and learning outcomes. But overall, the education system largely succeeds in limiting inequity and social segregation by implementing some steering and accountability mechanisms that apply to all schools. The attainment targets, far from being an imposed national curriculum, offer guidance to schools in maintaining quality. An inspectorate evaluates schools regularly and monitors their performance. There are no central examinations, but system- and school-level assessments of the education delivered in specific subjects allow for monitoring the overall quality of education. Public and private schools are treated the same way in the state's accountability and oversight mechanisms.

Diversity among and within schools in the Netherlands

Like the Flemish Community of Belgium, the Netherlands is a high-performing school system where more than two in three 15-year-old students attend publicly funded private schools. It is also a highly diversified system, with wide differences among schools in pedagogical approaches, religious denomination and socio-economic profile. But the between school variation in PISA science performance in 2015 was one of the largest among OECD countries (just over 65% of the performance variation is explained by between-school differences in performance).

The Netherlands has a highly decentralised school system. School autonomy is grounded in the principle of "freedom of education", guaranteed by the Dutch Constitution since 1917. This allows any person to set up a school, organise teaching, and determine the educational, religious or ideological principles on which teaching is based. In principle, parents can choose their child's school (although this is somewhat restricted by the guidance given by education professionals when students complete primary school); but local authorities control enrolments to some extent in order to mitigate imbalances in school composition or weight student funding to support greater social diversity in schools.

In 2011, about one in three primary students was enrolled in a public school, one in three was enrolled in a Catholic school, one in four attended a Protestant school, and the remainder were enrolled in other types of government-dependent private schools. While public schools are open to all students, government-dependent private schools may refuse students whose parents do not subscribe to the school's profile or principles.

A distinctive feature of the Dutch system is the institution of school boards. These bodies are given far more powers than the schools they govern. The boards oversee the implementation of legislation and regulations in the school, and employ teachers and other staff. While in the past public schools were governed mostly by local authorities, governance has increasingly been devolved to independent school boards. The school governors who make up the boards may be volunteers (laypersons receiving an honorarium) or professionals (who receive a salary).

The role of the school boards is a subject of debate in the Netherlands. A recent OECD review[21] calls for strengthening the governance capacity and accountability of school boards by improving transparency and rebalancing decision-making powers between the board and school leaders.

Since the 1980s, the government has devolved additional responsibilities to schools. Private foundations have assumed responsibility for schools managed by local authorities (although the schools themselves remain public) and lump-sum financing has been introduced, which gives school boards the freedom to make their own spending decisions. Conversely, some re-centralisation has taken place through the establishment of national learning objectives and examination programmes. Mergers of school boards have been promoted, as larger school boards are considered to be more professional and financially stable.

In the decentralised Dutch education system, religious organisations and associations of citizens receive public funding for the schools for which they are responsible, provided they meet government regulations. Public and private schools receive the same amount of public funding in the form of a lump-sum allocation based on the number of enrolled students. Since the mid-1980s, additional subsidies are assigned for disadvantaged students, reflecting the higher cost of teaching them. Since 2006, these voucher weights have been based on parents' educational attainment, replacing previous criteria based on students' immigrant background.

Although publicly funded private schools are not allowed to charge mandatory tuition fees or operate for profit, state-funded schools can supplement their funding with voluntary contributions from parents or businesses. Private schools receive significantly more of such contributions than public schools do. Publicly funded private schools are not allowed to engage in selective admissions, but parents of prospective students may be required to subscribe to the school's profile or principles.

Similar to that of the Flemish Community of Belgium, the education system of the Netherlands manages to offer parents a wide choice, and fund private entities that organise schools with public resources in a way that is generally seen as fair. The overall high quality of the system can partly be attributed to its diversity, the degree of competition among schools, and the high level of autonomy enjoyed by school boards, school leaders and teachers. While the Netherlands shows large between-school variations in PISA performance, it succeeds – better than the Flemish Community of Belgium does – in maintaining equity in its system. The accountability system works well; teachers are regarded, and work, as professionals; and the relative consistency in the quality of schools allows for examinations to be centrally designed.

Choosing schools

In contrast to successful choice-based school systems such as those in Belgium, Hong Kong and the Netherlands, in Chile and Sweden the introduction of choice-based mechanisms seems to have led to a widening of social disparities without overall improvements in results. In May 2015, we published a report about this for Sweden, which I presented with Minister of Education Gustav Fridolin and then-Minister for Upper Secondary School, Adult Education and Training, Aida Hadžialić.[22] Five years earlier, in May 2010, I had given a keynote at the Summit of European Mayors in Stockholm where I had presented data that highlighted how Sweden's emphasis on autonomy and choice, which wasn't balanced with a strong regulatory framework and the capacity to intervene, was threatening Sweden's long-standing success in quality and equity in education. I was surprised, then, when Swedish mayors told me that they were prioritising choice over other considerations in response to demands from their residents.

It is worth taking a closer look at the data, and also to consider the political economy of the issues involved. The degree of choice that parents enjoy and the level of competition in school systems vary widely between countries and within countries among different social groups. Across 18 countries with comparative data in the PISA 2015 assessment, the parents of 64% of students reported that they had a choice of at least one other school available to them, but this percentage varies widely among countries.[23] Parents of students who attend rural and disadvantaged schools reported having less choice than parents of students in urban and advantaged schools.

PISA also asked parents to report how much importance they gave to certain criteria when choosing a school for their child. These were mainly related to school quality, financial considerations, the school's philosophy or mission, and distance between their home and the school. Across the 18 education systems, parents were more likely to consider important that there is a safe school environment, that the school has a good reputation and that the school has an active and pleasant climate – even more than the academic achievement of the students in the school.[24]

It is noteworthy that the parents of children who attend disadvantaged, rural and/or public schools were considerably more likely than the parents of children in advantaged, urban and/or private schools to report that the distance between the home and the school is important. The children of parents who assigned more importance to distance scored considerably lower in the PISA science assessment, even after accounting for the students' and schools' socio-economic profile. This was also observed among students whose parents considered low expenses to be important or very important. These students scored 30 points lower in science (roughly the equivalent of a school year) than students whose parents considered low expenses to be only somewhat important or not important. Again, the parents of students in disadvantaged and public schools were more likely than the parents of students in advantaged and private schools to consider low expenses important when they choose a school for their child. It seems that struggling families often have a hard time making choices based on student outcomes even if they have access to information about schools. They may not have the time to visit different schools, they may not have the transportation needed to get their children to the school of choice, or they may not have the time to get them to a school located further from their home or to pick them up at the end of the school day.

The degree of competition in a school system and the rate of enrolment in private schools can be related, but they are not the same thing. On average across OECD countries, about 84% of 15-year-old students attend public schools, about 12% attend government-dependent private schools, and slightly more than 4% attend government-independent private schools. Of the 12% of students who are enrolled in private government-dependent schools, around 38% of them attend schools run by a church or other religious organisation, 54% attend schools run by another non-profit organisation, and 8% attend schools run by a for-profit organisation. In Ireland, all 15-year-old students in private government-dependent schools attend a religious school; in Austria, all students enrolled in private government-dependent schools attend those run by another non-profit organisation; and in Sweden, over half of students in private government-dependent schools attend one run by a for-profit organisation.[25]

Public, private and public-private

Greater enrolment in private schools is often referred to as the privatisation of education, and is regarded as a move away from the notion of education as a public good. But we are often too quick to make that link. In many countries where large parts of the school system operate under private legal statutes, such schools are seen as legally private but functionally public. This means that, even though they are private entities, they contribute to fulfilling public missions and functions, and they see themselves as part of public education. For example, they can partly or completely follow the national curriculum and serve the public mission of education by providing quality education. There are also many cases in which private schools provide access to education for underserved communities and have equity-related missions.

As in other sectors of public policy, the distinction between public and private education is often blurred. Public-private partnerships are an accepted reality in various other public policy sectors, and there is no reason why education should be an exception. For me, the more relevant question is: how can public policy objectives, such as providing high-quality education for all students, be achieved?

Many critics of school choice claim that the prevalence of private schools would have a negative impact on the quality of education. But PISA data show that there is no relationship between the share of private schools in a country and the performance of an education system. After accounting for the socio-economic profile of schools, there is little difference in performance between public and private schools in most countries; where such differences are observed, they are mostly in favour of public schools.

At the system level, equity also seems virtually unrelated to the percentage of students enrolled in private schools. The positive association between the percentage of students enrolled in government-dependent private schools and student performance is mainly explained by the greater levels of autonomy these schools enjoy. This is noteworthy because opponents to school choice often argue that a larger share of private schools would turn education systems into quasi education "markets", with increased competition and segregation among schools. They also argue that extending the possibilities for private schools to be integrated into a functionally public system and receive public funding fosters disparities among schools, leading to greater between-school variations in learning outcomes. But again, at the country level, there is no correlation between the share of private schools in an education system and the percentage of the variation in PISA scores that is explained by that share.

Perhaps the most contentious issue is how much public funding should go to private schools. In Finland, Hong Kong, the Netherlands, the Slovak Republic and Sweden, principals of privately managed schools reported that over 90% of school funding comes from the government; in Belgium, Germany, Hungary, Ireland, Luxembourg and Slovenia, between 80% and 90% of funding for privately managed schools does. By contrast, in Greece, Mexico, the United Kingdom and the United States, 1% or less of funding for privately managed schools comes from the government; in New Zealand, between 1% and 10% does.[26] What is noteworthy here is that in countries where privately managed schools receive larger proportions of public funding, there is less of a difference in the socio-economic profiles of publicly and privately managed schools (*FIGURE 4.5*). Across OECD countries, 45% of the variation in this difference can be explained by the level of public funding devoted to privately managed schools; across all participating countries, 35% of the variation in this difference can be accounted for in this way.

In order to mitigate the potential negative effects of school choice and public funding of private schools, particularly segregation and social stratification, various governments have implemented compensatory financing mechanisms. For example, Chile, the Flemish Community of Belgium and the Netherlands have instituted weighted student-funding schemes, whereby funding follows the student on a per-student basis, and the amount provided depends on the socio-economic status and education needs of each student. These schemes target disadvantaged students and, in doing so, make these students more attractive to schools competing for enrolment.

Specific area-based support schemes, such as the "zones of educational priority" found in France and Greece, are observed in school systems with large between-school variations in performance and a concentration of low-performing schools in certain locations. In Belgium, government-dependent private schools, which constitute a majority of the market, receive almost the same amount as public schools, and they are forbidden from charging tuition fees or selecting students.

▪ The vexing issue of vouchers

It is also important to pay due attention to the mechanisms by which public funding is provided to private schools. One way is through vouchers, which assist

FIGURE 4.5: PUBLIC FUNDING CAN MAKE PRIVATE EDUCATION AFFORDABLE FOR ALL STUDENTS

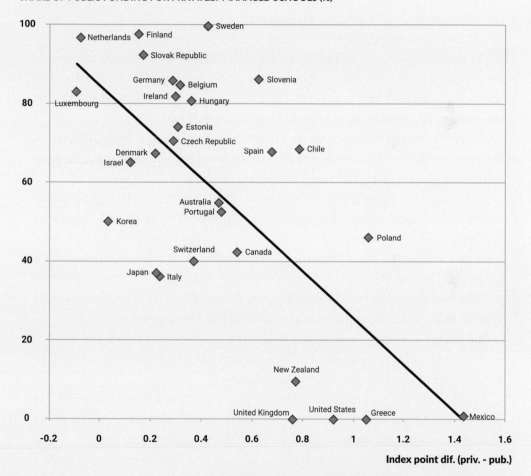

SHARE OF PUBLIC FUNDING FOR PRIVATELY MANAGED SCHOOLS (%)

Index point dif. (priv. - pub.)

DIFFERENCE BETWEEN THE SOCIO-ECONOMIC PROFILE OF PUBLICLY
AND PRIVATELY MANAGED SCHOOLS (PRIV. - PUB.)

Source: OECD, PISA 2009 Database.

parents directly. As of 2009, 9 out of 22 OECD countries with available data reported that they use vouchers to facilitate enrolment in government-dependent private primary schools. In five of these countries, the voucher programme was restricted to disadvantaged students. At the lower secondary level, 11 out of 24 countries reported using voucher schemes, 7 of which targeted disadvantaged students. At the upper secondary level, 5 of 11 voucher programmes were means-tested. Of the surveyed OECD countries, seven reported that they provide vouchers from primary through upper secondary school.[27] Tuition tax credits, which allow parents to deduct expenses for private school tuition from their tax liabilities, are used less frequently than vouchers. As of 2009, only 3 out of 26 OECD countries with available data reported using tax credits to facilitate enrolment in government-dependent private schools.[28]

Between universal voucher systems, in which vouchers are available to all students, and targeted voucher systems, in which vouchers are provided only to disadvantaged students, there are large differences in their role in mitigating the adverse effects of school choice. Vouchers that are available for all students can help expand school choice and promote competition among schools. School vouchers that target only disadvantaged students can help improve equity in access to schools. An analysis of PISA data shows that, when comparing systems with similar levels of public funding for privately managed schools, the difference in the socio-economic profiles between publicly managed schools and privately managed schools is twice as large in education systems that use universal vouchers as in systems that use targeted vouchers.

The design of voucher schemes is thus a key determinant of their success. For example, regulating private school pricing and admissions criteria seems to limit the social inequities associated with voucher schemes.[29]

Beyond that, the international evidence suggests that schools that are selective in their admissions tend to attract students with greater ability and higher socio-economic status, regardless of the quality of the education they provide. Given that high-ability students are less costly to educate and their presence can make a school more attractive to parents, schools that can control their intake wind up with a competitive advantage. Allowing private schools to select their students thus gives these schools an incentive to compete on the basis of exclusiveness rather than on their intrinsic quality. That, in turn, can undermine the positive effects of competition.

The evidence also shows that selective admissions can be a source of greater inequality and stratification within a school system. However, there are few studies that have investigated whether these effects vary, depending on the selection criteria – for example, interviews with parents compared to results of aptitude tests. It is also important to keep in mind that students are selected not only based on explicit admissions criteria but also because of parents' self-selection, selective expulsion and more subtle barriers to entry. Policies that aim to reduce segregation in a school system should therefore also identify and address overly complex application procedures, expulsion practices, lack of information and other factors that prevent some students and parents from exercising their right to choose a school.

Critics also argue that allowing publicly funded private schools to charge tuition fees gives these schools an unfair advantage over public schools and undermines the principle of free school choice. Like selective admissions, imposing substantial add-on fees tends to skim the top students from the public sector and increase inequalities in education. Some policy interventions that limited fees for low-income families have been effective in reducing segregation; but I have found few empirical studies in developed countries that have determined the effect of fees as distinct from that of selective admissions and other confounding factors.

Relatively little is known about whether there is a threshold of household contributions beyond which lower-income families will be deterred from choosing subsidised private schools. However, both simulations and empirical evidence confirm that public funding might fail to widen access to private schools unless it is accompanied by restrictions on tuition fees. If private schools invest public resources to improve their quality, rather than to broaden access, subsidies can exacerbate inequities across schools. This is one of the reasons why abolishing substantial add-on fees, along with offering targeted vouchers, can help reduce disparities in achievement between advantaged and disadvantaged students.

I have concluded from all this that school choice, in and of itself, neither assures nor undermines the quality of education. What seem to matter are smart policies that maximise the benefits of choice while minimising the risks, and establishing a level playing field for all providers to contribute to the school system. Well-crafted school-choice policies can help school systems deliver education tailored to a diverse student population, while limiting the risk of social segregation. When market mechanisms are introduced or expanded in education systems, the role of public policy needs to shift from overseeing the quality and efficiency of public schools to ensuring that oversight and governance arrangements are in place to guarantee that every child benefits from accessible, high-quality education.

It is clear that school choice will only generate the anticipated benefits when the choice is real, relevant and meaningful, that is, when parents can choose an important aspect of their child's education, such as the pedagogical approaches used to teach him or her. If schools are not allowed to respond to diverse student populations, and to distinguish themselves from each other, choice is meaningless.

In turn, private schools might need to accept the public steering and accountability mechanisms that ensure the attainment of public-policy objectives in exchange for the funding they receive from the public purse. All parents must be able to exercise their right to choose the school of their preference; that means government and schools need to invest in developing their relationships with parents and local communities, and help parents make informed decisions. Successful choice-based systems have carefully designed checks and balances that prevent choice from leading to inequity and segregation.

Last but not least, the more flexibility there is in the school system, the stronger public policy needs to be. While greater school autonomy, decentralisation and a more demand-driven school system seek to devolve decision making to the frontline, central authorities need to maintain a strategic vision and clear guidelines for education, and offer meaningful feedback to local school networks and individual schools. In other words, only through a concerted effort by central and local education authorities will school choice benefit all students.

Big city, big education opportunities

More than half of the world's population now lives in cities and this ratio is projected to increase to seven out of ten people by 2050. Urban environments attract people from rural areas and foreign countries hoping for better economic prospects and easier access to public services, such as education and health care, and a wider variety of cultural institutions. Major urban areas have already seen their populations grow to equal or surpass those of many countries. Mexico City's population of over 20 million, for example, is larger than that of Denmark, Hungary or the Netherlands.

The concentration of human talent can stimulate research and development, making cities regional hubs for growth and innovation. The concentration of resources found in cities makes it easier to conduct business. In cities, companies are closer to more clients and customers, they have immediate access to transport, and they have access to a skilled labour force. Cities often share certain characteristics that distinguish them from the rest of the country. This means that cities in two very different countries – New York City and Shanghai, for example – may have more in common with each other than with the rural communities in their own countries.

But while urban areas concentrate productivity and employment opportunities, they can also contain high levels of poverty and labour-market exclusion. These difficult conditions can unravel social networks and loosen family and community ties, which, in turn, can engender social alienation, distrust and violence. Many of these problems tend to show up at the school gate.

Still, cities offer significant advantages to schools, such as a richer cultural environment, a more attractive workplace for teachers, more school choice, and better job prospects that can help motivate students. Indeed, major cities have also been among the star performers in education. Countless policy makers and researchers have flocked to observe the education systems of Hong Kong, Shanghai and Singapore, which have consistently ranked among the top performers in PISA assessments.[30] Many visitors have been particularly impressed by how these education systems succeed in embracing the social diversity in student populations that is intrinsic to large urban environments – something that many other education systems struggle to achieve.

PISA results confirm that, in several countries, students from urban areas (defined here as cities with over one million inhabitants) do as well as students in PISA's top performing city-states, even if the different push and pull factors of urban environments play out very differently across countries.[31]

For example, students in urban centres in Japan can compare their science performance with top-performer Singapore. Students in major urban centres in Portugal, a country that performs around the OECD average, can compare with the average student in Finland. And students in urban centres in Poland can compare with the average student in South Korea. More generally, students in large urban areas in OECD countries outperform students in rural schools by the equivalent of more than one year of education.

These differences in performance between students living in rural areas and those in big cities can sometimes be linked to the socio-economic disparities between their populations. But PISA results show that differences in social background explain only part of the story; much of the performance gap remains even after accounting for socio-economic status. So there does seem to be something distinct about education in large cities.

What seems most striking is how willing cities are to expose and share their strengths and weaknesses across cultural and linguistic borders. In a way, cities seem to engage with global opportunities much more than countries as a whole do. Whenever I meet with city leaders, I find them outward-looking and keenly interested to learn from other cities, wherever on the globe these may be located. Rarely do they ask whether they can or should learn from other cities and cultures the way that national education leaders often do.

But not everywhere do students in large cities do better. While the performance of most countries improves when only the scores of students in urban environments are considered, the opposite effect is seen in a few countries. In Belgium and the United States, for example, the performance of students in large urban areas drags down the overall national score. This might be because, in these countries, not all students enjoy the advantages that large urban centres offer. They might, for example, come from socio-economically disadvantaged homes, speak a different language at home than the one in which they are taught at school, or have only one parent to turn to for support and assistance.

The large difference in performance in Poland, for example, reflects the wide gap in socio-economic levels between urban and rural areas. And those differences are made manifest in how educational resources, and cultural and educational facilities, are distributed, depending on the socio-economic profile of a geographic area. All of these can have an impact on student performance.

So while moderate PISA performers like Israel, Poland and Portugal can take some pride in knowing that their students living in urban areas now perform on par with students in the best-performing education systems, these countries need to address inequities in the distribution of educational resources and opportunities, and in learning outcomes insofar as they are associated with students' backgrounds.

In particular, isolated communities in these countries might need targeted support and policies to ensure that students attending schools in these areas reach their full potential. Conversely, those countries whose urban students underperform will have to figure out how to enable these students to tap into the cultural and social advantages that urban environments provide, otherwise these countries will continue to fall short in excellence in education.

Targeted support for immigrant students

In March 2004, the president of the German commission for immigration and integration, Rita Süssmuth, and I reported on the educational achievement of students with an immigrant background.[32] At the time, the commission showed its concern about how well schools help students integrate into their new communities, but the topic did not rise to the top of the policy agenda until much later. In those years, Germany, like many other countries, lost valuable time to prepare the country for a more diverse school population.

More than a decade later, in January 2016, when I met with Filippo Grandi, United Nations High Commissioner for Refugees, the issue of migration had taken on an entirely new dimension. Tens of thousands of migrants and asylum-seekers – including an unprecedented number of children – were flooding into Europe to seek safety and a better life.

Even before that influx, the population of immigrant students in OECD countries had grown from 9.4% of the population of 15-year-old students in 2006 to 12.5% of that population in 2015. But despite media-stoked concern, this growth did not lead to a decline in the education standards in host communities.[33] That may be surprising, but only at first glance. While it is true that migrants often endure economic hardship and precarious living conditions, many immigrants bring to their host countries valuable knowledge and skills. On average across OECD countries, the majority of the first-generation immigrant students taking part in the PISA 2015 assessment had at least one parent who had attended school for as many years as the average parent in the host country.

Equally striking is the remarkable cross-country variation in performance between immigrant students and students without an immigrant background, even after accounting for their socio-economic status (*FIGURES 4.6 AND 4.7*). Even if the culture and the education acquired before migrating have an impact on student performance, the country where immigrant students settle seems to matter much more.

But designing education policies to address immigrant students' needs – particularly language instruction – is not easy, and education policy alone is insufficient. For example, immigrant students' performance in PISA is more strongly (and negatively) associated with the concentration of disadvantaged students in schools than with the concentration of immigrants or of students who speak at home a language that is different from the language of instruction.[34] Reducing the concentration of disadvantage in schools might require changes in other social policy, such as housing or welfare, to encourage a more balanced social mix in schools.

Consider this: When the influx of low-skilled immigrants to Europe began to grow rapidly in the 1970s, the Netherlands chose to accommodate the migrants in large, specially constructed urban housing blocks. The neighbouring Flemish-speaking community of Belgium, whose schools are run on policies very similar to those in the Netherlands, chose to give vouchers to migrant workers to supplement the amount that they would otherwise have to spend on housing. They could use these vouchers wherever they wished. The result was that there were fewer Flemish schools composed entirely of the sons and daughters of migrant workers.

Years later, the Netherlands faced an enormous challenge to educate students from the public housing projects whom they had not been able to integrate into their education system and who continued to be low achievers. By contrast, in Flemish-speaking Belgium, where the migrants had been more dispersed, students from immigrant families were doing far better than their counterparts in the Netherlands, where housing segregation had led to school segregation.

Many children with an immigrant background face enormous challenges at school. They need to adjust quickly to different academic expectations, learn in a new language, forge a social identity that incorporates both their background and their adopted country of residence – and withstand conflicting pressures from family and peers. These difficulties are magnified when immigrants are segregated in poor neighbourhoods with disadvantaged schools. It should thus come as no surprise that PISA data have consistently shown a performance gap between students with an immigrant background and native-born students.

However, this should not mask the finding that many immigrant students overcome these obstacles and excel academically. Despite the considerable challenges they face, they succeed in school, a testament to the great drive, motivation and openness that they and their families possess.

In 1954, the United States opened its borders to an immigrant from Syria. His son, Steve Jobs, became one of the world's most creative entrepreneurs who revolutionised six industries: personal computers, film, music, telephony, tablet computing and digital publishing. Jobs's life story may sound like a fairy tale, but it is firmly rooted in reality. While immigrants are over-represented among poor performers in PISA, they are not under-represented among top performers, certainly not when accounting for socio-economic status. In many countries, the share of disadvantaged immigrants who attain high scores in PISA is as large as the share of disadvantaged students without an immigrant background who are high performers. In fact, in a number of countries there is a larger share of immigrants than non-immigrants among the highest-achieving disadvantaged students.[35]

These highly motivated students, who manage to overcome the double disadvantage of poverty and an immigrant background, have the potential to make exceptional contributions to their host countries. Most immigrant students and their parents hold an ambition to succeed that in some cases surpasses the aspirations of families in their host country.[36] For example, parents of immigrant students in several countries are more likely to expect that their children will earn

FIGURE 4.6: IMMIGRANT STUDENTS CAN PERFORM AS WELL AS THEIR NATIVE PEERS

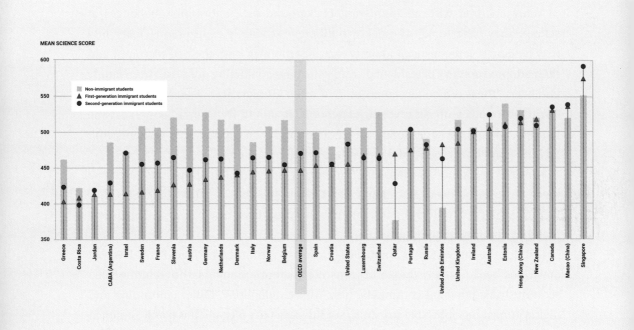

Notes: Only countries where the percentage of immigrant students is higher than 6.25% are shown. CABA (Argentina) refers to Ciudad Autónoma de Buenos Aires (Argentina).

Countries and economies are ranked in ascending order of the mean science score of first-generation immigrant students.

Source: OCDE, PISA 2015 Database, Table 1.7.4a

StatLink ᴍꜱ￫ http://dx.doi.org/10.1787/888933432903

FIGURE 4.7: IMMIGRANT STUDENTS ARE NOT DOOMED TO POOR PERFORMANCE

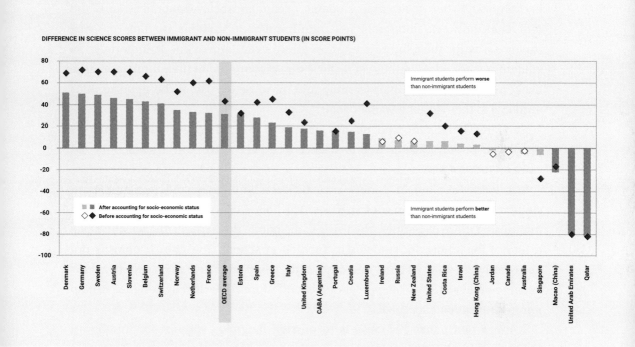

Notes: *Only countries where the percentage of immigrant students is higher than 6.25%, and with available data on the PISA index of economic, social and cultural status are shown. CABA (Argentina) refers to Ciudad Autónoma de Buenos Aires (Argentina). Statistically significant differences are marked in a darker tone.*

Countries and economies are ranked in descending order of the difference in science performance related to immigrant background, after accounting for students' socio-economic status.

Source: OECD, PISA 2015 Databases, Table I.7.4a.

StatLink http://dx.doi.org/10.1787/888933432915

a university-level degree than the native-born parents of native-born students. That is remarkable, given that immigrant students in these countries are more disadvantaged and do not perform as well as students without an immigrant background. When comparing students of similar socio-economic status, the difference between immigrant and non-immigrant students in their parents' expectations for their future education grows even larger. This is important, as students who hold ambitious yet realistic expectations about their future are more likely to put effort into their learning and make better use of the opportunities available to them to achieve their goals.

Similarly, immigrant students are 50% more likely than their non-immigrant peers who perform just as well in science to expect to work in a science-related career (**FIGURE 4.8**).

The large variation in performance between immigrant and non-immigrant students in different countries suggests that policy can play a significant role in minimising those disparities. The key is to dismantle the barriers that usually make it harder for immigrant students to succeed at school. The crunch point is not necessarily the point of entry, but afterwards, when educators and school systems decide whether or not to offer programmes and support specifically designed to help immigrant students succeed.

A quick-win policy response is to provide language support for immigrant students with limited proficiency in the language of instruction. Common features of successful language-support programmes include sustained language training across all grade levels, centrally developed curricula, teachers who are specifically educated in second-language acquisition, and a focus on academic language. Integrating language and content learning has also been proven effective.[37]

Since language development and general intellectual growth are intertwined, I also learned that it is best not to postpone teaching the mainstream curriculum until students fully master their new language. What is important is to ensure close co-operation between language teachers and classroom teachers, an approach that is widely used in countries that seem most successful in educating immigrant students, such as Australia, Canada and Sweden.

FIGURE 4.8: IMMIGRANT STUDENTS ARE MORE APT TO EXPECT TO PURSUE A SCIENCE CAREER

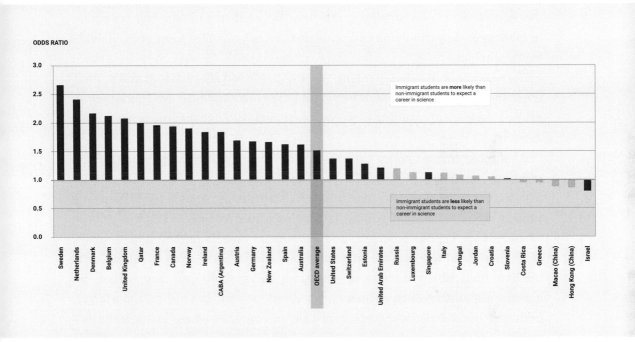

Notes: *The figure shows the likelihood of immigrant students expecting a career in science, compared with non-immigrant students, after accounting for science performance. Only countries/economies where the percentage of immigrant students is higher than 6.25% are shown. CABA (Argentina) refers to Ciudad Autónoma de Buenos Aires (Argentina).*

Countries and economies are ranked in descending order of the likelihood that immigrant students expect a career in science, after accounting for science performance.

Source: *OECD PISA 2015 database, Table 1.7.7.*

StatLink ᴍᵀˢᴸ *http://dx.doi.org/10.1787/888933432964*

Offering high-quality early childhood education, tailored to language development, is another policy response. Participating in early education programmes can improve the chances that immigrant students start school at the same level as non-immigrant children. Targeted home visits can encourage enrolment in early childhood education and can help families support their child's learning at home.

But research shows that spending on early childhood education, in and of itself, is not enough.[38] Key to success is helping children from disadvantaged backgrounds develop the kinds of cognitive, social and emotional skills that they might not acquire at home.

A third high-impact policy option is to build specialist knowledge in the schools receiving immigrant children. This can involve providing special education for teachers to better tailor instructional approaches to diverse student populations and support second-language learning. It can also help if teacher turnover is reduced in schools serving disadvantaged and immigrant populations, and if high-quality and experienced teachers are encouraged to work in these schools. Hiring more teachers from ethnic minority or immigrant backgrounds can help reverse the growing disparity between an increasingly diverse student population and a largely homogeneous teacher workforce, especially in countries where immigration is a more recent phenomenon.

The harder challenge is avoiding concentrating immigrant students in the same, underachieving schools. Schools that struggle to do well for domestic students will struggle even more with a large population of children who cannot speak or understand the language of instruction. Countries use different ways to address the concentration of immigrant and other disadvantaged students in particular schools. One way is to attract other students to these schools, including more advantaged students. A second is to better equip immigrant parents with information on how to select the best school for their child. A third is to limit the extent to which advantaged schools can select students.

A second set of options is related to limiting the use of selection policies, including ability grouping, early tracking and grade repetition. Tracking students into different types of education, such as vocational or academic, seems to be especially disadvantageous for immigrant students, particularly when it occurs at an early age. Early separation from mainstream students may prevent immigrant students from developing the linguistic and culturally relevant skills they need to perform well at school.

Extra support and guidance for immigrant parents can also help. While immigrant parents may have high aspirations for their children, they may feel limited in their capacity to support their children if they have poor language skills or an insufficient understanding of the school system. Programmes to support immigrant parents can include home visits to encourage these parents to participate in educational activities, employing specialised liaison staff to improve communication between schools and families, and reaching out to parents to involve them in school-based activities.

The stubbornly persistent gender gap in education

Technically, the industrialised world had closed the gender gap in education – as measured in average years of schooling – by the 1960s. That has made a huge difference, as about half of the economic growth in OECD countries over the past 50 years has been due to higher educational attainment, mainly among women. But women still earn 15% less than men, on average in OECD countries, and 20% less among the highest-paid workers. Some people say that this is because men and women who do similar work are not paid the same. But a more important factor is that men and women pursue different careers; and those career choices are made much earlier than commonly thought.[39]

We found that, even though boys and girls show similar performance on the PISA science test, on average across OECD countries, around 5% of 15-year-old girls contemplate pursuing a career as a science or engineering professional, compared with 12% of boys (*FIGURE 4.9*).

We may need to look at even younger ages in the search for solutions to these disparities. When Education and Employers, a charity in the United Kingdom, asked 20 000 children between the ages of 7 and 11 to draw their future,[40] over 4 times the number of boys as girls indicated that they wanted to become engineers; nearly double the number of boys as girls drew a scientist as the profile of their future career.

FIGURE 4.9: GENDER DIFFERENCES IN CAREER CHOICES TAKE ROOT IN CHILDHOOD

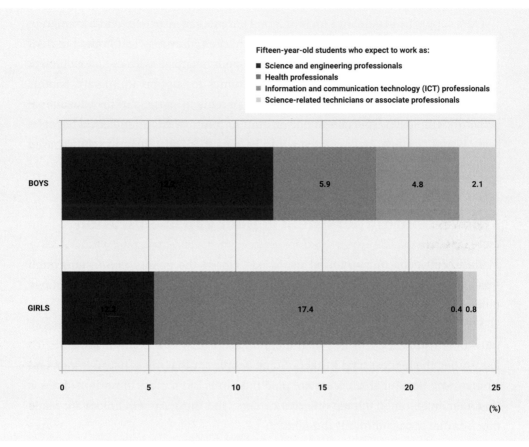

Note: OECD average.

Source: OECD, PISA 2015 Database, Tables I.3.11a-d.

To be fair, many countries have done a lot to level the playing field, and this is seen in the similarity of performance on the PISA 2015 science test between 15-year-old boys and girls. But while claiming victory in having closed gender gaps in girls' and boys' cognitive abilities, we may have lost sight of other social and emotional dimensions of learning that could have a stronger impact on children as they think about what they want to be when they grow up.

Providing more science lessons may therefore miss the point. The question is rather how to make science learning more relevant to children and young people. One answer may be to broaden their views of the world by giving them greater exposure to a wider range of occupations.

In most countries, teachers and schools need to do better to help girls see science and mathematics not just as school subjects, but as pathways to careers and life opportunities. This is significant not only because women are severely under-represented in the science, technology, engineering and mathematics (STEM) fields of study and occupations, but also because graduates of these fields are in high demand in the labour market and jobs in these fields are among the most highly paid.

Secondary-school career counselling comes far too late. It is clear from the drawings made by the 7-11 year-olds that children arrive at school with strong assumptions based on their own day-to-day experiences, which are often shaped by stereotypes regarding gender, ethnicity and social class. Those who still have doubts should watch the two-minute "Redraw the Balance" film which shows 66 child-drawn pictures of firefighters, surgeons and fighter pilots – 61 of which were represented by men and just five by women.[41]

There is another dimension to this. While gender differences in student performance overall are modest, it is striking that 6 out of 10 low achievers in all three of the subjects that PISA assesses – reading, mathematics and science – are boys. These low achievers seem to be stuck in a vicious cycle of low performance, disengagement and low motivation. At the same time, the top performers in mathematics and science are mostly boys.

We have known for a while that even the highest-performing girls are less confident in their abilities in mathematics and science than high-performing boys, but the PISA data also suggest that they do not seem to be getting much encouragement from their parents either. In all countries and economies surveyed on this question, parents were more likely to expect their sons, rather than their daughters, to work in a STEM field – even when boys and girls perform equally well in mathematics and science. In 2012, some 50% of parents in Chile, Hungary and Portugal reported that they expect their sons to have a career in science, technology, engineering or mathematics, but less than 20% held such expectations for their daughters. Interestingly, in South Korea, the difference in parents' expectations of a STEM career for their child, based on whether the child is a girl or boy, is just seven percentage points.

The good news is that narrowing these gender gaps does not require expensive reform. Rather, it requires concerted efforts by parents, teachers and employers to become more aware of their own conscious or unconscious biases so that they give girls and boys equal chances for success at school and beyond.

For example, PISA shows clearly that boys and girls have different reading preferences. Girls are far more likely than boys to read novels and magazines for enjoyment while boys prefer comic books and newspapers. If parents and teachers gave boys a greater choice in what they read, boys might be more successful in at least narrowing the wide gender gap in reading performance.

PISA also finds that boys spend more time playing video games and less time doing homework than girls. While excessive video gaming is shown to be a drag on student performance, a moderate amount of video gaming is related to boys' better performance in digital reading than in print reading (although boys still lag behind girls in both types of reading). Anyone with teenage children will know how difficult it is to tell them how to spend their free time; but all parents should be aware that convincing their children that completing their homework comes before playing video games will significantly improve their children's life chances.

One of the most revealing findings from PISA 2012 is that teachers consistently give girls better marks in mathematics than boys, even when boys and girls perform similarly on the PISA mathematics test. That might be because girls are "good students" – attentive in class and respectful of authority – while boys may have less self-control. But while higher marks may mean success at school, they are not necessarily an advantage for girls in the long run, particularly when they lead to lowered aspirations. Labour markets reward people for what they know and what they can do with what they know, not for their grades at school.

And when it comes to the entering the labour market, PISA shows that girls are more likely than boys to get information about future studies or careers through Internet research, while boys are more likely than girls to get hands-on experience, by working as interns, job shadowing, visiting a job fair or speaking to career advisers outside school. This implies that employers and guidance counsellors can do far more to engage girls in learning about potential careers.

Perhaps surprisingly, the large gender gap in reading performance observed among 15-year-olds virtually disappears among 16-29 year-olds.[42] Why? Data from the Survey of Adult Skills show that young men are much more likely than young women to read at work – and at home. Once again, this suggests that there are many ways to narrow or even eliminate gender gaps in education and skills, as long as we enlist parents, teachers, school leaders and employers in giving boys and girls the same opportunities and encouragement to learn.

Education and the fight against extremism

Whoever has a hammer sees every problem as a nail. Those in the security business tend to see the answer to radicalism and terrorism in military power, and those in the financial business, in cutting flows of money. It is only natural for educators to view the struggle against extremism as a battle for hearts and minds. So I should not have been surprised when around 90 education ministers at the 2016 Education World Forum in London repeatedly touched on this issue in their conversations.

At the same time, the terrorist attacks in Europe, in particular, have brought home that it is far too simplistic to depict extremists and terrorists as victims of poverty or poor education. More research on the background and biographies of extremists and terrorists is badly needed, but it is clear that these people often do not come from the most impoverished parts of societies. Radicals are also found among young people from middle-class families who have completed their formal education. Ironically, those terrorists seem to be well-equipped with the entrepreneurial, creative and collaborative skills that have become the bedrock of a 21st-century education.

But that is no reason to give up on education as the most powerful tool for building a fairer and more humane and inclusive world. We know that extremism flourishes in splintered societies. Young people become receptive to extremist ideas when their self-image, self-confidence and trust in others are threatened by conflicting world views.

Some countries do so much better than others not just in equipping disadvantaged and immigrant children with strong academic skills, but also in helping them integrate fully into society. In the PISA 2012 assessment, 9 out of 10 Norwegian 15-year-old students with an immigrant background said they felt a sense of belonging at school, compared with fewer than 4 out of 10 immigrant students in France. The well-being of immigrant students is affected not just by cultural differences between the country of origin and the host country, but also by how schools and communities in the host country help immigrant students handle the daily problems of living, learning and communicating.

Still, having good academic and social skills does not seem to prevent people from using those skills to destroy, rather than advance, their societies. So how can education combat extremism? It comes down to the heart of education: teaching the values that can give students a reliable compass and the tools to navigate with confidence through an increasingly complex, volatile and uncertain world.

Of course, that is treacherous territory. As my colleague Dirk Van Damme explains, to make one's way through it, one has to strike a balance between strengthening common values in societies, such as respect and tolerance, which cannot be compromised, and appreciating the diversity in our societies and the plurality of values that diversity engenders. Leaning too far in either direction is risky: enforcing an artificial uniformity of values is detrimental to people's capacity to acknowledge different perspectives; and overemphasising diversity can lead to cultural relativism that questions the legitimacy of any core value. But avoiding this issue in discussions about the curriculum just means that it becomes another problem put on the shoulders of classroom teachers without any adequate support.

As difficult as it is to get that balance right, educators need to prepare students for the culturally diverse and digitally connected communities in which they will work and socialise. It is important to begin reflecting on how well education systems deliver on that broader notion of citizenship in the 21st century. In 2013, governments asked PISA to explore the possibility of developing metrics on this in its international assessments. They called it "global competency" – the set of skills that enables people to see the world through different eyes and appreciate different ideas, perspectives and values.[43]

What we mean when we talk about "global competence"

PISA defines global competence[44] as "the capacity to analyse global and intercultural issues critically and from multiple perspectives, to understand how differences affect perceptions, judgements, and ideas of self and others, and to engage in open, appropriate and effective interactions with others from different backgrounds on the basis of a shared respect for human dignity". According to PISA, global competence includes the ability to:

- **Examine issues of local, global and cultural significance.** This refers to the ability to combine knowledge about the world with critical reasoning whenever people form their opinions about a global issue. Globally competent students can draw on and combine the disciplinary knowledge and modes of thinking acquired in school to ask questions, analyse data and arguments, explain phenomena, and develop a position regarding a local, global or cultural issue. They can also access, analyse and critically evaluate messages delivered through the media, and can create new media content.

- **Understand and appreciate the perspectives and world views of others.** This highlights a willingness and capacity to consider global problems from multiple viewpoints. As individuals acquire knowledge about other cultures' histories, values, communication styles, beliefs and practices, they begin to recognise that their perspectives and behaviours are shaped by many influences, that they are not always fully aware of these influences, and that others have views of the world that are profoundly different from their own. Engaging with different perspectives and world views requires individuals to examine the origins and implications of others' and their own assumptions. People who acknowledge and appreciate the qualities that distinguish individuals from one another are less likely to tolerate acts of injustice in their daily interactions. In contrast, people who fail to develop this competence are considerably more likely to internalise stereotypes, prejudices and false heuristics about those who are "different".

- **Engage in open, appropriate and effective interactions across cultures.** Globally competent people can adapt their behaviour and communication to interact with individuals from different cultures. They engage in respectful dialogue, want to understand the other, and try to include marginalised groups. This dimension emphasises individuals' capacity to bridge differences with others by communicating in ways that are open, appropriate and effective. "Open" interactions mean relationships in which all participants demonstrate sensitivity towards, curiosity about, and a willingness to engage with others and their perspectives. "Appropriate" refers to interactions that respect the cultural norms of both parties. In "effective" communication, all participants can make themselves understood and understand the other.

- **Take action for collective well-being and sustainable development.** This dimension focuses on young people's role as active and responsible members of society, and refers to individuals' readiness to respond to a given local, global or intercultural issue or situation. It recognises that young people can have an impact on personal and local situations. Competent people in this sense create opportunities to take informed, reflective action and have their voices heard. Taking action may imply standing up for a schoolmate whose human dignity is in jeopardy, initiating a global media campaign at school, or disseminating a personal opinion about the refugee crisis through social media.

The PISA assessment of global competence offers a way to provide countries with the data they need to build more sustainable societies through education. It will provide a comprehensive overview of education systems' efforts to create learning environments that encourage young people to understand one another and the world beyond their immediate environment, and to take action towards building cohesive and sustainable communities. It can help the many teachers who work every day to combat ignorance, prejudice and hatred, which are at the root of disengagement, discrimination and violence.

Naturally, global competence can be developed in many contexts; but schools can play a crucial role in this regard. Schools can provide opportunities for young people to critically examine developments that are significant to both the world at large and to their own lives. They can teach students how to use digital information and social media platforms critically and responsibly. Schools can also encourage intercultural sensitivity and respect by encouraging students to engage in experiences that nurture an appreciation for diverse peoples, languages and cultures.

School as a venue for constructive debate

Since the end of the Second World War, liberal societies have engaged confidently in the global battlefield of ideas. But in the 21st century, it seems that liberal and democratic ideals and values are facing a fresh onslaught, and will have to prove their worth once again against competing world views.

This is where education comes in. Universities and schools – and their online learning programmes – are important venues in which these ideas and values can be shared and debated. It is important to support and strengthen education in its role as a global exchange of ideas.

The five million students who cross international borders each year to get the best possible education are also champions of intercultural dialogue and global understanding. There could even be many more of them if we invest in education sufficiently to be able to offer attractive opportunities for bright people in countries where the ideological battles for young people's hearts and minds are becoming increasingly fierce and the stakes alarmingly high.

5. Making education reform happen

Why education reform is so difficult

As discussed in previous chapters, without substantial change, the gap between what education systems provide and what our societies demand is likely to widen further. There is a risk that education becomes our next steel industry, and schools a relic of the past. But to transform schooling at scale, we need not just a radical, alternative vision of what is possible, but also smart strategies that help make change in education happen.

Policy makers face tough choices when evaluating policy alternatives; they need to weigh the potential impact against the economic and political cost of change. Should they pursue what is most technically feasible? What is most politically and socially feasible? What can be implemented quickly? What can be sustainable over a sufficient time horizon?

The good news is that our knowledge about what works in education has improved vastly (see Chapter 3). It is true that digitalisation has contributed to the rise in populism and "post-truth" societies that can work against rational policy making. But the very same forces, whether in the form of more and better data or new statistical and analytical tools, have also massively expanded the scope and power of social research to create a more evidence-based environment in which policies can be developed. PISA is a good example of that. The first assessment in 2000 was able to explain about 30% of the performance variation among schools across the participating countries; by 2015, that figure had risen to 85%. That means that most of the performance differences among schools can now be statistically associated and explained with the data that PISA collects from students, parents, teachers and school principals.

Still, knowledge is only as valuable as our capacity to act on it. The reality is that many good ideas get stuck in the process of policy implementation. Governments are under pressure to deliver results in education services while ensuring that citizens' tax dollars are spent wisely and effectively. They set ambitious reform agendas and develop strategic plans to achieve them. But in my conversations with education ministers around the world, the challenges they most commonly cite are not about designing reforms, but about how reforms can be put into practice successfully.

So what is holding back change in education and why do great plans fall by the wayside? My colleagues at the OECD, Gregory Wurzburg, Paulo Santiago and Beatriz Pont, have studied the implementation of education reform over many years, and have developed important insights into how plans are turned into practice.[1]

One reason for the difficulty in reforming education is simply the scale and reach of the sector. Schools, colleges, universities and other educational institutions are among the biggest recipients of public spending. And because everyone has participated in education, everyone has an opinion about it. Everyone supports education reform – except when it might affect their own children. Even those who promote change and reform often revise their views when they are reminded what change actually entails.

The laws, regulations, structures and institutions on which policy makers tend to focus when reforming education are just like the small, visible tip of an iceberg. The reason why it is so hard to move education systems is that there is a much larger, invisible part under the waterline. This invisible part is composed of the interests, beliefs, motivations and fears of the people who are involved. This is where unexpected collisions occur, because this part tends to evade the radar of public policy. Policy makers are rarely successful with education reform unless they help people recognise what needs to change, and build a shared understanding and collective ownership for change; unless they focus resources, build capacity, and create the right policy climate with accountability measures designed to encourage innovation and development, rather than compliance; and unless they tackle institutional structures that too often are built around the interests and habits of educators and administrators rather than learners.

The potential loss of advantages or privileged positions is of particular importance in education reform, because the vast structure of established, usually public, providers means that there are extensive vested interests. As a result, the status quo has many protectors – stakeholders in education who stand to lose a degree of power or influence if changes are made. It is difficult to ask the frogs to clear the swamp. Even small reforms can involve massive reallocations of resources, and touch the lives of millions. This rules out "reform by stealth" and makes it essential to have broad political support for any proposed reform. In essence, education reform will not happen unless educators implement and own it.

Education ministries have been at the frontline of some of the most visible public policy reforms on issues related to improving the quality and status of teachers, strengthening accountability, ensuring sufficient school places, and controlling and financing higher education. Education policy makers know only too well the difficulty of securing stable financing for expanding tertiary education, whether by reallocating funding from other areas of public expenditure, or imposing tuition fees. Reforms that entail more testing of students often encounter resistance from teachers; reforms to vocational education might be resisted by parents who are sceptical about the promised benefits.

There is often uncertainty about who will benefit from reforms and to what extent. This uncertainty is acute in education because of the range of people involved, including students, parents, teachers, employers and trade unions. Uncertainty about costs is problematic because education infrastructure is large and involves multiple levels of government, each often trying to minimise or shift the costs of reform. Assessing the relative costs and benefits of reform in education is also difficult because of the large number of intervening factors that can influence the nature, size and distribution of any improvements. The investment may be expensive over the long term, while in the short term it is rarely possible to predict clear, identifiable results from new policies, especially given the time lags between implementation and effect.

Teachers are generally viewed positively by the public, even when there is great dissatisfaction with education systems. Teachers also tend to command greater public trust than politicians, so any resistance to reform on their part is likely to be effective. Even when parents have a poor opinion of the education system, they will generally view their children's school and its teachers positively.

Implementing reforms is therefore often impossible without the co-operation of education staff. They can easily undermine reforms in the implementation phase, while blaming policy makers for having attempted misguided reforms in the first place. And teachers in many countries are well organised. But in fairness, many teachers have suffered from years of incoherent reforms that disrupt rather than improve education practice because they prioritise variable political interests over the needs of learners and educators. Many of these efforts to reform do not draw on the expertise and experience of teachers themselves. So teachers know that the easiest approach for them may be simply to wait out attempts at reform.

Timing is also relevant to education reform, and in more than one sense. Most significantly, there is a substantial gap between the time at which the initial cost of reform is incurred, and the time when it is evident whether the benefits of reform will actually materialise. While timing complicates the politics of reform in many domains, it seems to have a greater impact on education reform, where the lags often involve many years. It is a long way to successful reform implementation; failure is often just one small step away. As a result, the political cycle may have a direct impact on the timing, scope and content of education reform. Education reform becomes a thankless task when elections take place before the benefits of reform are realised. Policy makers may lose an election over education issues, but they rarely win an election because of education reform. That may also be why, across OECD countries, only about one in 10 reforms is followed by any attempt to evaluate its impact.[2]

The toughest challenge to policy implementation goes back to the way in which we manage and govern educational institutions. Public education was invented in the industrial age, when the prevailing norms were standardisation and compliance, and when it was both effective and efficient to educate students in batches and to train teachers once for their working lives. The curricula that spelled out what students should learn were designed at the top of the pyramid, then translated into instructional material, teacher education and learning environments, often through multiple layers of government, until they reached and were implemented by individual teachers in the classroom.

This structure, inherited from the industrial model of work, makes change a very slow process. Even the most agile countries revise their curriculum only every six to seven years. But the rapid pace of change in most other domains makes that response far too slow. Digital technologies that have revolutionised nearly every aspect of our lives have entered our children's classrooms surprisingly slowly. Even when there are attempts to use new technology, it often seems to be misaligned with the needs of the curriculum.

In short, the changes in our societies have vastly outpaced the structural capacity of our current governance systems to respond. And when fast gets really fast, being slower to adapt makes education systems seem glacial and disconnected. Top-down governance through layers of administrative structures is no longer working. The challenge is to build on the expertise of the hundreds of thousands of teachers and tens of thousands of school leaders and to enlist them in the design of superior policies and practices. When we fail to engage them in designing change, they will rarely help implement it.

What successful reform requires

Successful policy implementation requires mobilising the knowledge and experience of teachers and school leaders, the people who can make the practical connections between the classroom and the changes taking place in the outside world. That is the fundamental challenge of policy implementation today.

There are strong countervailing forces pushing for a shake-up of the status quo. At an individual level, education plays an increasingly important role in determining individual well-being and prosperity; at a macro level, education is associated ever more strongly with higher levels of social inclusion, productivity and growth. The emergence of the knowledge society and the upward trend in skill requirements only increase the importance of education. The cost of underperformance and underinvestment in education is rising.

As a result, the circle of those who feel they are directly affected by the outcomes of education has broadened beyond parents and students to employers and virtually anyone who has a stake in social and economic welfare. These forces also make stakeholders more demanding.

Strategies to overcome resistance to education reforms are similar in certain respects to those adopted in other areas. Reform is more easily undertaken in "crisis" conditions, although the meaning of "crisis" might be somewhat different in education. The shock involved is likely to be something that alters perceptions of the education system (see Chapter 1) rather than an event that suddenly affects its ability to function.

"Crisis" in education can be slow-building, but relentless, pressures imposed by demographic changes. For example, rapidly shrinking school-age populations forced the Estonian and Portuguese governments to face the tough challenge of consolidating rural schools. This tends to be one of the most difficult reform issues because closing a school in a village means taking the heart out of that village. But such a move can also open up new opportunities, such as creating a broader array of courses for students, strengthening teacher collaboration and professional development, or simply freeing up resources for other investments in education. Some observers attribute the rapid improvement of education outcomes in Portugal's rural areas to the change dynamic unleashed by these reforms. But that dynamic has not played out the same way in all countries. I have seen many half-empty primary schools in Japan, drained by declining birth rates and bled of much-needed resources. The fewer the students and teachers who remain in these schools, the harder it becomes to pursue any real change.

In Germany, smaller populations of school-aged children forced some *Länder* (states) to merge different types of secondary school, the *Realschule* (secondary middle schools geared towards both vocational and general programmes) and *Hauptschule* (secondary middle schools mainly geared towards basic vocational programmes). The important side-effect of these changes was a reduction in the degree of tracking and stratification in the German school system and, by implication, a weakening of the impact that social background has on learning outcomes.

Similarly, the prospect of fewer upper secondary school graduates forced the government of Finland, only a few years after it created a new polytechnic sector, to launch ambitious reforms to reduce the number of tertiary institutions and alter how they were governed and financed.

As in other sectors, co-ordinated reforms in different parts of education systems have proved to be mutually reinforcing. Sometimes real opportunities are disguised as insoluble problems. This was the case in Scotland when the government, intending to initiate sweeping reforms to the curriculum, testing and leadership, started with an overhaul of teacher education, induction and pay. The success of reforms to the curriculum and testing were seen as dependent on prior reforms that would have an influence on who teaches and how they are educated.

But given that education systems involve multiple levels of government, implementation of "comprehensive reform" is often difficult to co-ordinate. Denmark faced this problem when it proved difficult to synchronise reforms to strengthen national testing with the pre- and in-service education of teachers employed by municipalities. Local and regional entities often do not have sufficient capacity to implement national policies.

Federal education systems, such as those in Australia, Austria, Belgium, Brazil, Canada, Germany, Switzerland, the United Kingdom and the United States, share a different dilemma. Though the federal government in the United States, for example, can require states to set quality standards as a condition for receiving federal money for education, it cannot determine what those standards are. In 2009, state school officials and governors in the United States agreed on the principle of establishing national, common standards in core subjects;[3] but in 2015, these standards were still insufficiently implemented to affect teachers' practice in the classroom at scale.

Germany was more successful in implementing national standards,[4] even though it too has a federal government. The unsatisfactory results of the PISA 2000 assessment created huge pressure on policy makers to establish more rigorous and coherent school standards across the states, and to advance from traditional content-based curricula towards competency-based learning. Constantly prodded by federal authorities and an increasingly demanding public, the states progressively agreed and implemented such standards.

Why was the effort so much more successful in Germany than in the United States? First of all, Germany took time to engage a wide range of stakeholders in the development, trial and implementation of the standards. Second, along with the standards, the states developed a range of resources to implement them in classrooms, including guidelines for instructional design, lesson plans and pedagogy. Capacity to implement the standards was developed at all levels of the education system.

Unlike the United States, the German states also put a premium on the improvement, rather than the accountability, function of these standards. While national tests were introduced, they were based on samples of schools; this avoided comparisons of individual schools. By implication, the immediate stakes for teachers in implementing new standards were intentionally kept low, while the stakes for policy makers responsible for state-level performance were high. In addition, teachers, schools and communities were provided with a range of methods by which they could monitor progress at the local level.

It is not only difficult to co-ordinate policy development across levels of government, it is also hard to align the perspectives of different government departments. But if education is to be developed over a lifetime, then a broad range of policy fields need to be involved, including education, family, employment, industrial and economic development, migration and integration, social welfare and public finance. A co-ordinated approach to education policies allows policy makers to identify policy trade-offs, such as between immigration and labour-market integration, or between spending on early education or investing in welfare programmes later on.

Creating linkages between different policy fields is also important to ensure efficiency and avoid duplication of effort. But a whole-of-government approach to education is not easy to achieve. Ministries of education will naturally focus on building strong education foundations for life, with due emphasis on transferring knowledge, skills and values. Ministries of employment, by contrast, are mainly concerned with getting unemployed workers into work through short-term, job-specific training. Ministries of the economy might be more interested in the skills needed to secure long-term competitiveness.

These competing interests were clearly evident in Portugal, where the government struggled to consolidate two parallel systems of vocational education and training, one run by the Ministry of Education that was school-based and focused on foundation skills, the other run by the Ministry of Employment that focused on work-based learning. We were called in to help Portugal develop a coherent national skills strategy [5] We found a lot of goodwill among the different ministries to work together, but it took time to establish a common language and framework that centred on what young people should learn, rather than on how that learning should be provided and who should provide it.

More generally, I have found several aspects particularly important when implementing reform:

- Policy makers need to build **broad support** about the aims of education reform and engage stakeholders, especially teachers, in formulating and implementing policy responses. External pressures can be used to build a compelling case for change. All political players and stakeholders need to develop realistic expectations about the pace and nature of reforms.

- **Capacity development.** Efforts to overcome resistance to reform will be wasted if education administrations do not have state-of-the-art knowledge, professional know-how and adequate institutional arrangements for the new tasks and responsibilities included in the reforms. Successful reform might require significant investment in staff development, or clustering reforms to build capacity in related institutions. This also means that reform needs to be backed by sustainable financing.

- **The right governance in the right place.** Education systems extend from local schools to national ministries. The responsibilities of institutions and different levels of government vary from country to country, as do the relative importance and independence of private providers. Reforms need to take into account the respective responsibilities of different players. Some reforms may only be possible if responsibilities are well aligned or reallocated. Layers of regional government might be good at identifying local needs, but they might not be the right vantage point from which to monitor progress towards overall goals and objectives. They may also have insufficient scientific, technical and infrastructure capacity to design and implement education policies that are consistent with national goals and objectives.

- **Use of performance data.** As obtaining, managing and accessing information have become easier and cheaper, education systems can capitalise on collecting better and more relevant data to track individual and institutional performance, locally, nationally and internationally. Evidence from national surveys and inspectorates as well as comparative data and assessments can be used to catalyse change and guide policy making. Such evidence is most helpful when it is fed back to institutions along with information and tools about how they can use the information.

- There needs to be progression from initial reform initiatives towards building **self-adjusting systems** with feedback at all levels, incentives to react and tools to strengthen capacities to deliver better outcomes. Investment in change-management skills is essential. Teachers need reassurance that they will be given the tools to change. Their motivation to improve their students' performance should be recognised too.

- **"Whole-of-government"** approaches can include education in more comprehensive reforms.

It is worth looking at these aspects in greater detail.

Different versions of the "right" approach

The diversity of views on education reform makes policy making particularly challenging, especially given that policy makers often represent one of the stakeholder groups: government authorities. For example, in the choice of teacher-appraisal methods, there is a particularly contentious debate about the relative merits of summative (evaluation of performance) and formative (providing continuous feedback for improvement) appraisals. On the one hand, policy makers and parents tend to value quality assurance and accountability. They make the point that schools are public institutions, supported by taxpayers' money, and that the public has a legitimate interest in the quality of teaching. Summative teacher appraisal provides a way for school principals to reward excellence and commitment, and the public, their legislators, local boards of education and administrators with the means to monitor and ensure the quality of teaching. But teachers and their organisations often reject summative appraisals as tools for control; they favour more formative approaches.

But there are also many examples where divergent views have been successfully reconciled. The Czech Republic, for example, began developing a standardised section of the school-leaving examination in 1997, but the section was only introduced 14 years later, in 2011. During the intervening time, several models were developed, pilot versions were implemented, and fundamental features were modified several times. The reforms were hotly debated, particularly among the country's political parties, which could not reach consensus on the approach to the examination.[6]

Setting the direction

Another priority is to clearly communicate a long-term vision of what is to be accomplished for student learning. Individuals and groups are more likely to accept changes that are not necessarily in their own interests if they and society at large understand the reasons for these changes and can see the role they should play within the broad strategy. To achieve this, the evidence base of the underlying policy diagnosis, research findings on alternative policy options and their likely impact, and information on the costs of reform versus inaction should be disseminated widely in a language that is accessible to all.

For instance, in order to convince teachers of the need to reform standardised student tests, it is critical that teachers understand and support the broader goals of the assessment, and the standards and frameworks underlying the assessment. Establishing clear goals and standards, and communicating them to teachers, mitigates such behaviour as "teaching to the test", as teachers have a clearer sense of the kinds of student outcomes they should be trying to achieve.

Resistance to reform is often due to incomplete information about the nature of the proposed policy changes, their impact, or whether or not the stakeholders involved – including the general public – will be better or worse off. Opposition to change can also signal that the public has not been sufficiently briefed on or prepared for reform; it can also indicate a lack of social acceptance of policy innovations. This highlights the importance of making the underlying evidence available to convince educators and society at large. It involves raising awareness about how difficult decisions were made, enhancing the national debate and sharing evidence on the impact of different policy alternatives. That is the way to build a solid consensus.

Building a consensus

There is extensive evidence of the importance of consensus if policy reforms are going to be successful. At the same time, given the diversity of stakeholders in education, consensus might wind up meaning agreement at the level of the lowest common denominator; and that may be insufficient to lead to genuine improvement. Hence, strategic leadership is at the heart of successful education reform (see also Chapter 6).

Consensus can be fostered through consultations and feedback that allow concerns to be taken into account, and thus reduce the likelihood of strong opposition by some stakeholder groups. Regular involvement by stakeholders in policy design helps build capacity and shared ideas over time. Engaging stakeholders in the development of education policy can cultivate a sense of joint ownership about the need, relevance and nature of reforms.

The experience of OECD countries suggests that regular and institutionalised consultations – which are inherent in consensual policy making – help develop trust between the various stakeholder groups and policy makers, and help them reach consensus.

For example, in Chile, the Teachers' Act of 1991, designed to introduce teacher-evaluation systems in elementary and secondary schools, allowed employers to dismiss teachers who had negative evaluations two years in a row. But this evaluation system had not been implemented because of objections from the Teachers' Association about the composition of the evaluation committees, and the fact that the system focused on punishment rather than improvement.

Nevertheless, teacher evaluation continued to be a topic of public and political concern throughout the 1990s. In response, Chile's Ministry of Education established a technical committee composed of representatives of the ministry, the municipalities and the Teachers' Association. After several months, the committee reached agreement on a model for teacher evaluation. At the same time, its members agreed to prepare guidelines for standards of professional performance, and to implement a pilot project in several areas of the country to evaluate and adjust the procedures and instruments to be used.

After wide consultations throughout the country and agreement with the teaching profession, a framework for performance standards was developed and officially approved. The pilot project for teacher-performance evaluation was applied in four regions. In June 2003, the ministry, the municipalities and the Teachers' Association signed an agreement that established the progressive application of the new evaluation system.[7]

Several countries have established teaching councils that provide teachers and other stakeholder groups with a forum for policy development. For example, the Teaching Council in Ireland, established in 2006, seeks to promote and maintain best practice in the teaching profession and in teacher education.[8] As a statutory body, the council regulates the professional practices of teachers, oversees teacher-education programmes and enhances teachers' professional development. Through these activities, the council provides teachers with a large degree of professional autonomy and thus enhances the professional status and morale of teachers. Some of the main functions of the Teaching Council are to establish, publish and maintain a code of professional conduct; establish and maintain a register of teachers; determine the education requirements for teacher registration; promote teachers' continuing education and professional development; and conduct inquiries into the fitness of teachers and impose sanctions on underperforming teachers, where appropriate.

The Council is composed of representatives from various parties involved in education, including registered teachers and representatives from teacher-education institutions, school-management organisations, national parents' associations, industry and business, and ministerial nominees.

Critically, these kinds of councils also offer mechanisms for profession-led standard setting and quality assurance in teacher education, teacher induction, teacher performance and career development. These bodies aim to establish the kind of autonomy and public accountability for the teaching profession that has long characterised other professions, such as medicine, engineering and law.

Our review of assessment and evaluation frameworks found numerous examples of how effective consensus building has resulted in the successful implementation of reform.[9]

In Denmark, following the 2004 OECD recommendations on the need to establish an evaluation culture, all major stakeholder groups agreed on the importance of working to that end.[10] In fact, there is a tradition in Denmark of involving the relevant interest groups in developing policies for primary and lower secondary schools (*Folkeskole*). The key interest groups include education authorities at the national level, municipalities (local government), teachers (Danish Union of Teachers), school leaders/principals (Danish School Principals' Union), parents (National Parents' Association), students, the association for municipal management in the area of schools, associations representing the interests of the independent (private) primary schools in Denmark, and researchers.

The Council for Evaluation and Quality Development of Primary and Lower Secondary Education is the most prominent platform for discussing evaluation and assessment policies. But there are other initiatives promoting dialogue, including one on developing national student tests that, each month, selects and celebrates a school that has achieved excellent results, and one that encourages municipalities to work together to improve the *Folkeskole*.[11]

At the heart of the New Zealand education system is trust in the professionalism of staff and a culture of consultation and dialogue. It was collaborative work, rather than prescriptions imposed from above, that was responsible for developing the country's evaluation and assessment system. I admit that I had been sceptical that New Zealand would be successful in developing a high-stakes assessment system that would remain entirely teacher-graded. But they succeeded because of the time and effort they invested in educating teachers and fostering peer collaboration. At the end of the process, they not only obtained reliable student performance data, but teachers also had a good understanding of the nature of the assessment and how students responded to the different tasks. Perhaps most important, teachers had a better sense of how teachers in other classrooms and other schools were grading similar student work.

As a result of this participative approach, schools now show considerable support for and commitment to evaluation and assessment strategies. While there are, of course, differences of views, there seems to be an underlying consensus on the purposes of evaluation and an expectation among stakeholders to participate in shaping the national agenda.

Policy making in Norway is characterised by a high level of respect for local ownership. This is evident in the development of the national evaluation and assessment framework. Schools have a high degree of autonomy regarding school policies, curriculum development, and evaluation and assessment. There is a shared understanding that democratic decision making and buy-in from those concerned by evaluation and assessment policy are essential for successful implementation. In addition, the government does a lot to build and strengthen capacity at local levels and to bring local communities together to compare notes.

In Finland, the objectives and priorities for education evaluation are determined in the Education Evaluation Plan, which is crafted by the Ministry of Education and Culture in collaboration with the Education Evaluation Council, the Higher Education Evaluation Council, the National Board of Education and other key groups. The members of the Education Evaluation Council represent the education administration, teachers, students, employers, employees and researchers.

A monitoring commission in the French Community of Belgium was given a key role in monitoring the education system. It has two main missions: co-ordinate and review the coherence of the education system, and follow the implementation of pedagogical reforms. Its membership reflects all the relevant actors in the education system: school inspectors, school organisers, researchers, teachers' unions and parents' representatives. When new policies are introduced, a combination of top-down and bottom-up initiatives can generally build consensus. The involvement of practitioners – teachers, other education staff and their unions – in producing, interpreting and translating research evidence into policy can give these practitioners a strong sense of ownership and strengthen their confidence in the reform process.

Engaging teachers to help design reform

The process of developing policy is more likely to yield consensus if there is a range of stakeholders involved from the outset. Regular interactions help build trust and raise awareness of the concerns of others, creating a climate of compromise. When politics becomes managing mistrust, and when clinging to positions becomes more important than using common sense, we lose the capacity to change and develop ideas based on dialogue. Where teachers are not genuinely involved in the design of reforms, they are unlikely to help with their implementation. This needs to be more than lip-service. In fact, I have sometimes heard policy makers talk in somewhat patronising ways about the lack of teacher capacity, and their intention to address that by rolling out more teacher-training programmes. But the bigger problem is that policy makers often do not have much of a sense of the capacity and expertise that is dormant among their teachers, because all their efforts focus on getting government prescription into classrooms, rather than getting the good practice from great classrooms into the education system.

We have learned a lot about the dynamics involved from our review of evaluation and assessment practices. In fact, evaluation policy has much to gain from forging a compromise from different perspectives rather than imposing one view over all others. For instance, teachers will accept evaluation more easily if they are consulted as the process is being designed. In addition, this is a good way to recognise and capitalise on their professionalism, the importance of their skills and experience, and the extent of their responsibilities. If teacher-appraisal procedures are designed and implemented only from "above", there will be a "loose coupling" between administrators and teachers. It could mean teachers are less engaged and less willing to identify any potential risks in the procedures.

Engaging teachers and school leaders in their own appraisal, such as by setting objectives, self-appraisal and preparing individual portfolios, can create a stronger sense of empowerment among teachers and school leaders and, therefore, ensure that the process is successfully implemented. Education authorities have a lot to gain from listening to the advice of experienced teachers. These teachers can identify good teaching practices and the best ways to evaluate their peers. An evaluation system is more likely to be successful if it is accepted by professionals and is perceived as useful, objective and fair.

The need to engage the teaching profession extends beyond politics and pragmatism. One of the main challenges for policy makers in an increasingly knowledge-based society is how to maintain teacher quality and ensure that all teachers continue to engage in professional learning. Research on the characteristics of effective professional development indicates that teachers need to be involved in analysing their own practice in light of professional standards, and in analysing their students' progress in light of standards for student learning.

Introducing pilot projects and continuous evaluation

Experimenting with policy and using pilot projects can help build consensus, allay fears and overcome resistance by evaluating proposed reforms before they are fully introduced. It is equally important to review and evaluate reform processes periodically after full implementation. Teachers and school leaders are more likely to accept a policy initiative if they know that they will be able to express their concerns and provide advice on making adjustments.

In New Zealand, the Ministry of Education commissions independent evaluations to monitor national policies. For example, the implementation of the curriculum in English medium schools was monitored by the Education Review Office. National standards were monitored by the ministry and the Education Review Office, using samples of schools, in a project run by a contracted evaluation team. The information obtained from these reviews was complemented by survey data, information from reports of the Education Review Office, and results from national and international assessments.

In a range of countries, external evaluators typically collect feedback from schools and other stakeholders on their experience with the evaluation process in order to monitor the implementation of that process.

Building capacity in the system

One of the biggest obstacles to reform is inadequate capacity and resourcing, often because the resource implications are underestimated in scope, nature and timing. The main shortcoming is often not a lack of financial resources, but a dearth of human capacity at every level of the system.

The Alberta Initiative for School Improvement, in Alberta, Canada, was created in 1999 to address exactly this kind of problem. It encourages teachers, parents and the community to work together to introduce innovative projects to meet local needs. The initiative's platform allows schools and school districts to improve teachers' professional capacity in curriculum and pedagogic development through a process of collaborative inquiry.

The initiative was the result of the close partnership between the Alberta Teachers' Association, the Alberta government and other professional partners, such as the Alberta School Boards Association. The Alberta Teachers' Association spends around half of its budget on professional development, education research and public advocacy to build a stronger and more innovative teaching profession.[12]

The OECD Teaching and Learning International Survey (TALIS) of 2013 clearly shows Alberta's strong commitment to teacher professionalism. Alberta's teachers were more likely to report participating in professional learning than teachers in other TALIS-participating countries and economies: 85% reported participating in courses and workshops (the TALIS average was 71%); almost 80% participated in education conferences (the TALIS average was 44%); nearly two in three teachers belong to a professional network (the TALIS average was just over one in three); and almost 50% were involved in individual or collaborative research (the TALIS average was 31%). Only 4% of Alberta's teachers reported that they had never participated in professional learning activities compared with the TALIS average of 16%.[13]

Teachers need to have time not only to reflect on their own practices, but to avail themselves of professional development activities when they are offered. Teacher education for reform is also often needed to ensure that all stakeholders are equipped and prepared to assume the new roles and responsibilities that are required of them.

Timing is everything

A week is a long time for a political leader, but successful education reform often takes years. First of all, as I mentioned before, there is often a substantial gap between the time at which the initial cost of reform is incurred, and the time when the intended benefits of reforms materialise. I have often asked myself why underinvestment in early childhood education and care is so persistent, despite the extensive evidence that these investments have particularly large social returns and a significant influence on what happens in subsequent schooling. In Germany, parents must pay a fee for enrolling their child in pre-school programmes, but it has proved impossible to impose even the most modest fees on Germany's university students, where there would be much stronger justification for doing so. The reason is not just that children have no lobby behind them, it is also because it takes such a long time for the fruits of improvements in early childhood education to become apparent. That is also why we tend to try to find a way to afford the most expensive medical treatment when foregoing it would immediately compromise our health, while we are all too often ready to accept serious shortcomings in education services when their consequences won't be apparent for years.

In addition, reform measures are often best introduced in a specific sequence. For example, one element – curriculum reform – may require prior reform in pre-service and in-service teacher education in order to be effective.

It is also crucial that there is, from the outset, a clear understanding of the timing of intended, implemented and achieved reforms. Time is also needed to learn about and understand the reform measures, build trust, and develop the necessary capacity to move on to the next stage of policy development. Sir Michael Barber examines the design and implementation of reform trajectories, the sequencing of reform steps, and ways to leverage principles of best-in-class performance management in his book, *Deliverology*.[14] But what has been eloquently described in print is rarely put into practice.

Making teachers' unions part of the solution

To put the teaching profession at the heart of education reform, there must be a fruitful dialogue between governments and the teaching profession. A survey conducted in 2013 among 24 unions in 19 countries by the Trade Union Advisory Committee to the OECD[15] revealed that this dialogue is in many countries already well developed.

The large majority of respondents to this survey indicated that they at least partially engage with governments on developing and implementing education policies. However, while most unions reported that governments had established arrangements for consultation, half of the respondents felt only partially engaged in these consultation structures. Moreover, unions considered themselves generally more engaged in policy development than in implementation.

This suggests that the mere existence of formal structures alone does not guarantee actual engagement. Perspectives sometimes varied between unions in the same country, reflecting the fact that governments may have different relations with unions representing different sectors of the workforce.

Union representatives were also asked to identify those areas of education policy that were under discussion. Almost all respondents mentioned teachers' professional development, followed by working conditions and equity issues. Issues concerning the curriculum, pay, support for students with special needs, teacher evaluation, student assessment and institutional evaluation were also mentioned by a majority of unions. One in three reported that there are productive discussions on student behaviour. Issues rarely mentioned were education research, school development and teaching councils.

Similar questions were asked about training policies. More unions reported that they are not engaged in discussions about the implementation of training policy than reported full engagement. Fewer said that they were able to engage governments when they considered it necessary. Asked to cite areas of training policy where there were productive discussions, the majority of unions identified the curriculum, followed by professional development, equity issues, pay, adult learning and working conditions. Less consultation was reported on strategies for training youth and funding for training.

In general, this union survey presented an encouraging picture of involvement in most OECD countries, particularly on teacher and skills policies. But there is room for improvement, especially when it comes to establishing union-government dialogue across the board. Governments need to play a more active role in encouraging a dialogue with unions by recognising and supporting such initiatives.

This is not easy to do, because there are many thorny issues that separate teachers and policy makers. There are opponents of teachers' unions who see the unions as interfering with promising school-reform programmes by giving higher priority to their own bread-and-butter issues than to what the evidence suggests students need to succeed. But many of the countries with the strongest student performance also have strong teachers' unions. There seems to be no relationship between the presence of unions in a country, including and especially teachers' unions, and student performance. But there may be a relationship between the degree to which teachers' work has been professionalised and student performance. Indeed, the higher a country ranks on the PISA league tables, the more likely it is that the country works constructively with its teachers' organisations and treats its teachers as trusted professional partners.

In Ontario, Canada, the government signed a four-year collective bargaining agreement with the four major teachers' unions in 2014. In reaching the accord, the ministry was able to negotiate items that were consistent with both its education strategy and the unions' interests, thus providing a basis for pushing forward the education agenda while creating a sustained period of labour peace that allowed for a continuous focus on improving education.

I have observed that the nature of the relationship between governments and teachers' unions often reflects the work organisation in education. A highly industrialised work organisation, where the government focuses on prescribing and justifying, and where teachers are expected to do the same work that their counterparts decades ago did, and for similar pay, inadvertently encourages unions to focus on pay and working conditions. That, in turn, tends to lead to stakeholder relationships that are top-down and antagonistic.

By contrast, a highly professional work organisation, where the government enables and offers incentives to teachers, and where the teaching profession is characterised by diverse careers, ownership and innovative ways of working, is conducive to developing a strategic, principled and professional working relationship between the government and unions. In that sense, every education system gets the teachers' unions it deserves.

So in the wake of the results from the PISA 2009 assessment, the US Secretary of Education, Arne Duncan, Fred Van Leeuwen from Education International (the international federation of teachers' unions) and I organised the first International Summit on the Teaching Profession. Secretary Duncan had been a great supporter of PISA and international collaboration on education, in general, and he knew that implementing change on the ground would always hinge on engaging teachers' organisations. The idea was to bring together ministers and unions from around the world to address issues that are difficult to tackle nationally, often because of entrenched stakeholder interests. We felt that it was time for governments, teachers' unions and professional bodies to redefine the role of teachers, and to create the support and collaborative work organisation that can help teachers grow in their careers and meet the needs of 21st-century students. Since then, we have invited ministers and teachers' union leaders from the best-performing and most rapidly improving education systems each year in a unique global effort to raise the status of the teaching profession.

Of course, both ministers and union leaders had had many international meetings before, but what makes the International Summit on the Teaching Profession unique is that they are sitting next to each other. They can listen to ministers and union leaders from other countries who might have successfully broken the stalemates in which they are stuck in their own country. In fact, one of the ground rules that we established was that no country could join the summit unless it was represented by both the minister and the national union leader. Consensus might be too ambitious a goal for these summits, but a lively – not to say provocative and passionate – discussion has proved extremely valuable for everyone involved.

6. What to do now

Educating for an uncertain world

The backdrop to 21st-century education is our endangered environment. Growing populations, resource depletion and climate change compel all of us to think about sustainability and the needs of future generations. At the same time, the interaction between technology and globalisation has created new challenges and new opportunities. Digitalisation is connecting people, cities, countries and continents in ways that vastly increase our individual and collective potential. But the same forces have also made the world volatile, complex and uncertain.

Digitalisation is a democratising force: we can connect and collaborate with anyone. But digitalisation is also concentrating extraordinary power. Google creates more than a million US dollars for every employee – ten times more than the average American company, showing how technology can create scale without mass, leaving people out of the equation. Digitalisation can make the smallest voice heard everywhere. But it can also quash individuality and cultural uniqueness. Digitalisation can be incredibly empowering: the most influential companies that were created over the past decade all started out with an idea, and they had the product before they had the financial resources and physical infrastructure for delivering that product. But digitalisation can also be disempowering, when people trade their freedom in exchange for convenience and become reliant on the advice and decisions of computers.

But while digital technologies and globalisation can have disruptive implications for our economic and social structure, those implications are not predetermined. As Tom Bentley notes, it is the nature of our collective responses to these disruptions that determines their outcomes – the continuous interplay between the technological frontier and the cultural, social, institutional and economic contexts and agents that we mobilise in response.[1]

In this environment, the Sustainable Development Goals, set by the global community for 2030, describe a course of action to end poverty, protect the planet and ensure prosperity for all. These goals are a shared vision of humanity that provides the missing piece of the globalisation puzzle, the glue that can counter the centrifugal forces in the age of accelerations.[2] The extent to which those goals will be realised will depend in no small part on what happens in today's classrooms. It is educators who hold the key to ensuring that the underlying principles of the Sustainable Development Goals become a real social contract with citizens.

2030 is also the date when today's primary school pupils will be finishing their compulsory schooling. So we need to be thinking about their future in order to shape what primary school pupils are learning today.

In the social and economic sphere, the questions turn on equity and inclusion. We are born with what political scientist Robert Putnam calls "bonding social capital" – a sense of belonging to our family or other people with shared experiences, cultural norms, common purposes or pursuits.[3] But it requires deliberate and continuous efforts to create the kind of "bridging social capital" through which we can share experiences, ideas and innovation, and build a shared understanding among groups with diverse experiences and interests, thus increasing our radius of trust to strangers and institutions. Societies that value bridging social capital and pluralism have always been more creative, as they can draw on the best talent from anywhere, build on multiple perspectives, and nurture creativity and innovation.

Yet there is growing disenchantment with the values of pluralism and diversity. We see this in shifting political landscapes, including the rise of inward-looking populist parties.

Perhaps this should not surprise us. While better integration with the world economy has brought significant improvements in overall standards of living, it has also widened the gap in job quality between those with better and worse knowledge and skills.[4] The Survey of Adult Skills (PIAAC) shows that there are over 200 million workers in OECD countries who do not even have the most basic foundation skills – in essence, they do not read as well as we would expect a 10-year-old child to read.[5] That is where the education agenda circles back to the agenda of inclusiveness.

How unequal can communities become before trust erodes, social capital weakens and the conditions for a thriving civil society are undermined? Taking advantage of an international labour market, cheap travel and social media networks, many choose to spend their lives in transit, changing jobs and swapping values. Others are forced to leave home by war and poverty: Mexican families heading north into the United States; Eastern Europeans moving west; those fleeing from war-torn Syria; and many hundreds of thousands more. Staying or leaving, millions of people are struggling to adapt to changing environments. Angered and confused by the flux of contemporary living, they wonder about their identity – who they are and where they stand. We will need to redouble our efforts to close the opportunity gap with imagination and innovation rather than simplistic solutions. We need to do better to figure out our common humanity.

Sustainability is another dimension of the challenge. The goal declared by the Brundtland Commission[6] some 30 years ago – calling for development that meets the needs of the present without compromising the ability of future generations to meet their own needs – is more relevant today than ever, in the face of environmental degradation, climate change, overconsumption and population growth. Many of our best minds are already focused on building sustainable cities, developing green technologies, redesigning systems and rethinking individual lifestyles. For the young, the challenges encapsulated in the Sustainable Development Goals are not just urgent, but often also personal and inspiring.

While sustainability aims to put the world into balance, resilience looks for ways to cope in a world that is in constant disequilibrium. Strengthening cognitive, emotional and social resilience and adaptability is perhaps the most significant challenge for modern education, as it affects virtually every part of the education system. It starts with the understanding that resilience is not a personality trait, but a process that can be learned and developed. In the 21st century, education can help people, communities and organisations to persist, perhaps even thrive, amid unforeseeable disruptions.

There is one more element that is worth considering in this context. As discussed in Chapter 1, the Survey of Adult Skills shows that more education is not only related to better social and economic outcomes, but also to improved social and civic participation and to trust (see *FIGURE 1.2*). While the roots of the relationship between education, identity and trust are complex, these links matter, because trust is the glue of modern societies. Without trust in people, governments, public institutions and well-regulated markets, public support for innovative policies is difficult to mobilise, particularly where short-term sacrifices are involved and where long-term benefits are not immediately evident. Less trust can also lead to lower rates of compliance with rules and regulations, and therefore lead to more stringent and bureaucratic regulations. Citizens and businesses may avoid taking risks, delaying decisions regarding investment, innovation and labour mobility that are essential to jump-start growth and social progress.

Ensuring fairness and integrity in policy development and implementation, rendering policy making more inclusive, and building real engagement with citizens all depend upon people having the knowledge, skills and character qualities to participate. Education will be key to reconciling the needs and interests of individuals, communities and nations within an equitable framework based on open borders and a sustainable future.

So we have an obligation to cultivate human potential far more equitably. This is a moral and social obligation; it is also a huge opportunity. A growth model based on human potential can produce a more dynamic economy and a more inclusive society, since talent is far more equally distributed than opportunity and financial capital. As I discussed in Chapter 4, a more equitable distribution of knowledge and skills has a complementary impact on reducing gaps in earnings. And it has this impact while also expanding the size of the economy. More inclusive progress made possible through better skills therefore has tremendous potential to ensure that the benefits of economic and social development are shared more equitably among citizens which, in turn, leads to greater overall social and economic progress.

The times when we could address inequalities mainly through economic redistribution are gone, not just because this is an uphill struggle economically, but more important, because it does not address the much more pressing issue of social participation, where an increasingly complex world with blurring boundaries between life and work demands high levels of cognitive, social and emotional skills from all citizens. Perhaps one day machines will be able to do much of the work that is now occupying humans and reduce the demand for many skills at work. But the demands on our skills to contribute meaningfully to an increasingly complex social and civic life will keep rising.

Economic and social inequality in much of the world keeps growing, inhibiting progress and tearing societies apart.[7] Equity in opportunity became a fundamental education goal because in the industrial age, everyone was needed and had a role to play, so school systems were designed to deliver the same education for all students, even if they did not deliver on that goal. As Israeli historian Yuval Noah Harari notes, liberalism succeeded because there was abundant political, economic and military sense in ascribing value to every human being.[8] But, as he further explains, humans are in danger of losing their economic value, as biological and computer engineering make many forms of human activity redundant and decouple intelligence from consciousness. So time is of the essence if we want to broaden the goal of equity in education opportunities from providing everyone with the literacy and numeracy skills for employment, towards empowering all citizens with the cognitive, social and emotional capabilities and values to contribute to the success of tomorrow's world.

We need to address the sources of social and economic inequality, and these lie to a significant extent in the ways in which we develop and use people's talents. Every economic age has its core asset. In the agricultural age that asset was land; in the industrial age it was capital; and in our times, it is the knowledge, skills and character qualities of people. This core asset remains largely untapped and undervalued. It's time for us to change that.

Education as the key differentiator

Prior to the Industrial Revolution, neither education nor technology mattered much for the vast majority of people. But when technology raced ahead of education during that period, vast numbers of people were left behind, causing unimaginable social pain.[9] It took a century for public policy to respond with the gradual push to provide every child with access to schooling. That goal is now within reach for much of the world; but in the meantime, the world has changed, and neither access to schooling nor a degree guarantees success. In the digital age, technology is once again racing ahead of people's skills, and rising unemployment among graduates in much of the industrialised world is raising anxiety.

Some say that accelerating digitalisation will leave the majority of people with nothing to do. At times, it does seem as though we are living in the first age in which technology destroys jobs faster than it creates them. Even where we are creating new jobs, these are not necessarily jobs that humans perform better than machines.[10]

Still, I'm sceptical. When I was in high school, I had to write an essay about *The Weavers*, a play written in 1892 by the German playwright Gerhart Hauptmann. The play portrays a group of Silesian weavers who staged an uprising during the 1840s against the Industrial Revolution. It is true that the Industrial Revolution eliminated the tasks carried out by those weavers, but it did not end employment in the clothing business. In fact, once people were equipped with the new knowledge, skills and mindset needed in the industrial age, there were more and higher-paying jobs in the weaving industry than ever before – and the changes in work allowed more people to have more and better clothes than ever before. History suggests, though it has many dark twists and reversals, that our capacity for imagination and adaptation is unlimited.

However, while education has won the race with technology throughout history, there is no guarantee for that to continue. Those children who grow up with a great smartphone but a poor education will face unprecedented challenges. The least we can do now is use our capacity to reimagine the education they will need.

Developing knowledge, skills and character for an age of accelerations

The dilemma for educators is that routine cognitive skills, the skills that are easiest to teach and easiest to test, are exactly the skills that are also easiest to digitise, automate and outsource. David Autor, professor of economics at the Massachusetts Institute of Technology, has produced impressive data on this.[11] There is no question that state-of-the-art knowledge and skills in a discipline will always remain important. Innovative and creative people generally have specialised skills in a field of knowledge or a practice. As much as "learning-to-learn" skills are important, we always learn by learning something. However, success in education is no longer about reproducing content knowledge, but about extrapolating from what we know and applying that knowledge creatively in novel situations; it is also about thinking across the boundaries of disciplines. Everyone can search for – and usually find – information on the Internet; the rewards now accrue to those who know what to do with that knowledge.

The results from PISA show how learning strategies dominated by memorisation help students less and less as the tasks students are asked to complete become more complex and involve more non-routine analytic skills (**FIGURE 6.1A**)[12] – which is exactly where digitalisation is taking our real-life tasks.[13] In turn, learning strategies framed around elaboration – the process of connecting new knowledge to familiar knowledge, thinking divergently and creatively about novel solutions or about how knowledge can be transferred – are more likely to help students complete the more demanding PISA tasks that are more predictive of tomorrow's world (**FIGURE 6.1B**).[14]

It is likely that future work will pair computer intelligence with humans' social and emotional skills, attitudes and values. It will then be our capacity for innovation, our awareness and our sense of responsibility that will enable us to harness the power of artificial intelligence to shape the world for the better. That is what will enable humans to create new value, which involves processes of creating, making, bringing into being and formulating, and can generate outcomes that are innovative, fresh and original, contributing something of intrinsic positive worth. It suggests entrepreneurialism in the broadest sense – of being ready to try, without being afraid of failing. In this light, it is not surprising that employment in Europe's creative industries, that is, industries that specialise in the use of talent for commercial purposes, grew at 3.6% during the crucial period between 2011 and 2013, a time when many European sectors were shedding jobs or showing stagnant employment rates, at best. In several leading European countries, the growth of creative jobs outpaced job creation in other sectors, including manufacturing.[15]

FIGURE 6.1A: MEMORISATION IS LESS USEFUL AS TASKS BECOME MORE COMPLEX

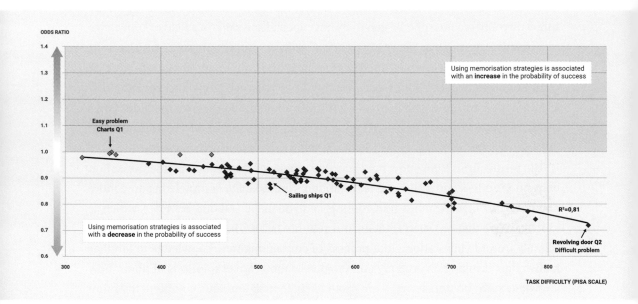

Notes: Average across 48 education systems. Diamonds in a darker tone indicate a statistically significant odds ratio. Memorisation strategies include rehearsal, routine exercises, drills and practice and/or repetition. "Easy problem" refers to the specific task, "Charts QI", which was the easiest task in the PISA 2012 mathematics assessment. "Difficult problem" refers to the specific task, "Revolving door Q2" , which was the most difficult task in the assessment.

Source: OECD, PISA 2012 Database.

StatLink ⬛🖳 *http://dx.doi.org/10.1787/888933414854*

FIGURE 6.1B: ELABORATION STRATEGIES ARE MORE USEFUL AS PROBLEMS BECOME MORE COMPLEX

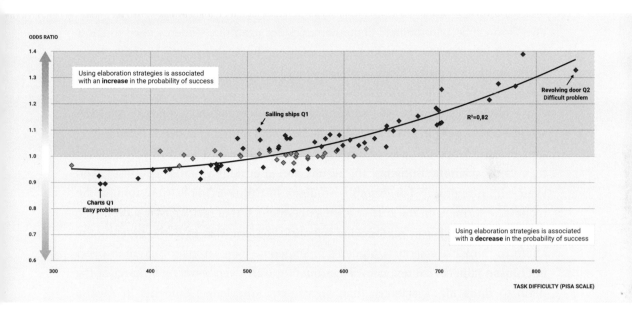

Notes: Average across 48 education systems. Diamonds in a darker tone indicate a statistically significant odds ratio. Elaboration strategies for learning include using analogies and examples, brainstorming, using concept maps and seeking alternative ways to find solutions. "Easy problem" refers to the specific task, "Charts Q1", which was the easiest task in the PISA 2012 mathematics assessment. "Difficult problem" refers to the specific task, "Revolving door Q2", which was the most difficult task in the assessment.

Source: OECD, PISA 2012 Database.

StatLink ⛁ http://dx.doi.org/10.1787/888933414903

Similarly, the more rapidly content knowledge in a subject evolves, the more important it is for students to understand the structural and conceptual foundations of a discipline ("know how"), rather than just master content with a limited shelf life ("know that"). In the field of mathematics, for example, students need to know how and why we study mathematics (epistemic beliefs), be able to think like a mathematician (epistemic understanding) and grasp the practices associated with mathematics (methodological knowledge).

We made epistemic beliefs, knowledge and understanding a focus of the PISA science assessment in 2015, assessing not just what students know, for example in the field of science, but also whether they could think like a scientist and whether they value scientific thinking. The results varied strikingly across countries, and even within regions.[16] For example, students in Chinese Taipei were among the highest performers on the 2015 science assessment, but in relative terms, they were significantly stronger in reproducing scientific content than in demonstrating the ability to think like scientists. Students in Singapore were stronger than their peers in Chinese Taipei in content knowledge, but they were even better on tasks requiring them to think like a scientist than on content knowledge. Students in Austria were stronger in the knowledge of scientific facts than in understanding scientific concepts, while their French counterparts were stronger in conceptual knowledge.

Such variations, even among otherwise similarly performing countries, suggest that education policy and practice can make a difference in student learning. The results should encourage policy makers and educators to reframe curricula and instructional systems so that they place greater emphasis on deep conceptual and epistemic understanding.

None of this is new; in fact, learning that focuses on thinking skills has been with us for thousands of years. In September 2016, I joined Israel's Education Minister Naftali Bennet on a visit to the Hebron *Yeshiva*. Headed by a handful of orthodox rabbis, including Yosef Hevroni and Moshe Mordechai Ferberstein, this *yeshiva* was considered one of the flagship institutions for those studying traditional Jewish texts and legal codes.

In contrast to conventional classroom learning, in which a teacher lectures and students are the consumers of that knowledge, students at the *yeshiva* learn in pairs, with occasional advice or guidance from a teacher. Among the 1 400 students who were learning in one giant classroom, I could detect no more than two dozen teachers, so this was all about learning, not about teaching. The learning experiences I saw there asked students to challenge each other, analyse and explain the material together, point out errors in their partner's reasoning, question and develop each other's ideas, and arrive at new insights into the meaning of the text they studied. The word *hevruta* is ancient Aramaic and is translated as "pair" or "couple", so collaborative learning is the essential learning format – except when one *hevruta* fails to crack a challenge or understand a text, in which case it turns to the two people sitting next to it forming a group of four, which could then grow to six or eight – until they resolve the challenge. Then the students return to their original pairs.

Here, the learning was loud and animated, as the study partners debated and argued their points of view. It was the complete opposite of a traditional Western library where only the eyes work in an atmosphere of absolute quiet. The idea is to help students keep their minds focused on learning, sharpen their reasoning powers, organise thoughts into logical arguments, and understand another person's viewpoint, rather than memorising anything. The goal is not to come up with "the correct" interpretation, but rather to develop a deeper understanding about the argument. Why do viewpoints differ? What are the possible outcomes from disagreement? What proofs are offered to substantiate the views? The best students are those who can ask a question that challenges the teacher's ability to respond. In a way, this seems to be the mother of enquiry-based learning and modern pedagogy.

And yet, like so many other innovations in education, this approach to learning has made few inroads into regular classrooms, either in Israel or elsewhere. It remains frozen in time and limited to religious texts and the complex legal codes of traditional Jewish law. That seems to be one of the fundamental difficulties about education reform: education's industrial work organisation helps us get ideas into schools and classrooms, but it is not as good in moving ideas from classrooms and schools into the system as a whole, to scale and spread promising practice.

▨ Connecting the dots

Innovation and problem solving also depend increasingly on being able to bring together disparate elements, and then synthesise them to create something different and unexpected. This involves curiosity, open-mindedness, and making connections between ideas that previously seemed unrelated. It requires being familiar with knowledge in a range of fields. If we spend our whole life in the silo of a single discipline, we will not gain the imaginative skills to connect the dots and develop the next life-changing invention. Again, the PISA assessment reveals how difficult it is for students to think across the boundaries of school disciplines and solve cross-curricular tasks.

Still, some countries have been trying to develop cross-curricular capabilities. Japan's network of Kosen schools is one example. Its president, Isao Taniguchi, showed me around the Tokyo campus in early 2018. At first sight, the campus looks like a vocational school, since much of the learning is hands-on, collaborative and project-based. But for those who associate hands-on learning with an academically less-rigorous curriculum, Kosen is profoundly different. In fact, the 51 Kosen schools are among Japan's most selective high schools and colleges, and the curriculum is as much about liberal arts as about technical and scientific studies. Some 40% of the graduates will continue studying at university; those who choose to enter the labour market directly can expect an average of 20 job offers as Japan's most sought-after innovators and engineers.

What makes the Kosen schools different is their unique blend of classroom-based and hands-on project-based learning, where learning is cross-curricular and student-centred, and where teachers are mainly coaches and mentors. This is not about the kind of contrived one-week projects that have now become fashionable in many schools around the world; students will typically work for several years on developing and realising their big idea. Riki Ishikawa, a student specialising in electrical engineering, invited me to an amazing virtual-reality experience of white-water rafting. Daisuke Suzuki, a chemistry student, was working on a low-cost solution to purify soil from heavy metal pollution. Unlike most other school projects, the fruits of their work don't typically end up in a bin, but often in an incubator where they find their way to market as one of Japan's many innovations. None of the students I met knew anyone who had dropped out of this demanding programme. While project-based learning has only recently gained widespread traction, the Kosen schools have been in operation since the early 1960s.

In the late 1990s, Japan tried to introduce a cross-curricular approach to learning in its regular schools too, through the course of integrated studies.[17] Its impact was limited, however, because the course was insufficiently embedded in teachers' practice, particularly in secondary schools where exams focus on knowledge of single disciplines.

More recently, Finland has made project-based and cross-disciplinary learning central to all students' education. Confronted with problems similar to those found in real life, students are required to, for example, think like a scientist, like an historian and like a philosopher, all at the same time.[18] But even teachers in Finland find it difficult to meet this standard. Students will only learn to think in multidisciplinary ways when teachers themselves have sufficient knowledge about different disciplines and can collaborate across them. But the fragmented organisation of school days and teachers' work means that there is often limited room for such collaboration across subjects.

In addition, the world is also no longer divided into specialists, who know a lot about very little, and generalists, who know a little about a lot. Specialists generally have deep skills and narrow scope, giving them expertise that is recognised by peers but not always valued outside their domain. Generalists have broad scope but shallow skills. What counts today are people who are able to apply a depth of knowledge to new situations and experiences, gaining new skills, building new relationships and assuming new roles in the process: people who are capable of constantly learning, unlearning and relearning in a fast-changing world when the contexts change. Helping students develop effective learning strategies and metacognitive abilities, such as self-awareness, self-regulation and self-adaptation, will become increasingly important, and should be a more explicit goal in curricula and instructional practice.

Learning to be critical consumers of information

The more knowledge that technology allows us to search and access, the more important becomes deep understanding and the capacity to make sense out of content. Understanding involves knowledge and information, concepts and ideas, practical skills and intuitions. But fundamentally, it involves bringing them together, integrating and applying them, in ways that are appropriate to the learner's context. It also involves the capacity to inform our aspirations for the future with an understanding of the past: the challenges that societies have faced, the solutions they have discovered, and the values they have developed and defended over time.

In the "post-truth" climate in which we now find ourselves, quantity seems to be valued more than quality when it comes to information. Assertions that "feel right" but have no basis in fact become accepted as fact. Algorithms that sort us into groups of like-minded individuals create social media echo chambers that amplify our views, leaving us uninformed of and insulated from opposing arguments that may alter our own beliefs. These virtual bubbles homogenise opinions and polarise our societies; and they can have a significant – and adverse – impact on democratic processes. Those algorithms are not a design flaw; they are how social media work. There is scarce attention, but an abundance of information. We are living in this digital bazaar where anything that is not built for the network age is cracking apart under its pressure.

To what extent should we approach the issue from a consumer-protection angle, that is, restricting providers of information, or from a skills angle, that is, strengthening the capacity of people to better navigate through a tidal wave of information? It is interesting that we haven't touched knowledge products in the same way that we address consumer-protection issues with physical products. People have sued McDonalds when they suffered from obesity or Starbucks when they burned themselves with hot coffee.[19] But it seems very hard to fight against fake news, because tinkering with free speech tends to be regarded as an assault on democratic principles.

Rather than protecting people from information, it may be more fruitful to strengthen people's capacity to sort through the information they receive. Students need to be able to distinguish between credible and untrustworthy sources of information, between fact and fiction. They need to be able to question or seek to improve the accepted knowledge and practices of our times. Literacy in the 20th century was about extracting and processing pre-coded information; in the 21st century, it is about constructing and validating knowledge. In the past, teachers could tell students to look up information in an encyclopaedia, and to rely on that information as accurate and true. Nowadays, Google, Baidu or Yandex presents us with millions of answers to any question, and the task of readers is to triangulate, evaluate and build knowledge.

The growing complexity of modern living, for individuals, communities and societies, suggests that the solutions to our problems will also be complex: in a structurally imbalanced world, the imperative of reconciling diverse perspectives and interests, in local settings with sometimes global implications, will require young people to become adept in handling tensions, dilemmas and trade-offs. Striking a balance between competing demands – equity and freedom, autonomy and community, innovation and continuity, efficiency and democratic process – will rarely lead to an either/or choice or even a single solution. Individuals will need to think in a more integrated way that recognises interconnections. Underpinning these cognitive skills are empathy (the ability to understand another's perspective and to have a visceral or emotional reaction); adaptability (the ability to rethink and change one's perceptions, practices and decisions in the light of fresh experience, new information and additional insight); and trust.

Dealing with novelty, change, diversity and ambiguity assumes that individuals can "think for themselves". Creativity in problem solving requires the capacity to consider the future consequences of one's actions, evaluate risk and reward, and assume accountability for the products of one's work. This suggests a sense of responsibility, and moral and intellectual maturity, with which a person can reflect upon and evaluate his or her actions in the light of their experiences and personal and societal goals. The perception and assessment of what is right or wrong, good or bad in a specific situation is about ethics. It implies asking questions related to norms, values, meanings and limits, such as: What should I do? Was I right to do that? Where are the limits? Knowing the consequences of what I did, should I have done it? Central to this is the concept of self-regulation, which involves self-control, self-efficacy, responsibility, problem-solving and adaptability. Advances in developmental neuroscience show that a second burst of brain plasticity takes place during adolescence, and that the brain regions and systems that are especially plastic are those implicated in the development of self-regulation.

▨ Collaborating with others

We also need to think more about teaching and rewarding collaboration in addition to individual achievement. In today's schools, students typically learn individually, and at the end of the school year we test and certify their individual achievements. But the more interdependent the world becomes, the more we need effective collaborators. Innovation today is rarely the product of individuals working in isolation but an outcome of how we mobilise, share and link knowledge.

To help develop agency among learners, educators need to recognise not just learners' individuality, but also the wider set of relationships – with their teachers, peers, families and communities – that influence student learning. At the heart of this is "co-agency" – the interactive, mutually supportive relationships that help learners progress. In this sense, everyone should be considered a learner, not only students but also teachers, school managers, parents and communities.

We often overlook the fact that collaborative learning is also a great way to inspire self-regulated and enquiry-based learning. For a time, massive open online courses, known as MOOCs, seemed to offer an attractive alternative to expensive instruction; but completion rates for MOOCs have remained dismal. Part of the reason for this is that we have not yet figured out reliable methods of accreditation, so that it is difficult for learners to convert their MOOC experience into qualifications that are relevant in the labour market.

But the bigger part of the problem is the "read-only" mode of many of these online courses: they replicate the lecture format but without the benefit of a motivating teacher. Holm Keller, former vice president of Leuphana University in Germany, developed an interesting collaborative variant of a MOOC for PISA, called PISA4U.[20] He asked potential learners, most of them professional educators, to subscribe to a course and then grouped them based on an algorithm so that members of the group shared common aspirations about their education goals, but were as diverse as possible in virtually every other way. Those diverse groups then identified and worked on problems collaboratively, with each individual supported by an online mentor, and each group supported by an experienced tutor. Over 6 000 teachers from 172 countries took part in piloting PISA4U. Completion rates were high; and most participants said that the key to their enthusiasm was working with people from different countries and cultures, with different interests and experiences. The pilot was so successful that we are now building a permanent digital platform for it.

In 2015, PISA carried out the world's first international assessment of collaborative problem-solving skills, defined as the capacity of students to solve problems by pooling their knowledge, skills and efforts with others.[21] As one would expect, students who have stronger reading or mathematics skills also tend to be better at collaborative problem solving, because managing and interpreting information, and complex reasoning are always required to solve problems. The same holds across countries: top-performing countries in PISA, like Japan, Singapore and South Korea in Asia, Estonia and Finland in Europe, and Canada in North America, also came out on top in the PISA assessment of collaborative problem solving.

But there are countries where students did much better in collaborative problem solving than what one would predict from their performance in the PISA science, reading and mathematics assessments. For example, Japanese students did very well in those subjects, but they did even better in collaborative problem solving. The same holds for students in Australia, New Zealand and South Korea. Students in the United States also did much better in collaborative problem solving than one would expect from their average performance in reading and science, and their below-average performance in mathematics. By contrast, students in the four Chinese cities and provinces that took part in PISA (Beijing, Shanghai, Jiangsu and Guangdong) did well in mathematics and science, but came out just average in collaborative problem solving. Likewise, in Lithuania, Montenegro, the Russian Federation, Tunisia, Turkey and the United Arab Emirates, students punched below their weight in collaborative problem solving. In a nutshell, while the absence of science, mathematics and reading skills does not imply the presence of social skills, social skills are not an automatic by-product of the development of academic skills either.

The results show that some countries do much better than others in developing students' collaborative problem-solving skills, but all countries need to make headway in preparing students for a much more demanding world. An average of only 8% of students can complete problem-solving tasks with fairly high collaboration complexity. These are tasks that require them to maintain awareness of group dynamics, take the initiative to overcome obstacles, and resolve disagreements and conflicts. Even in top-performer Singapore, just one in five students attained this level. Still, three in four students showed that they can contribute to a collaborative effort to solve a problem of medium difficulty and that they can consider different perspectives in their interactions.

Similarly, all countries need to do better in reducing gender disparities. When PISA assessed individual problem-solving skills in 2012, boys scored higher than girls in most countries. By contrast, in the 2015 assessment of collaborative problem solving, girls outperformed boys in every country, both before and after considering their performance in science, reading and mathematics. The relative size of the gender gap in collaborative problem-solving performance is even larger than it is in reading.

These results are mirrored in students' attitudes towards collaboration. Girls reported more positive attitudes towards relationships, meaning that they tend to be more interested in others' opinions and want others to succeed. Boys, on the other hand, are more likely to see the instrumental benefits of teamwork, and how collaboration can help them work more effectively and efficiently.

As positive attitudes towards collaboration are linked with the collaboration-related component of performance in the PISA assessment, this opens up one avenue for intervention. Even if the causal nature of the relationship is unclear, if schools foster boys' appreciation of others and their interpersonal friendships and relationships, then they may also see better outcomes among boys in collaborative problem solving.

There seem to be factors in the classroom environment that relate to those attitudes. PISA asked students how often they engage in communication-intensive activities, such as explaining their ideas in science class; spending time in the laboratory doing practical experiments; arguing about science questions; and taking part in class debates about investigations. The results show a clear relationship between these activities and positive attitudes towards collaboration. On average, valuing relationships and teamwork is more prevalent among students who reported that they participate in these activities more often.

Many schools can also do better in fostering a learning climate where students develop a sense of belonging, and where they are free of fear. Students who reported more positive student-student interactions scored higher in collaborative problem solving, even after considering the socio-economic profile of students and schools. Students who do not feel threatened by other students also scored higher in collaborative problem solving.

It is interesting that disadvantaged students see the value of teamwork often more clearly than their advantaged peers. They tended to report more often that teamwork improves their own efficiency, that they prefer working as part of a team to working alone, and that they think teams make better decisions than individuals. Schools that succeed in building on those attitudes by designing collaborative learning environments might be able to engage disadvantaged students in new ways.

Education does not end at the school gate when it comes to helping students develop their social skills. For a start, parents need to play their part. For example, students scored much higher in the collaborative problem-solving assessment when they reported that they had talked to their parents outside of school on the day prior to the PISA test, and also when their parents agreed that they are interested in their child's school activities or encourage them to be confident.

Collaborative problem-solving skills are, of course, just one facet of a much wider range of social and emotional skills that students need to live and work together throughout their lives. As I discussed in Chapter 1, these skills are related to the character qualities of perseverance, empathy, resilience, mindfulness, courage and leadership.

I gave the opening keynote at the 2016 OEB educational technology conference in Berlin on 21st-century skills.[22] Many fascinating views on the potential role of technology in education were offered at the conference, and sometimes the line between human and computer-based capacities seemed to blur. But Tricia Wang,[23] Global Technology Ethnographer and Co-Founder of Constellate Data, defined that line as the ability to take another person's perspective. She explained how that skill was growing in importance in the tech sector as computers were being asked to – and designed to – handle more and more cognitive tasks.

It's a tall order, but schools need to help students learn to be autonomous in their thinking and develop an identity that is aware of the pluralism of modern living. At work, at home and in the community, people will need a broad comprehension of how others live, in different cultures and traditions, and how others think, as scientists, mathematicians, social scientists and artists. Not least, the ability to read and understand diversity, and to recognise the core liberal values of our societies, such as tolerance and empathy, may also be one of the most powerful responses to extremism. In short, schools now need to enable students to think for themselves and act with and for others.

All this has motivated us to integrate the concept of global competence into PISA, by assessing a set of capabilities that enable people to see the world through different eyes and appreciate different ideas, perspectives and values. PISA conceives of global competence as a multidimensional, lifelong learning goal. Globally competent individuals can examine local, global and intercultural issues, understand and appreciate different perspectives and world views, interact successfully and respectfully with others, and take responsible action toward sustainability and collective well-being (see Chapter 4).

It is a formidable scientific challenge to measure global competence, as such a construct of social and civic inclusion involves so many varied cognitive, social and emotional components. But the more striking aspect is how difficult it has been to gather political support for the effort among countries that participate in PISA. Only a minority of countries has so far agreed to implement this component of the PISA assessment.

The value of values

That brings me to the toughest challenge in modern education: how to incorporate values into education. Values have always been central to education, but it is time that they move from implicit aspirations to explicit education goals and practices in ways that help communities shift from situational values – meaning "I do whatever a situation allows me to do" – to sustainable values that generate trust, social bonds and hope. As New York Times columnist Thomas Friedman puts it, "points of view, traditions and conventional wisdom that looked to be as solid as an iceberg, and just as permanent, can now suddenly melt away in a day, in ways that used to take a generation". And as he notes further, "if society doesn't build foundations under people, many will try to build walls, no matter how self-defeating that would be".[24]

In 2011, when I visited the areas of northeast Japan that had been devastated by the tsunami a few months earlier, I saw how well-established cities could disappear overnight, and how people and schools are suddenly confronted with an entirely new set of challenges. But I also saw how strong societal foundations and resilient communities can meet such challenges.

I had been to Japan more than 50 times before, but this visit to Iwate prefecture made a profound impression on me. Driving for hours along the coastline through endless areas where entire villages had been swept away when the tsunami hit on 11 March 2011, I could see nothing left except the foundations of houses. In some places, one ruin after the other was marked with circles and red crosses, signalling where people had lost not just their homes but also their loved ones.

While temporary housing had been erected and public infrastructure repaired at impressive speed, re-establishing civic life proved to be a much greater challenge. The principals of Funakoshi and Ohtsuchi elementary schools, who were running the temporary Rikuchu-Sanriku school, showed the dynamism and creativity that Japan's educators can bring to bear, if they choose to unleash it. In fact, just before I met them I had visited the remains of the old Funakoshi Elementary School, a school that looked like just about any other in the world, with long dark corridors, classrooms and a teachers' room upstairs.

But the Rikucho-Sanriku temporary school was different. The gymnasium hosted three classes in an open learning space and the teachers' rooms faced the "classroom". Together, students and teachers found creative solutions to ease the difficult conditions, fostering mutual respect and responsibility at the same time.

As the head teacher explained, when one class had a music lesson, the others would go outside for sports. The teachers could not preserve much from the old school library, but community groups had chipped in to donate books and whatever else was needed; and there seemed nothing that you couldn't build from cardboard. In some ways, the tsunami had transformed a school of the past into a learning environment for the future.

The most moving reports were those from teachers. Even in normal times, Japan is a country where there seems no boundary between the public and private lives of teachers. Teachers there feel a deep commitment not just to the intellectual development of their students, but also to their students' social and emotional lives at school and at home. The crisis only amplified this, with teachers taking on an incredible amount of additional responsibility with little material and psychological support.

Many teachers had risked their lives to save their students. One high school teacher recounted how he had reached out to save a child being swept away by the violent floods, but missed the child's hand by just a few centimetres. Another teacher had rescued all the children in the school after the initial earthquake hit and brought them to higher ground. When the parents of one of the children arrived and demanded to take her home, the teacher was not convinced that it was the right thing to do, but didn't refuse. The child and her family died on their way down to the city when the tsunami struck.

I was deeply impressed by the more than 12 000 members of the Japan Teachers' Union who volunteered in the tsunami-hit area. Few people I have met share such a deep commitment to the future of Japan's children than the vice president of the JTU and her colleagues in Iwate prefecture.

The point is that if we want to stay ahead of technological developments, we have to find and refine the qualities that are unique to our humanity, and that complement, not compete with, capacities we have created in our computers.

Trying to limit education to the delivery of academic knowledge carries the risk that education ends up dumbing people down to compete with computers, rather than focusing on core human traits that will enable education to stay ahead of technological and social developments. Ask yourself why it is so much easier for digital technologies to replace today's office workers rather than yesterday's hunter-gatherers. The answer is that in Taylorising work organisation and specialising human skills, we have lost many of the human capabilities that may have no direct instrumental value at work.

In October 2016, I met Josh Yates, from the Institute for Advanced Studies in Culture in Virginia, the United States,[25] who proposes an intriguing framework of the key endowments needed for learning and human development. He speaks about the true (the realm of human knowledge and learning); the beautiful (the realm of creativity, aesthetics and design); the good (the realm of ethics); the just and well-ordered (the realm of political and civic life); and the sustainable (the realm of natural and physical health).

Singapore was the first country I came across that places values explicitly at the centre of its curriculum framework. It emphasises respect, responsibility, resilience, integrity, care and harmony in school. These values are meant to shape students' character qualities, such as self- and social awareness, relationship management, self-management and responsible decision making. In fact, this framework refers to character qualities as "values in action".[26]

As a whole, the Singaporean curriculum framework is designed to nurture a confident person, a self-directed learner, a concerned citizen and an active contributor. Singapore's schools use the framework to design curricular and co-curricular programmes that will help students develop the requisite competencies. In addition, every student is expected to participate in "Values-in-Action" programmes that help build a sense of social responsibility. Still, even in Singapore, much of this remains an aspiration that is at best only partially reflected in how students actually learn and teachers actually teach.

While the case for creating and implementing a new 21st-century curriculum is strong, there seems to be an equally strong alliance standing in the way of change. Parents who worry that their child will not pass an exam may not trust any approach that promises to achieve more with less. Teachers and their unions may worry that if they are asked to teach more subjective material, such as social and emotional skills, they will no longer be assessed just for what they teach but also for who they are. School administrators and policy makers may feel that they will no longer be able to manage schools and school systems when the metric for success shifts from easily quantifiable content knowledge to certain human qualities that may not reveal themselves in full until well after their students graduate. Developing convincing responses to these concerns will require a courageous approach towards the design of modern curricula and assessments. Devising school curricula for the next generation that move beyond past experience will therefore require extraordinary leadership. It will involve explaining and advocating for study plans and assessments that prioritise depth of understanding, and encourage breadth of engagement in learning across the community.

The changing face of successful school systems

Many countries have responded to new demands on what students should learn by layering more and more content on top of their curriculum, with the result that curricula have often become a mile wide but just an inch deep. Teachers are ploughing through a large amount of subject-matter content but with little depth. Adding new material provides an easy way to show that education systems are responding to emerging demands, while it is really hard to remove material from instructional systems. Some countries have looked to broaden the learning experience by integrating new subjects, topics and themes into traditional curriculum areas, often under the flag of an interdisciplinary approach. Other countries have reduced the amount of learning material to provide teachers with more space for depth (see also Chapter 3).

What is needed is a careful balance between a "negotiated" and a designed curriculum. In other words, there has to be both wide consultation and compromise in selecting what should be taught and a well-designed end product. That, in turn, will inspire public confidence and the engagement of the profession.

Finding the right balance is not easy. For example: the question many pose in this technology-rich world is whether today's students should learn coding. There are intriguing examples of schools all around the world that teach coding. But the risk is that we will again be teaching students today's techniques to solve today's problems. By the time those students graduate, those techniques may already be obsolete. The larger question this example poses is: how can we strengthen a deep understanding of and engagement with the underlying concepts of digitalisation without being distracted by today's digital tools?

What is important is to think more systematically about what we want to achieve from the design of curricula, rather than continuing to add more "stuff" to what is being taught. Twenty-first-century curricula need to be characterised by rigour (building what is being taught on a high level of cognitive demand); by focus (aiming at conceptual understanding by prioritising depth over breadth of content); and by coherence (sequencing instruction based on a scientific understanding of learning progressions and human development). Curricula need to remain true to the disciplines, while aiming at interdisciplinary learning and building students' capacity to see problems through multiple lenses.

Curricula need to balance knowledge of discipline content with knowledge about the underlying nature and principles of the disciplines. To help students address unknown future problems, curricula also need to focus on areas with the highest transfer value, in other words, they need to give priority to knowledge, skills and attitudes that can be learned in one context and applied to others. To bring teachers along with this idea, they need to be explicit about the theory of action for how this transfer value occurs. They need to balance cognitive, social and emotional aspects of learning, and help teachers make shared responsibility among students part of the learning process. They need to frame learning in relevant and realistic contexts, and help teachers use approaches that are thematic, problem-based, project-based and centred around co-creation with their colleagues and their students.

But how do we foster motivated, engaged learners who are prepared to meet the unforeseeable challenges of tomorrow, not to mention those they are confronted with today? In traditional school systems, teachers are dispatched to the classroom with instructions about what to teach. In top-performing school systems, a different model has emerged: teachers are given the tools and the support to create their own path to the same end. There are clear goals for what students should be able to do, but there is an expectation that teachers will use their professional independence to determine how to achieve this.

As I've mentioned many times before, countries need to look outward. It is no longer possible to ignore countries like China. As of this writing, the talent pools of well-educated people in Europe, the United States and China are roughly the same size. But in the next decade, China is going to move far ahead in numbers of well-educated youth. In 2017, eight million students graduated from Chinese universities – a ten-fold increase in just ten years, and twice as many as graduated in the United States. Within the next decade, the population of China's well-educated youth might exceed the number of all young people – well-educated and not – in Europe and North America combined.

It is time to explore the implications of all this for learners, educators and education leaders.

A different type of learner

The next generation of young citizens will create jobs, not seek them, and collaborate to advance humanity in an increasingly complex world. That will require curiosity, imagination, empathy, entrepreneurship and resilience, the ability to fail constructively, to learn from mistakes. The most obvious implication of a world that requires constant adaptation and growth from learners is the need to build the capacity and motivation for lifelong learning. We used to learn to do the work; now learning is the work – and that will require a post-industrial way of coaching, mentoring, teaching and evaluating that can build passion and capacity for learning.

The concept is not new. I recall a powerful speech given by then Finnish Education Minister Olli-Pekka Heinonen on lifelong learning at an OECD education ministers meeting in 1996. While the concept of lifelong learning was largely theoretical at that time, and gained little traction beyond issues around adult learning and continuing education and training, it now needs to be at the centre of education policy from the first years of life.

Early on in their school career, learners need to be able to appreciate the value of learning well beyond school, beyond graduation; they need to take responsibility for their learning and bring energy to the process of learning. Lifelong learning does not just require people to constantly learn new things but, and this tends to be far more difficult, to un-learn and re-learn when contexts and paradigms change. When I was young, I could eat whatever I liked without gaining weight. It hasn't been easy to quit old habits when I realised that my metabolism had changed.

Lifelong learning also builds on effective learning strategies and aspirations. PISA offers some interesting findings on the relationships – or lack thereof – among academic knowledge, students' learning strategies and students' career expectations. *FIGURE 6.2* shows the percentage of 15-year-old students who expect to work in science-related professional and technical occupations when they are 30 years old. The data show a whole range of countries and economies – Belgium, the four municipalities and provinces in China that participated in PISA, Estonia, Finland, Germany, Japan, Macao, the Netherlands, Poland, South Korea, Switzerland and Viet Nam – with high scores on the PISA science tests, but where students have just moderate aspirations to make science part of their future lives. In fact, there are just a few countries where students' science knowledge, their belief in scientific methods and the way they see science opening career opportunities align: Canada and Singapore and, among students who scored somewhat lower in science, Australia, Ireland, Portugal, Slovenia and the United Kingdom. Of course, the data also show the flipside of the story. For example, students in Israel, Spain and the United States are open to methods of scientific inquiry and aspire to careers in science, but they lack the scientific knowledge and skills to realise their dreams.

The bottom line is that academic success alone is not sufficient. PISA also offers some interesting insights into the link between knowledge and aspirations. When students do not enjoy learning science, better performance in science translates into only a marginally higher likelihood that these students expect to pursue a career in science (*FIGURE 6.3*). But when students do enjoy learning about science, better learning outcomes are closely linked with students' expectations of a science-related career. Again, this highlights the importance of developing more multidimensional approaches to learning and instructional design, and doing so explicitly rather than just hoping that the focus on improved performance will result in other desired outcomes.

One might be tempted to conclude that lifelong learning means shifting resources from learning during childhood towards learning in adulthood. But OECD data show how learning throughout life is remarkably closely related to learning outcomes at school.[27] Indeed, subsequent learning opportunities tend to reinforce early disparities in learning outcomes. Individuals who failed at school are unlikely to seek out subsequent learning opportunities, and employers are unlikely to invest in learners with weaker foundation skills. In short, lifelong learning as we currently know it does not mitigate, but rather tends to reinforce, initial differences in education. This just underlines both how important it is to get the foundations right, and that we need to become much better at designing effective learning opportunities that meet the diverse interests of adults later in life.

Still, there is a lot that governments and societies can do to help learners adapt. The easiest is telling young people the truth about the social and labour-market relevance of their learning, and to incentivise educational institutions to pay more

FIGURE 6.2: MOST 15-YEAR-OLDS DO NOT ASPIRE TO WORK IN A SCIENCE-RELATED CAREER

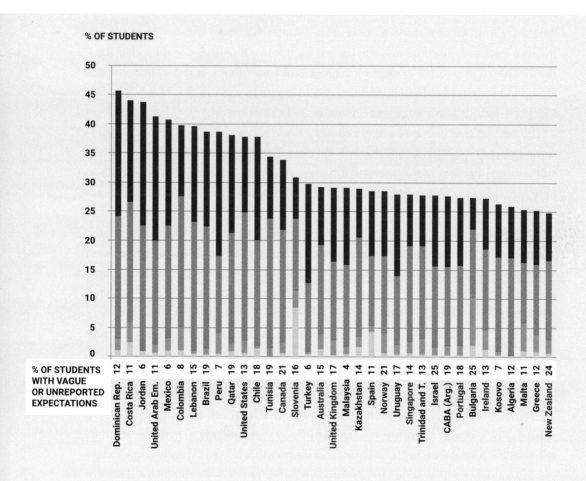

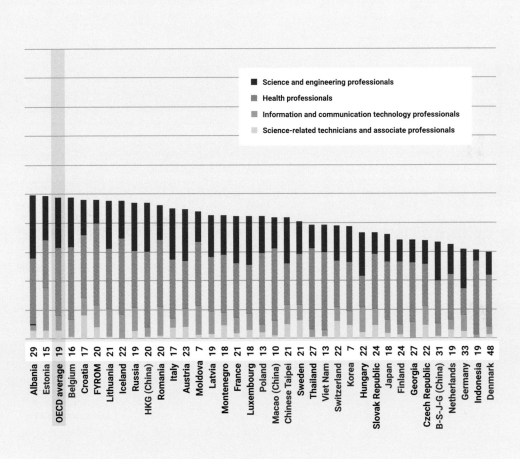

Notes: Percentage of students who expect to work in science-related professional and technical occupations when they are 30. Country/Economy names in dark pink were high performers in science in PISA 2015. CABA (Arg.) refers to Ciudad Autónoma de Buenos Aires (Argentina). Belgium refers only to the French and German-speaking communities. FYROM refers to the Former Yugoslav Republic of Macedonia. B-S-J-G (China) refers to Beijing-Shanghai-Jiangsu-Guangdong (China).

Source: OECD, PISA 2015 Database, Table I.3.10a.

FIGURE 6.3: WHEN STUDENTS ENJOY LEARNING SCIENCE, BETTER PERFORMANCE IS MORE STRONGLY ASSOCIATED WITH THE EXPECTATION OF PURSUING A SCIENCE CAREER

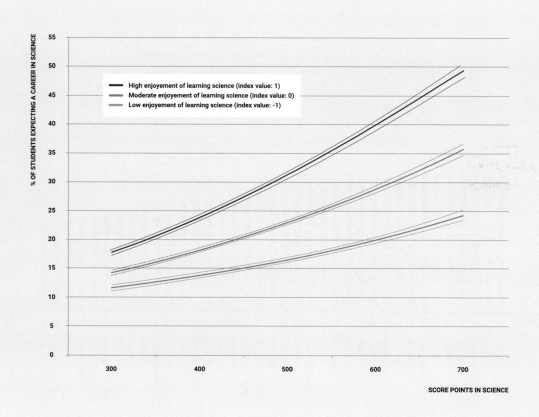

Notes: Estimate; OECD average, after accounting for gender and socio-economic status. The lines represent the predicted share of students expecting a career in a science-related occupation, based on a logistic model with the index of enjoyment of science, performance in science, their product, gender, and the PISA index of economic, social and cultural status introduced as predictors. The shaded area around the curves indicates the upper and lower bounds of the 95% confidence interval for these estimates.

Source: OECD, PISA 2015 Database, Table 1.3.13b.

StatLink ▐▊▅ *http://dx.doi.org/10.1787/888933432435*

attention to that too. When education systems help students choose a field of study that resonates with their passions, in which they can excel, and that allows them to contribute to society, they will put students on the path to success. But instead, many universities still focus on marketing study fields that are easy and cheap to provide.

More difficult, but at least equally important, is to shift from qualifications-based certification systems to more knowledge- and skills-based certification systems. That means moving from documenting education pathways towards highlighting what individuals can actually do, regardless of how and where they have acquired their knowledge, skills and character qualities. I am a good example of this. Many years ago, I acquired my degree in physics, and that remains the qualification recorded in my *curriculum vitae*. But if I were sent to a laboratory today, I would fail dismally at the work, both because of the rapid advances in physics since I earned my degree, and because I have lost some of the skills that I have not used for a long time. In the meantime, I have acquired many new skills that have not been formally certified.

Twenty-first century teachers

High and growing expectations for teachers

The expectations for teachers are high and rising each day (see Chapter 3). We expect them to have a deep and broad understanding of what they teach, whom they teach and how students learn, because what teachers know and care about makes such a difference to student learning. But we expect much more than what we put into the job descriptions of teachers. We expect teachers to be passionate, compassionate and thoughtful; to make learning central and encourage students' engagement and responsibility; to respond effectively to students of different needs, backgrounds and languages, and to promote tolerance and social cohesion; to provide continual assessments of students and feedback; and to ensure that students feel valued and included and that learning is collaborative. We expect teachers themselves to collaborate and work in teams, and with other schools and parents, to set common goals, and plan and monitor the attainment of goals. Not least, students are unlikely to become lifelong learners if they do not see their teachers as active lifelong learners, willing to extend their horizons and question the established wisdom of their times.

Teachers of today's "connected" learners must also meet the challenges that have arisen from digitisation, from information overload to plagiarism, from protecting children from online risks, such as fraud, violations of privacy or online bullying, to setting an adequate and appropriate media diet for their students. They are expected to help educate children to become critical consumers of Internet services and electronic media, to make informed choices and avoid harmful behaviours.

But there is more. Most successful people had at least one teacher who made a real difference in their life – because the teacher acted as a role model, or took a genuine interest in the student's welfare and future, or provided emotional support when the student needed it. These aspects of teaching are difficult to compare and quantify, but designing a work organisation and support culture that nurture these qualities will go a long way towards ensuring that every student succeeds.

Digital technology in support of teaching

While people have different views on the role that digital technology can and should play in schools, we cannot ignore how digital tools have so fundamentally transformed the world outside of school. Everywhere, digital technologies are offering firms new business models and opportunities to enter markets and transform their production processes. They can make us live longer and healthier, help us delegate boring or dangerous tasks, and allow us to travel into virtual worlds. People who cannot navigate through the digital landscape can no longer participate fully in our social, economic and cultural life.

Technology should therefore play an important role if we want to provide teachers with learning environments that support 21st-century methods of teaching and, most important, if we want to provide students with the 21st-century skills they need to succeed.

I am pretty relaxed when I hear people argue that digital technologies will make teachers redundant. The heart of teaching has always been relational, and teaching seems to be one of the most enduring social activities. So there will be more, not less, demand for people who are able to build and support learners throughout their life.

The value of teaching as a key differentiator is only bound to rise as digitalisation drives forward the unbundling of educational content, accreditation and teaching that makes up traditional schools. In the digital age, anything that we call our proprietary knowledge and educational content today will be a commodity available to everyone tomorrow. Accreditation still gives educational institutions enormous power, but just think a few years ahead. What will micro-credentialing do to accreditation when employers can directly validate specific knowledge and skills? Or think of employers' rapidly growing capacity to see through the degrees that prospective employees list on their CVs to the knowledge and skills they actually have. In the end, the quality of teaching seems the most valuable asset of modern educational institutions.

Still, as in many other professions, digital technologies are likely to assume many of the tasks now carried out by teachers. Even if teaching will never be digitised or outsourced to other places, routine administrative and instructional tasks that take valuable time away from teaching are already being handed over to technology.

In the health sector, we start by looking at the outcomes, we measure the blood pressure and take the temperature of a patient and then decide what medicine is most appropriate. In education, we tend to give everyone the same medicine, instruct all children in the same way, and when we find out many years later that the outcomes are unsatisfactory, we blame that on the motivation or capacity of the patient. That is simply no longer good enough. Digital technology now allows us to find entirely new responses to what people learn, how people learn, where people learn and when they learn, and to enrich and extend the reach of excellent teachers and teaching.

We need to embrace technology in ways that elevate the role of teachers from imparting received knowledge towards working as co-creators of knowledge, as coaches, as mentors and as evaluators. Already today, intelligent digital learning systems cannot just teach you science, but they can simultaneously observe how you study, how you learn science, the kind of tasks and thinking that interest you, and the kind of problems that you find boring or difficult. These systems can then adapt learning to suit your personal learning style with far greater granularity and precision than any traditional classroom setting possibly can. Similarly, virtual laboratories give you the opportunity to design, conduct and learn from experiments, rather than just learning about them.

Technology can enable teachers and students to access specialised materials well beyond textbooks, in multiple formats and in ways that can bridge time and space. Technology can support new ways of teaching that focus on learners as active participants. There are good examples of technology enhancing experiential learning by supporting project- and enquiry-based teaching methods, facilitating hands-on activities and co-operative learning, and delivering formative real-time assessments. There are also interesting examples of technology supporting learning with interactive, non-linear courseware based on state-of-the-art instructional design, sophisticated software for experimentation and simulation, social media and educational games. These are precisely the learning tools that are needed to develop 21st-century knowledge and skills. Not least, one teacher can now educate and inspire millions of learners and communicate their ideas to the whole world.

Perhaps the most distinguishing feature of technology is that it not only serves individual learners and educators, but it can build an ecosystem around learning that is predicated on collaboration. Technology can build communities of learners that make learning more social and more fun, recognising that collaborative learning enhances goal orientation, motivation, persistence and the development of effective learning strategies. Similarly, technology can build communities of teachers to share and enrich teaching resources and practices, and also to collaborate on professional growth and the institutionalisation of professional practice. It can help system leaders and governments develop and share best practice around curriculum design, policy and pedagogy. Imagine a giant crowdsourcing platform where teachers, education researchers and policy experts collaborate to curate the most relevant content and pedagogical practice to achieve education goals, and where students anywhere in the world have access to the best and most innovative education experiences.

But the reality in classrooms looks quite different from these promises. In 2015, we published a PISA report on students' digital skills and the learning environments designed to develop those skills.[28] The results showed that technology has not yet been widely adopted in classrooms. At the time of our 2012 PISA survey, only around 37% of schools in Europe had high-end equipment and high-speed Internet connectivity, ranging from 5% of schools in Poland to virtually all schools in Norway. But when asked, between 80% and 90% of school principals reported that their schools were adequately equipped when it comes to computers and Internet connectivity – even principals in the many countries where the equipment was clearly substandard. So is technology not that important? Or were school leaders not aware of the potential of digital technologies to transform learning?

More important, even where such technologies are used in the classroom, their impact on student performance seems mixed, at best. PISA measured students' digital literacy, and the frequency and intensity with which students use computers at school. Students who use computers moderately at school tend to have somewhat better learning outcomes than students who use computers rarely. But students who use computers very frequently at school do a lot worse in most learning outcomes, even after accounting for social background and student demographics (*FIGURE 6.4*). These findings hold for both skills in digital literacy and in mathematics and science.

PISA results also show no appreciable improvement in student achievement in the countries that had invested heavily in digital technology for education. Perhaps the most disappointing finding is that technology has been of little help in bridging the divide in knowledge and skills between advantaged and disadvantaged students. Put simply, ensuring that every child attains a baseline level of proficiency in reading and mathematics still seems to do more to create equal opportunities in a digital world than is currently achieved by expanding or subsidising access to high-tech devices in school.

One interpretation of all this is that building deep, conceptual understanding and developing higher-order thinking requires intensive teacher-student interactions, and technology sometimes distracts from such human engagement. Another is that we have not yet become good enough at the kind of pedagogies that make the most of technology, that adding 21st-century technologies to 20th-century teaching practices in a 19th-century school organisation will just dilute the effectiveness of teaching. If students use Google to copy and paste prefabricated answers to questions, that's certainly a less effective way to learn than through traditional teaching methods.

In short, while digital technologies can amplify great teaching, they rarely replace poor teaching. If we continue to dump technology on schools in a fragmented way, we won't be able to realise technology's potential. Countries need to have a clear plan and build teachers' capacity to make that happen; and policy makers need to become better at building support for such an approach. The future is with teachers who

FIGURE 6.4: STUDENTS WHO USE COMPUTERS AT SCHOOL THE MOST SCORE THE LOWEST IN READING DIGITAL AND PRINTED TEXT

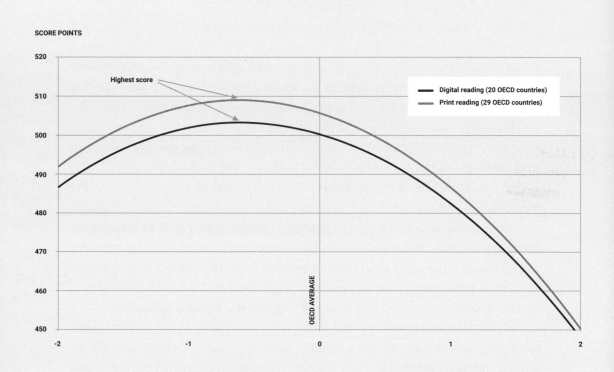

Notes: OECD average relationship, after accounting for the socio-economic status of students and schools. The lines represent the predicted values of the respective outcome variable, at varying levels of the PISA index of computer use at school

Source: OECD, PISA 2012 database, Table X.2

StatLink ⟦⟧ http://dx.doi.org/10.1787/888933253280

can harness the potential of technology and help students see the value of learning beyond acquiring content knowledge, who are designers of imaginative problem-based environments, and who nurture critical evaluation and metacognition

Creating a culture of sharing

There is another angle from which to consider technology in education. Big data could support the redesign of education as it has already done in so many other sectors. Imagine the power of an education system that could share all of its collective expertise and experience through new digital spaces.

But throwing education data into the public space does not, in itself, change how students learn, teachers teach and schools operate. That is the discouraging lesson from many administrative accountability systems. People may have data, but they may not do anything with it to change education practice.

Turning digital exhaust into digital fuel, and using data as a catalyst to change education practice requires getting out of the "read-only" mode of our education systems, in which information is presented as if inscribed in stone. This is about combining transparency with collaboration. Too often, educational institutions are run by experts sitting somewhere in a distant administration who determine the content, rules and regulations affecting hundreds of thousands of students and teachers. Few are able to figure out how those decisions were made.

If we could make the data on which those decisions are based available to all, and enable teachers at the frontline to experiment and become creators, then we could use big data to help cultivate big trust. I am always struck by the power of "collaborative consumption", where online markets are created in which people share their cars, and even their apartments, with total strangers. Collaborative consumption has made people micro-entrepreneurs – and the driving force behind it is trust between strangers. In the business world, trustworthy strangers are connected in all sorts of marketplaces. The reason this works is because behind these systems are powerful reputational metrics that help people know their counterparts and build trust. When we want to buy something from a stranger, we can see how other customers have rated the seller, and at the end of the purchase we can rate the seller ourselves. Similarly, the seller can rate us as trustworthy buyers.

It is worth considering the use of technology in Shanghai, the top-ranked education system in PISA 2012. Teachers there are judicious and selective in using technology in their classrooms, but they embrace technology when it comes to enhancing and sharing professional practice. When I visited Shanghai in 2013, I saw teachers using a digital platform to share lesson plans. That in itself is not unusual; what made it different from other places was that the platform was combined with reputational metrics. The more other teachers downloaded, or critiqued or improved lessons, the greater the reputation of the teacher who had shared them. At the end of the school year, the principal would not just ask how well the teacher had taught his or her students, but what contribution he or she had made to improve the teaching profession and the wider education system.

Shanghai's approach to curated crowdsourcing of education practice is not just a great example of how to identify and share best practice among teachers, it is also so much more powerful than performance-related pay as a way to encourage professional growth and development. It might even be fairer, too, since the assessments are based on the views of the entire profession rather than just on the views of a single superior who may be years removed from actual practice.

In this way, Shanghai created a giant open-source community of teachers and unlocked teachers' creativity simply by tapping into the desire of people to contribute, collaborate and be recognised for their contributions. This is how technology can extend the reach of great teaching, recognising that value is less and less created vertically, through command and control, but increasingly horizontally, by whom we connect and work with.

When parents are surveyed about the quality of their children's schooling, many rate the school system as poor, but the quality of their children's school as good, irrespective of schooling outcomes. We trust our children's schools because we know them, just as we trust the teachers in these schools because we know them. We have less trust in strangers. But the digital age allows us to create much more enriching and valuable social capital. What reputational metrics, such as those used in Shanghai, do is give those strangers faces and identities, and because so many other people are doing the same, we learn whom we can trust.

Obviously, once again, the devil can be in the detail. Successful collaboration depends deeply on relationships, and this may not automatically translate into having the right number of online badges or stars certifying someone is a good collaborator. There is also the risk that digital sharing platforms may become commercialised, limiting the free sharing of experience.

Owning their profession

The heart of great teaching is not technology, it is ownership. Successful education systems in the 21st century will do whatever it takes to develop ownership of professional practice by the teaching profession. I meet many people who say we cannot give teachers and education leaders greater autonomy because they lack the capacity and expertise to deliver on it. There may be some truth in that. But simply perpetuating a prescriptive model of teaching will not produce creative teachers: those trained only to reheat pre-cooked hamburgers are unlikely to become master chefs.

By contrast, when teachers feel a sense of ownership over their classrooms, when students feel a sense of ownership over their learning, that is when productive teaching takes place. So the answer is to strengthen trust, transparency, professional autonomy and the collaborative culture of the profession all at the same time.

When teachers assume ownership, it is difficult to ask more of them than they ask of themselves. In 2011, I studied how the Netherlands' Ministry of Education was developing teacher-led professional standards. Initially, there were concerns in the government that leaving this to the profession could sacrifice the necessary rigour and result in a set of professional standards based on the lowest common denominator. But the opposite happened. Then-State Secretary for the Ministry of Education, Culture and Science, Sander Dekker, told me later that no government in the Netherlands would have ever been able to impose such demanding standards for the profession as the profession itself had developed. The same holds in other professions: think of barriers to entry in the medical profession or in law. Sometimes professionalism and professional pride seem far better regulators than governments.

I learned many things from this experience. First of all, involving teachers in the development of professional standards is a great way to build professional knowledge. Indeed, for teaching standards to be relevant and owned by the profession, it is essential that teachers play a lead role in designing them. Similarly, as I discussed in Chapter 5, it is essential that teachers participate in designing methods for teacher appraisal if the appraisal system is to be effective.[29] Inviting teachers to participate is a way of recognising their professionalism, the importance of their skills and experience, and the extent of their responsibilities. Teachers will also be more open to being appraised if they are consulted in the process. Thus designers of appraisal systems need to work with teachers' professional organisations and outstanding teachers from across the system. In the end, teachers, like other professionals, have a genuine interest in safeguarding the standards and reputation of their profession.

But most important, teachers must assume ownership of the profession because of the pace of change in 21st-century school systems. Even the most urgent efforts to translate a government-established curriculum into classroom practice typically drag out over a decade, because it takes so much time to communicate the goals and methods through the different layers of the system, and to build them into teacher-education programmes. When what and how students learn changes so rapidly, this slow implementation process leads to a widening gap between what students need to learn, and what and how teachers teach.

The only way to shorten that timeframe is to professionalise teaching, ensuring that teachers have a deep understanding not only of the curriculum as a product, but of the process of designing a curriculum and the pedagogies that will best communicate the ideas behind the curriculum.

Schools face a tough challenge in responding to what will be valuable for young people in the future. Subject-matter content will be less and less the core and more and more the context of good teaching. Many of today's curricula are designed to equip learners for a static world that no longer exists. Those types of curricula could be delivered with an industrial approach in hierarchical bureaucracies; they do not require teachers to have advanced professional insights into instructional design. But that is no longer good enough. Curricula now need to account for fast-moving flows of knowledge creation.

Paradoxically, the highly standardised industrial work organisation of teaching has often left teachers alone in the classroom. Zero percent school autonomy has meant one hundred percent teacher isolation behind closed classroom doors.

As the prescriptive approach weakens, the position of the classroom practitioners needs strengthening. While governments can establish directions and curriculum goals, the teaching profession needs to take charge of the instructional system, and governments need to find ways to enable and support professionalism. However, increased professional autonomy also implies challenging idiosyncratic practice. It means moving away from every teacher having his or her own approach towards the common use of practices agreed by the profession as effective, making teaching not just an art but also a science. That is what the above example of teacher collaboration in Shanghai is really about.

We should not take freedom as an argument to be unconventional for its own sake. If you were a pilot, and you would announce to your passengers you were taught to land against the wind but, this time, you want to try to land with the wind, your passengers would start to feel rather anxious. Of course, it is not easy for school leaders to balance the fact that teachers may feel that landing with the wind is a good idea, on the one hand, and promoting their autonomy and ownership over the profession, on the other. Because so many areas of teaching do not yet have clear standards of practice, teachers may infer that there should be complete autonomy in all areas, even in those where the evidence base is well established. So when there is not common agreement on professional practice, teachers may feel disempowered when leaders steer them towards selected evidence.

Finding out which pedagogical approaches work best in which contexts takes time, an investment in research, and collaboration so that good ideas spread and are scaled into the profession. Achieving that will require a major shift from an industrial work organisation to a truly professional work organisation for teachers and school leaders, in which professional norms of control replace bureaucratic and administrative forms of control. In turn, more professional discretion accorded to teachers will allow them greater latitude in developing student creativity and critical thinking skills that are central to success in the 21st century, and that are much harder to develop in highly prescriptive learning environments. Supporting such a shift is what we should expect from 21st-century education policy.

Encouraging innovation in and outside of school

When other sectors see flat-lining productivity they look to innovation; that is happening in education too. Comparisons point to levels of innovation in education that are pretty much in line with those in other sectors of the economy.[30] But the issue is less the volume of innovation than its relevance and quality, and the speed from idea to impact. Innovation is happening, but too little of it focuses on the heart of learning; when it does, it spreads too slowly.

Innovative change can be more difficult in hierarchical structures that are geared towards rewarding compliance with rules and regulations. One policy approach to foster innovation in education has been to increase autonomy, diversity and competition among educational institutions. But evidence of the benefits of this approach remains patchy.

To reconcile flexibility and innovation with equity, school systems need to devise checks and balances that prevent choice from leading to inequity and segregation, and do whatever it takes so that all parents can choose the school of their preference. That means government and schools must invest in developing their relationships with parents and local communities, and help parents make informed decisions. As I discussed in Chapter 4, the more flexibility there is in the school system, the stronger public policy needs to be. While greater school autonomy, decentralisation and a more demand-driven school system seek to devolve decision making to the frontline, public policy needs to maintain a strategic vision and clear guidelines for education, establish effective mechanisms for mobilising and sharing knowledge, and offer meaningful feedback to local school networks and individual schools. In other words, only through a concerted effort by central and local education authorities will school choice benefit all students.

Innovation in governance is one challenge, innovation in the instructional system another. There is a long history of introducing new methods in education – whether it was television, video, digital whiteboards or computers – in the hope of radically improving teaching and the effectiveness of schooling, only to find, at best, incremental change achieved at higher cost and complexity. I have asked myself many times why education has not kept up with innovation in other areas. I have found no good answers except, perhaps, that it would disrupt the current business model of governments, academia and textbook publishers.

It may also be that the education industry is too weak and fragmented to accept this particular challenge. Keep in mind that public health-research budgets in OECD countries are 17 times larger than education-research budgets.[31] That says a lot about the role that we expect knowledge to play in advancing practice.

But the bigger issue is that, even where good education research and knowledge exists, many practitioners just do not believe that the problems they face can be solved by science and research. Too many teachers believe that good teaching is an individual art based on inspiration and talent, and not a set of skills you can acquire during a career. Yet it would be a mistake to blame just teachers for that. This problem often goes back to policy, because there is a lack of incentives and resources to codify professional knowledge and knowhow. In many countries, the room for non-teaching working time is far too limited for teachers to engage in knowledge creation. Because education has not been able to build a professional body of practice or even a common scientific language as other professions have, practice remains unarticulated, invisible, isolated and difficult to transfer. Investing in better knowledge – and disseminating that knowledge widely – must become a priority; it promises to deliver huge rewards.

It is also important to create a more level playing field for innovation in schools. Governments can help strengthen professional autonomy and a collaborative culture where great ideas are refined and shared. Governments can also help with funding, and can offer incentives that raise the profile of, and demand for, what works. But governments alone can only do so much. Silicon Valley works because governments created the conditions for innovation, not because governments do the innovating. Similarly, governments cannot innovate in the classroom; they can only help by opening up systems so that there is an innovation-friendly climate where transformative ideas can bloom. That means encouraging innovation within the system and making it open to creative ideas from outside. More of that needs to be happening.

Policy makers often view education industries as providers of goods and services to schools. They tend to underappreciate that innovation in education is also changing the very environment in which schools operate. In particular, technology-based innovations open up schools to the outside world, both the digital world and the social environment. They also bring new actors into the system, including the education industries with their own ideas, views and dreams about what a brighter future for education could hold.

It is difficult for education systems to treat industry as a valuable partner. Fears of a perceived "marketisation" of education, or the displacement of teachers by computers, often endanger what could be a fruitful dialogue. At the same time, we should be more demanding of the education industry. Most of our children would not voluntarily play with the kinds of software that companies are still able to sell to schools. Is innovation in the education industry as dynamic as it should or could be? Can we break the cartel of a few large suppliers of educational resources who use an army of salespeople to sell their services to a fragmented market? Can we overcome the slow sales cycles, where buyers have to deal with layers and layers of people all "in charge"?

Is it possible to create a business culture for managing innovation in school systems? At the moment, it is so much easier for administrators to buy new tools and systems, and use existing staff because this costs them "nothing". The treatment of teacher time as a sunk cost means people see no benefit to saving this time. It is worthwhile to explore how industry can help the education sector close the productivity gap with new tools and new practices, organisations and technology.

It is surprising to me how entrepreneurship in the education sector remains so limited. Yes, there are large organisations producing textbooks, learning materials and online courses, and there are countless private schools and universities. But these are highly fragmented. It was not until June 2013 that I met Indian entrepreneur Sunny Varkey,[32] who had the ambition to transform the education sector by shifting gears from private-versus-public to private-with-public. What makes his mission different from others is that it is not about education as part of something else, but about putting education first.

Perhaps we should stop seeking the "killer app" or the "disruptive" business model that will somehow turn existing practices upside down. Perhaps, instead, we should learn how to identify, interpret and cultivate a capacity for learning across the entire ecosystem that produces education outcomes. To deliver on the promises offered in the digital age, countries will need much more convincing strategies to build teachers' capacity to use the new tools; and policy makers will need to become better at building support for this agenda. Given the uncertainties that accompany all change, educators will often opt to maintain the status quo. To mobilise support for more innovative schools, education systems need to become better at communicating the need and building support for change. Investing in capacity development and change-management skills will be critical; and it is vital that teachers become active agents for change, not just in implementing technological innovations, but in designing them too (see Chapter 5).

Education systems need to better identify key agents of change and champion them; and they need to find more effective ways of scaling and disseminating innovations. That is also about finding better ways to recognise, reward and celebrate success, to do whatever is possible to make it easier for innovators to take risks and encourage the emergence of new ideas. One of the most devastating findings from our first survey of teachers (TALIS) was that three in four teachers in the industrialised world consider their workplace an environment that is essentially hostile to innovation.[33] Nothing will change if we don't change that perception.

Cultivating effective system leadership

Changing education bureaucracies can be like moving graveyards: it is often hard to rely on the people out there to help, because the status quo has so many protectors. The bottom line is that school systems are rather conservative social systems. Everyone supports education reform – unless it affects their own children. Parents may measure the education of their children against their own education experiences. Teachers may teach how they were taught, rather than how they were taught to teach. But the real obstacle to education reform is not conservative followers but conservative leaders: leaders who exploit populism to preserve the status quo; leaders who stick to today's curriculum rather than adapt pedagogical practice to a changing world, because it is so much easier to stay within everybody's comfort zone; leaders who invest in popular solutions, like smaller classes, rather than take the time to convince parents and teachers of the benefits of spending money more effectively, including through investing in greater teacher professionalism.

Effective leadership is central to virtually every aspect of education, particularly when there is little coherence and capacity. While there are many amazing teachers, schools and education programmes in every education system, it takes effective leadership to build a great education system. As Michael Fullan, an authority on education reform, notes, programmes do not scale; it is culture that scales, and culture is the hallmark of effective leadership. Culture is about system learning, system-wide innovation, and purposeful collaboration that can lead to large-scale and ongoing improvement. If you want to effect real and lasting change, do not ask yourself how many teachers support your ideas, ask yourself how many teachers are capable of and engage in effective co-operation.

The education crisis, reflected in flat education outcomes despite rising investment, is partly a leadership crisis. Finding adequate and forward-looking responses to the inter-related changes in technology, globalisation and the environment is ultimately a question of leadership. Effective leadership is vital to creating an environment where institutions, educators, researchers and other innovators can work together as professionals. These kinds of leaders should help people recognise what needs to change, mobilise support and share leadership responsibilities throughout the system.

As Michael Fullan explains, leaders who want to make forward-looking changes in their school systems have to do more than issue orders and try to impose compliance. They need to build a shared understanding and collective ownership, make the case for change, offer support that will make change a reality, and remain credible without being populist. They need to focus resources, build capacity, change work organisations, and create the right policy climate with accountability measures designed to encourage innovation and development, rather than compliance. And they need to go against the dynamics of turf and hierarchical bureaucracies that still dominate educational institutions.

System leaders need to tackle institutional structures that too often are built around the interests and habits of educators and administrators rather than learners.

Most of our school systems are designed to sort and weed out people, not to open opportunities and address the diverse needs of learners. That might have been an efficient and effective approach for the industrial age, when education was about finding and training a small minority of leaders, and equipping everyone else with just basic knowledge and skills. But in a modern society, where we need to capitalise on everyone's talents and ensure equitable access to learning, such an approach is a barrier to success. Incentives and support are needed so that schools can meet the needs of all of their pupils, rather than gain an advantage by shifting difficult learners elsewhere.

For schools to be entrepreneurial and able to adapt, system leaders need to be able to mobilise the human, social and financial resources needed for innovation. They need to be able to build strong linkages across sectors and countries, and establish partnerships with government leaders, social entrepreneurs, business executives, researchers and civil society.

It will be important for education policy to get beyond the unproductive wrangling between forces pushing for greater decentralisation and those aiming for greater centralisation of the school system. That debate detracts from the real question of what aspects of education are best managed at what level of the education system, and the overriding principle of subsidiarity, where every layer of the school system should continuously ask itself how it can best support learners and teachers at the frontline.

That also means that teachers, schools and local authorities recognise that certain functions, particularly those regarding the establishment of curriculum frameworks, course syllabi, examinations and teaching standards require a critical mass of capacity, and therefore tend to be best supported by some level of centralisation. The test of truth is a coherent instructional system that is available to all students, and in which world-class education standards feed into well-thought-out curriculum frameworks that guide the work of teachers and publishers of education materials.

Countries with an unregulated market for textbooks, where schools or districts are choosing what is taught in classrooms, will consider Japan's approach, where the Ministry of Education takes a strong role in guiding the development and review of textbooks, as overly centralised. But ask Japanese teachers about this, and they will tell you about the years of consultation and involvement of the profession that precede the development and publication of that textbook. They will also tell you about the extensive professional development that builds capacity around interpreting and implementing the goals of the curriculum. The result can be far greater ownership by the profession and far greater autonomy at the frontline than an approach where schools or districts purchase a textbook that is then handed to teachers to deliver in the classroom. In short, we need to stop considering centralisation and decentralisation as opposing ends of one spectrum.

System leaders need to be aware of how organisational policies and practices can either facilitate or inhibit transformation. They need to be ready to confront the system when it inhibits change. They need to be able to recognise emerging trends and patterns and see how these might benefit or obstruct the innovation they want to achieve. They need to be politically savvy in working with other organisations and people. They need to use their knowledge about what motivates people to convince others to support their plans for change; and they need to use their understanding of power and influence to build the alliances and coalitions needed to get things done.

Singapore's success in education, for example, is a story about leadership and alignment between policy and practice; setting ambitious standards; building teacher and leadership capacity to develop vision and strategy at the school level; and about a culture of continuous improvement that benchmarks education practices against the best in the world.

At the institutional level, both policy coherence and fidelity of implementation are brought about by a strategic relationship between the Ministry of Education, the National Institute of Education, which educates teachers, and the schools. Those aren't just words. The reports I received from policy makers, researchers and teachers in Singapore were always consistent, even where they represented different perspectives. The leader of the National Institute of Education meets the education minister every few weeks. Its professors are regularly involved in ministry discussions and decisions, so it is easy for the Institute's work to be aligned with ministry policies; and school principals learn about major reform proposals directly from the minister. In April 2014, I spoke at one of the regular meetings where Singapore's then-Education Minister, Heng Swee Keat, discussed plans for school reform with all of Singapore's secondary school principals. It would never have occurred to him to announce an education reform through the media; he was well aware that nothing would get done until school leaders owned the goals and methods of the envisaged changes.

What I learned from this is how important it is for education leaders to be transparent with teachers and school leaders about where reform is heading and what it means for them. Success depends on having an inclusive style of leadership that fosters collaboration and allows staff to take risks. That encourages staff to have the confidence to see problems from multiple perspectives and come up with new solutions. This is about achieving consensus without giving up on reform.

As a physicist, I found it at first challenging to recognise the different approach needed for system design in education. In physics, we tend to understand the world through complex models and then examine how altering one part of the model modifies the outcome. But education systems have become so fluid that that is no longer good enough. The strongest education systems will be those that can make their own constant adaptations to changing demands, mobilising, sharing and spreading the knowledge, insights and experience of students and teachers.

Many teachers and schools are ready for that. To encourage their growth, policy needs to inspire and enable innovation, and identify and share best practice. That shift in policy will need to be built on trust: trust in education, in educational institutions, in schools and teachers, in students and communities. In all public services, trust is an essential part of good governance. Successful schools will always be places where people want to work, and where their ideas can be best realised, where they are trusted and where they can put their trust.

We know too little about how trust is developed in education and sustained over time, or how it can be restored if broken. But trust cannot be legislated or mandated; that is why it is so hard to build into traditional administrative structures. Trust is always intentional; it can only be nurtured and inspired through healthy relationships and constructive transparency. That is the lesson we can all learn from Finland, where opinion polls consistently show high levels of public trust in education. At a time when command-and-control systems are weakening, building trust is the most promising way to advance and fuel modern education systems.

Redesigning assessment

The way students are tested has a big influence on the future of education too, because it signals the priorities for the curriculum and instruction. Tests will always focus our thinking about what is important, and they should. Teachers and school administrators, as well as students, will pay attention to what is tested and adapt the curriculum and teaching accordingly.

Some maintain that assessments are limiting as they only capture selected dimensions of learning outcomes. That is obviously true, but it is also true for any other form of measurement, including observation. Ask police investigators about divergences among the testimonies of witnesses, or consider teacher biases about gender or social background and you will see how limiting and subjective even direct observation can be.

The question is rather how we can get assessment right and ensure that it is one of several perspectives on student learning that can help teachers and policy makers track progress in education. Assessments need to be redesigned as curricula and instructional practices are reformed.

The trouble is that many assessment systems are poorly aligned with the curriculum, and with the knowledge and skills that young people need to thrive. Large parts of today's school tests can be answered in seconds with the help of a smartphone. If our children are to be smarter than their smartphones, then tests need to look beyond whether students can reproduce information to determine, instead, whether they can extrapolate from what they know, and apply their knowledge creatively to novel situations. Assessments also need to be able to reflect social and emotional skills.

As of this writing, most tests do not allow students to connect to the Internet, based on the fear that students may look up the answers to the test questions. The challenge for future assessments is whether they can encourage students to go on line to connect with the world's most advanced knowledge without jeopardising the validity and reliability of results.

Similarly, one of the worst offences in test taking is to consult with another student. But given that innovation is now more often based on sharing knowledge, future tests should not disqualify students for collaborating with other test-takers, but find ways that they can do so. The PISA assessment of collaborative problem-solving skills showed clearly that proficiency in individual problem solving only partially predicts the ability to work with others to solve problems (see above).

When designing assessments, we often trade gains in validity for gains in efficiency, and relevance for reliability. We do that because it makes results seemingly more objective and thus reduces the risk that they will be contested. Some education ministers have lost their job because of disputes around examination results; few have been challenged for poor validity and relevance in test results.

But prioritising reliability and efficiency has a price. The most reliable test is one where we ask students similar questions in a format that allows for little ambiguity – typically a multiple-choice format. A relevant test is one where we test for a wide range of knowledge and skills that is considered important for success in education. To do this well requires multiple response formats, including open formats, which elicit more complex responses. Necessarily, such formats may introduce variations in interpretation that require more sophisticated marking processes. Similarly, if the number of students to be assessed is large and/or if we want to test students frequently, efficiency becomes important, which again favours simple response formats that are easy to code.

For these reasons, one of the first decisions we took for PISA was to limit the assessment to a sample of schools and students, and not report results at the level of individual students or schools where the stakes become high. That has allowed us to prioritise validity and relevance in the assessments. The comparatively small sample sizes allow us to use more complex and expensive response formats.

Beyond that, assessments need to be fair, technically sound and fit for purpose. They also need to ensure adequate measurement at different levels of detail so they can serve decision-making needs at different levels of the education system. International assessments, like PISA, face the added challenge of ensuring that the outcomes are valid across the cultural, national and linguistic boundaries over which they are conducted, and that samples of schools and students from the participating countries are comparable. PISA has invested significant time and effort to ensure these standards are met.[34]

We also need to work hard to bridge the gap between summative and formative assessments. Summative assessment usually means testing students at the end of a course unit; formative assessment is a more diagnostic approach, carried out while students are studying and intended to show what needs to be improved at that moment.

We need to find more creative ways to combine elements of both approaches to testing, as it is now possible to create coherent multi-layered assessment systems that extend from students to classrooms to schools to regional to national and even international levels. Good tests should provide a window into students' thinking and understanding, and reveal the strategies a student uses to solve a problem. Digital assessments, such as PISA, now make that possible, in that they do not just measure the degree to which students' responses are correct, they also show the paths students have taken to arrive at their solutions.

Assessments should also provide productive feedback, at appropriate levels of detail, to fuel improvement decisions. Teachers need to be able to understand what the assessment reveals about students' thinking. School administrators, policy makers and teachers need to be able to use this assessment information to determine how to create better opportunities for student learning. Teachers will then no longer see testing as separate from instruction, taking away valuable time from learning, but rather see it as an instrument that adds to learning.

How PISA evolves

Of course, all of this also applies to PISA. While the results from PISA have no immediate consequences for individual students, teachers or schools, PISA is viewed as an important measure of the success of school systems. As such, PISA needs to lead education reform, not hold it back by being constrained with too limited a range of metrics. So it is no surprise that there is considerable debate among the countries that participate in PISA, at both policy and technical levels, about the extent to which PISA can and should evolve.

Some argue that if a test is to measure progress and change in education, then we cannot change the measure. They argue for the test to be a fixed point. But PISA has taken a different tack, recognising that if we do not continually develop the measures, we will wind up evaluating students by what was considered important at some point in the past, rather than measuring students against what they will need to thrive in their future.

The use of computer-delivered assessment for PISA means that a wider range of knowledge and skills can now be tested. The PISA 2012 assessment of creative problem-solving skills, the PISA 2015 assessment of collaborative problem-solving skills, and the PISA 2018 assessment of global competencies are good examples of this. It will be more challenging to measure social and emotional skills. But even in these domains, new research shows that many of their components can be measured meaningfully.[35]

PISA is also seeking to make results more open and more local. To that end, PISA has begun developing open-source instruments that schools can use to develop their own PISA scores. This new PISA-based test for schools[36] provides comparisons with other schools elsewhere in the world, schools that are similar to them or schools that are very different.

Schools are already beginning to use that data. In September 2014, I opened the first annual gathering of schools in the United States that had taken this test. It was encouraging to see how much interest there was among schools in comparing themselves not just with their neighbouring schools but with the best schools internationally. In Fairfax County, Virginia, ten schools had started a year-long discussion among principals and teachers based on the results of the first reports. With the help of district offices and the OECD, they were digging deeper into their data to understand how their schools compared with each other and with other schools around the world. Those principals and teachers were beginning to see themselves as teammates, not just spectators, on a global playing field. In other words, in Fairfax County, big data had begun to build big trust.

As the number of countries joining PISA keeps rising, it has also become apparent that the design needs to evolve for a more diverse set of participants, including a growing number of middle- and low-income countries. To make PISA more relevant to this wider range of countries, PISA is developing the test instruments to better measure a wider range of student capabilities; revising the contextual questionnaires so they are more relevant to low-income contexts; tackling financial and technical challenges through partnerships with donors and by capacity building; and extending outreach to local stakeholders in developing countries. This initiative, known as PISA for Development,[37] was successfully piloted in nine countries during 2016 and 2017.

Looking outward while moving forward

If I would add one more quality to the profile of responsive and responsible education leaders, particularly after considering assessment, it is the ability to look not just forward but also outward. It is not surprising that a strong and consistent effort to carry out international benchmarking and to incorporate the results of that benchmarking into policy and practice is a common characteristic of the highest-performing education systems.

This is not about copying and pasting solutions from other countries; it is about looking seriously and dispassionately at good practice in our own countries and elsewhere to become knowledgeable of what works in which contexts and applying it consciously.

Finland was benchmarking itself against the performance and practices of other education systems in the run-up to its own dramatic emergence as one of the world's top performers. Japan acquired its long-running status as one of the world's leading performers when its government, during the Meiji Restoration, visited the capitals of the industrialising West and decided to bring to Japan the best that the rest of the world had to offer. It has been doing so ever since.

In the latter half of the 20th century, Singapore did exactly what Japan had done a century earlier, but with even greater focus and discipline. Singapore's Economic Development Board, the nerve centre of the Singaporean government, is staffed with many engineers who view the government and administration of Singapore as a set of design challenges. Whenever Singapore seeks to create a new institution, it routinely benchmarks its planning against the best in the world. All of Singapore's educational institutions – from the National University of Singapore to individual schools – are encouraged to create global connections in order to develop "future-ready Singaporeans". They have never stopped learning from other countries as systematically as possible.

When Deng Xiaoping took the helm in China and began preparing for his country's re-emergence on the world stage, he directed China's educational institutions to form partnerships with the best educational institutions in the world, and to bring back to China the best of their policies and practices.

When Dalton McGuinty, then Premier of Ontario, visited us at the OECD in 2008, he made a point of saying that his own views about the right strategy for Ontario were shaped by the visits he made to other countries with successful education systems.

So a consistent effort to look outward and incorporate the results of that learning into policy and practice seems a common denominator of many high-performing countries.

Contrast this outward-looking attitude with that of those countries that prefer to cast doubt about PISA when test results show that their education system has been outperformed, and that consider it humiliating to make comparisons with what is happening in other countries.

This is likely to be a key distinction between the countries that will make progress in education and those that will not. The distinction may be between those education systems that feel threatened by alternative ways of thinking and those that are open to the world and ready to learn from and with the world's education leaders.

In the end, the laws of physics apply. If we stop pedalling, not only will we not move forward, our bicycles will stop moving at all and will fall over – and we will fall with them. Against strong headwinds, we need to push ourselves even harder.

But in the face of challenges and opportunities as great as any that have gone before, human beings need not be passive or inert. We have agency, the ability to anticipate and the power to frame our actions with purpose. I understood that when I saw the 10% most disadvantaged students in Shanghai outperforming the 10% wealthiest American students on the PISA 2012 mathematics assessment. I decided to write this book when I saw children from the poorest neighbourhoods of Shanghai learning – with joy – from Shanghai's best teachers. It was then that I realised that universal high-quality education is an attainable goal, that it is within our means to deliver a future for millions of learners who currently do not have one, and that our task is not to make the impossible possible, but to make the possible attainable.

NOTES

1. EDUCATION, THROUGH THE EYES OF A SCIENTIST

[1] *These students did not reach Level 2 on at least one of the PISA reading, mathematics or science scales, where students demonstrate elementary skills to read and understand simple texts, and master basic mathematical and scientific concepts and procedures. At Level 1, students can answer questions involving familiar contexts where all relevant information is present and the questions are clearly defined. They are able to identify information and carry out routine procedures according to direct instructions in explicit situations. They can perform actions that are almost always obvious and follow immediately from the given stimuli. At the next higher Level 2, students can interpret and recognise situations in contexts that require no more than direct inference. They can extract relevant information from a single source and make use of a single representational mode. Students at this level can use basic algorithms, formulae, procedures, or conventions to solve problems involving whole numbers. They are capable of making literal interpretations of the results. For more details and examples, see OECD 2016a.*

[2] *See Adams, 2002.*

[3] *See Chu, 2017.*

[4] *See https:/www.ccsso.org/.*

[5] *https://www2.ed.gov/programs/racetothetop/index.html.*

[6] *http://www.corestandards.org/.*

[7] *PISA – Der Ländertest, http://www.imdb.com/title/tt1110892/.*

[8] *As at May 2018, the 35 countries that are members of the OECD are: Australia, Austria, Belgium, Canada, Chile, the Czech Republic, Denmark, Estonia, Finland, France, Germany, Greece, Hungary, Iceland, Ireland, Israel, Italy, Japan, Latvia, Luxembourg, Mexico, the Netherlands, New Zealand, Norway, Poland, Portugal, the Slovak Republic, Slovenia, South Korea, Spain, Sweden, Switzerland, Turkey, the United Kingdom and the United States.*

[9] *See Hanushek, 2015a, 2015b.*

[10] *See Leadbeater, 2016.*

[11] *See also Griffin and Care, 2015.*

[12] *See OECD, 2017h.*

[13] *For data on historical attainment rates, see Barro and Lee, 2013.*

[14] *For data on current educational attainment, see OECD 2017a.*

[15] *Measured in terms of first-time upper secondary graduation rate; for data, see OECD 2017a.*

2. DEBUNKING SOME MYTHS

[1] For data, see Chapter 6 in OECD, 2016a.

[2] For data, see OECD, 2013d.

[3] For data, see OECD, 2016a.

[4] See OECD, 2017a.

[5] The ratios of teachers' salaries to earnings for full-time, full-year workers with tertiary education aged 25-64 are calculated using the annual average salaries (including bonuses and allowances) for teachers aged 25-64. For data and methodology, see OECD, 2017a.

[6] An analysis of PISA 2006 data shows that, across OECD countries, students who spend less than two hours per week in regular school lessons in science tend to score 15 points higher in science than students who do not spend any time learning science in regular school lessons; students who spend two to less than four hours per week tend to score 59 points higher; students who spend four to less than six hours per week tend to score 89 points higher; and students who spend six or more hours per week tend to score 104 points higher (Table 4.2a in OECD, 2011a).

[7] For data, see OECD, 2013b.

[8] The PISA assessment tested students but also asked them to report their school marks. In many countries and economies, marks tend to be higher for girls and socio-economically advantaged students, and are also sensitive to the academic context of the school, even after accounting for individual students' performance, attitudes and behaviours towards learning. The fact that marks are sensitive to factors that are unrelated to students' performance, engagement and learning habits signals that teachers may reward aspects that they feel are important but are not measured directly by PISA and that are strongly related to students' backgrounds. Teachers may also reward behaviours that are valued in the labour market and in other social environments. As marks constitute one of the most reliable and consistent indicators of students' own performance and potential, systematic inequalities in the allocation of marks may contribute to systematic inequalities in educational expectations, as discussed in the following chapter. For data and methodology, see OECD, 2012a.

[9] See Schleicher, 2017.

[10] See Hanushek, Piopiunik and Wiederhold, 2014.

[11] OECD, PISA 2015 Database, Tables II.5.9, II.5.18, II.5.22 and II.5.27.

[12] See Slavin, 1987.

3. WHAT MAKES HIGH-PERFORMING SCHOOL SYSTEMS DIFFERENT

[1] http://ncee.org/.

[2] See also http://ncee.org/what-we-do/center-on-international-education-benchmarking/ and OECD, 2011b.

[3] For data, see question ST111Q01TA in the PISA 2015 database.

[4] See Martin and Mullis, 2013.

[5] See Chen and Stevenson, 1995.

[6] See Good and Lavigne, 2018.

[7] See Bandura, 2012.

[8] See Weiner, 2004.

[9] See Carroll, 1963.

[10] See OECD, 2011b.

[11] The reform of the structure of the school system in the state of Hamburg was agreed between the governing coalition between Christian Democrats (CDU) and Greens (GAL) in their coalition contract of 17 April 2008. It was agreed by the parliament of Hamburg on 7 October 2009. It was significantly changed by a popular vote on 18 July 2010.

[12] See Figure IV.2.6a. in OECD, 2013b.

[13] http://www.phenomenaleducation.info/phenomenon-based-learning.html.

[14] See Table C6.1a in OECD, 2017a.

[15] See OECD, 2013a.

[16] See OECD, 2017i.

[17] It is possible, of course, that test anxiety is triggered by aspects of the tests other than their frequency that are not captured by the PISA questionnaires.

[18] See https://asiasociety.org/global-cities-education-network/japan-recent-trends-education-reform.

[19] See OECD, 2014b and OECD, 2017e.

[20] See Fadel, Trilling and Bialik, 2015.

[21] See Tan, 2017.

[22] See Barber, 2008.

[23] http://www.globalteacherprize.org/about/.

[24] See Good, 2018.

[25] See Hung, 2006.

[26] See OECD, 2014c.

[27] See OECD, 2009.

[28] See OECD, 2014c.

[29] See OECD, 2014c.

[30] See OECD, 2013c.

[31] https://www.gov.uk/government/news/network-of-32-maths-hubs-across-england-aims-to-raise-standards.

[32] See also http://www.bbc.co.uk/programmes/b06565zm and https://m.youtube.com/watch?v=DYGxAwRUpaI

[33] See OECD, 2016b.

[34] See OECD, 2016b.

[35] See http://ncee.org/what-we-do/center-on-international-education-benchmarking/top-performing-countries/shanghai-china/shanghai-china-instructional-systems/.

[36] For the data underlying this section, see OECD 2017f.

[37] See http://www.sici-inspectorates.eu/.

[38] See Pont, Nusche and Moorman, 2008.

[39] See OECD, 2014c.

[40] See OECD, 2013b.

[41] See Fullan, 2011.

[42] See OECD, 2013b.

[43] See OECD, 2014a.

[44] See OECD, 2015f.

[45] See Canadian Language and Literacy Research Network (2009), Evaluation Report: The Impact of the Literacy and Numeracy Secretariat, http://www.edu.gov.on.ca/eng/document/reports/OME_Report09_EN.pdf

[46] Singapore's vision of "Thinking Schools, Learning Nation" was first announced by then-Prime Minister Goh Chok Tong in 1997. This vision describes a nation of thinking and committed citizens capable of meeting future challenges, and an education system geared to the needs of the 21st century. See also https://www.moe.gov.sg/about.

[47] See OECD, 2016a.

[48] See OECD, 2016b.

[49] See OECD, 2013e for more details on teacher evaluation.

[50] See OECD, 2014c.

[51] https://www.cmec.ca/en/.

[52] https://www.kmk.org/.

[53] See OECD, 2017a.

[54] See OECD, 2017a.

4. WHY EQUITY IN EDUCATION IS SO ELUSIVE

[1] Hanushek and Woessmann, 2015b.

[2] http://www.nytimes.com/2012/03/11/opinion/sunday/friedman-pass-the-books-hold-the-oil.html.

[3] See OECD, 2013a.

[4] See OECD, 2017a

[5] See Paccagnella, 2015.

[6] See OECD, 2017a.

[7] Author of https://www.oecd.org/china/Education-in-China-a-snapshot.pdf.

[8] See OECD, 2016a.

[9] See Schleicher, 2014 http://oecdeducationtoday.blogspot.fr/2014/07/poverty-and-perception-of-poverty-how.html.

[10] See OECD, 2016a.

[11] See Prensky, 2016.

[12] https://surveys.quagliainstitute.org/.

[13] See OECD, 2017b.

[14] See Figure I.6.14 in OECD, 2016a.

[15] See OECD, 2011b.

[16] See Figure I.6.14 in OECD, 2016a.

[17] See OECD, 2016c.

[18] http://www.legislation.gov.uk/ukpga/2010/32/section/1.

[19] See Chapter 4 and https://www.gov.uk/education/pupil-premium-and-other-school-premiums.

[20] See http://www.oecd.org/edu/School-choice-and-school-vouchers-an-OECD-perspective.pdf.

[21] See OECD, 2016d.

[22] See OECD, 2015b.

[23] See OECD, 2016b.

[24] See OECD, 2016b.

[25] See OECD, 2016b.

[26] See OECD, 2012b.

[27] See OECD, 2017b

[28] See OECD, 2017b.

[29] See Epple, Romano and Urquiola, 2015.

[30] See OECD, 2016a.

[31] See OECD, 2016a.

[32] The Zuwanderungskommission *was established in 2000 by the German Parliament.*

[33] *See Figure I.7.13 in OECD, 2016a.*

[34] *See OECD, 2016a.*

[35] *See OECD, 2016a.*

[36] *See OECD, 2016a.*

[37] *See OECD, 2015g.*

[38] *See OECD, 2017j.*

[39] *See OECD, 2015e.*

[40] *https://www.educationandemployers.org/wp-content/uploads/2018/01/Drawing-the-Future-FINAL-REPORT.pdf.*

[41] *https://m.youtube.com/watch?v=kJP1zPOfq_0.*

[42] *See OECD, 2016e.*

[43] *PISA is using a two-part assessment consisting of a cognitive test and a background questionnaire. The cognitive assessment taps students' capacities to critically examine news articles about global issues; recognise outside influences on perspectives and world views; understand how to communicate with others in intercultural contexts; and identify and compare different courses of action to address global and intercultural issues. In a background questionnaire, students are asked to report how familiar they are with global issues; how developed their linguistic and communication skills are; to what extent they hold certain attitudes, such as respect for people from different cultural backgrounds; and what opportunities they have at school to develop global competence. In addition, school principals and teachers are asked to describe how education systems are integrating international and intercultural perspectives throughout the curriculum and in classroom activities.*

[44] *See https://www.oecd.org/education/Global-competency-for-an-inclusive-world.pdf.*

5. MAKING EDUCATION REFORM HAPPEN

[1] *See OECD, 2010a.*

[2] *See OECD, 2015a.*

[3] *http://www.corestandards.org/.*

[4] *https://www.bmbf.de/pub/Bildungsforschung_Band_1.pdf.*

[5] *See http://www.oecd.org/skills/nationalskillsstrategies/Diagnostic-report-Portugal.pdf.*

[6] *See OECD, 2013c.*

[7] *See OECD, 2005.*

[8] *See OECD, 2005.*

[9] *See OECD, 2013c.*

[10] Their efforts were documented in "The Folkeskole's response to the OECD".

[11] Danish Ministry of Education and Rambøll, 2011.

[12] See Alberta Education, 2014, and Hargreaves and Shirley, 2012.

[13] See OECD, 2014c.

[14] See Barber, 2010.

[15] Data provided by Education International and the Trade Union Advisory Committee to the OECD (2013), "Survey of Trade Unions' Engagement with Governments on Education and Training", in OECD, 2015a.

6. WHAT TO DO NOW

[1] Tom Bentley in "The responsibility to lead: Education at a global crossroads", Patron's Oration on 21 August 2017 at the Australian Council of Education Leadership.

[2] See http://www.un.org/sustainabledevelopment/sustainable-development-goals/.

[3] See Putnam, 2007.

[4] See OECD, 2017c.

[5] See OECD, 2016e.

[6] Brundtland Commission, 1987.

[7] See http://www.oecd.org/social/income-distribution-database.htm.

[8] See Harari, 2016.

[9] See Goldin and Katz, 2007.

[10] See OECD, 2017k.

[11] See Autor and Dorn, 2013.

[12] See Echazarra et al., 2016.

[13] Using memorisation instead of control and elaboration strategies results in a lower likelihood of answering correctly 78 of the 84 PISA mathematics items analysed. More important, the rate of success decreases as the difficulty of the item increases. While using memorisation appears to make little difference when answering the easiest items, a one-unit increase in the index of memorisation strategies is associated with a 10% decrease in the probability of answering problems of intermediate difficulty correctly (compared to using one of the other learning strategies), and with a more than 20% decrease in the probability of answering the most challenging items correctly. This implies that students who agreed with the statements related to elaboration or control strategies in all four questions on learning strategies are three times more likely to succeed in the five most challenging items in the PISA mathematics test than students who only agreed with the statements related to memorisation strategies.

[14] Using elaboration strategies more frequently is associated with less success in correctly solving the easiest mathematics problems (those below 480 points in difficulty). More important, for many of these simple items, memorisation is associated with better results than elaboration strategies. However, as

the items become more difficult, students who reported using elaboration strategies more frequently improve their chances of succeeding, especially when the items surpass 600 points in difficulty on the PISA scale. Elaboration strategies are associated with better results than memorisation strategies for items of intermediate difficulty; but they seem to be even better than control strategies for solving the most difficult items, especially those above 700 points on the PISA scale.

[15] European Union Labour Force Survey data; cited in Nathan, Pratt and Rincon-Aznar, 2015.

[16] See OECD, 2016a.

[17] In 1996, when the 15th Central Council for Education (中央教育審議会 *Chūō Kyōiku Shingikai*) was asked about what the Japanese education of the 21st century should be like, it submitted a report suggesting "the ability to survive" should be the basic principle of education. "The ability to survive" is defined as a principle that tries to keep the balance of intellectual, moral, and physical education. In 1998, the teaching guidelines were revised to reflect the council's report. Some 30% of the curriculum was cut and "time for integrated study" in elementary and junior high school was established.

[18] For an overview, see http://www.oph.fi/download/151294_ops2016_curriculum_reform_in_finland.pdf.

[19] See https://www.smh.com.au/lifestyle/health-and-wellness/fat-employee-sues-mcdonalds-wins-20101029-176kx.html;
http://fortune.com/2017/05/19/burned-woman-starbucks-lawsuit/.

[20] See https://www.pisa4u.org/.

[21] See OECD, 2017h.

[22] https://oeb.global/.

[23] For a profile, see https://www.triciawang.com/.

[24] Friedman, 2016.

[25] For an overview, see http://iasculture.org/.

[26] For an overview see https://www.moe.gov.sg/education/secondary/values-in-action.

[27] See OECD, 2017a.

[28] See OECD, 2015d.

[29] See also OECD, 2013c.

[30] See OECD, 2014a.

[31] OECD, forthcoming.

[32] See https://www.varkeyfoundation.org/.

[33] For data, see OECD, 2009.

[34] http://www.oecd.org/pisa/data/2015-technical-report/.

[35] See OECD, 2015c

[36] http://www.oecd.org/pisa/pisa-based-test-for-schools/.

[37] See http://www.oecd.org/pisa/aboutpisa/pisafordevelopment.htm.

REFERENCES

Adams, R. (2002), *Country Comparisons in PISA: The Impact of Item Selection*, Available at: http://www.findanexpert.unimelb.edu.au/individual/publication9377 [Accessed 26 August 2017].

Alberta Education (2014), *Teaching and Learning International Survey (TALIS) 2013: Alberta Report*, Alberta Education, Edmonton.

Autor, D. and D. Dorn (2013), "The Growth of Low-Skill Service Jobs and the Polarization of the US Labor Market", *American Economic Review*, Vol. 103/5, pp.1553-1597, https://doi.org/10.1257/aer.103.5.1553.

Bandura, A. (2012), *Self-efficacy*, W.H. Freeman, New York.

Barber, M. (2008), *Instruction to Deliver*, Methuen Publishing Ltd., London.

Barber, M., A. Moffit and P. Kihn (2011), *Deliverology 101: A Field Guide for Educational Leaders*, Corwin, Thousand Oaks, CA.

Barro, R. and J. Lee (2013), "A New Data Set of Educational Attainment in the World, 1950-2010", *Journal of Development Economics*, Vol. 104, pp.184-198, https://doi.org/10.1016/j.jdeveco.2012.10.001.

Borgonovi, F. and T. Burns (2015), "The Educational Roots of Trust", *OECD Education Working Papers*, No. 119, OECD Publishing, Paris, http://dx.doi.org/10.1787/19939019.

Brown, M. (1996), "FIMS and SIMS: The First Two IEA International Mathematics Surveys", in *Assessment in Education: Principles, Policy and Practice*, Vol. 3/2, 1996, https://doi.org/10.1080/0969594960030206.

Brundtland Commission (1987), *Our Common Future*, Oxford University Press, Oxford.

Carroll, J. (1963), "A Model of School Learning", *Teachers College Record*, Vol. 64/8, pp. 723-733.

Chen, C. and H. Stevenson (1995), "Motivation and Mathematics Achievement: A Comparative Study of Asian-American, Caucasian-American, and East Asian High School Students", *Child Development*, Vol. 66/4, p.1215, https://doi.org/10.1111/j.1467-8624.1995.tb00932.x.

Chu, L. (2017), *Little Soldiers: An American Boy, a Chinese School, and the Global Race to Achieve*, Harper Collins Publishers, New York.

Echazarra, A. et al. (2016), "How teachers teach and students learn: Successful strategies for school", *OECD Education Working Papers*, No. 130, OECD Publishing, Paris, http://dx.doi.org/10.1787/5jm29kpt0xxx-en.

Epple, D., E. Romano and M. Urquiola (2015), *School Vouchers*, National Bureau of Economic Research, Cambridge, MA.

Fadel, C., B. Trilling and M. Bialik (2015), *Four-Dimensional Education: The Competencies Learners Need to Succeed*, The Center for Curriculum Redesign, Boston.

Fullan, M. (2011), *Change Leader: Learning to Do What Matters Most*, Jossey-Bass, San Francisco.

Friedman, T.L. (2016), *Thank You for Being Late: An Optimist's Guide to Thriving in the Age of Accelerations*, Farrar, Straus and Giroux, New York.

Goldin, C. and L. Katz (2007), *The Race between Education and Technology*, National Bureau of Economic Research. Cambridge, MA.

Goldin, I. and C. Kutarna (2016), *Age of Discovery: Navigating the Risks and Rewards of Our New Renaissance*, St. Martin's Press, New York.

Good, T. and A. Lavigne (2018), *Looking in Classrooms*, Routledge, New York.

Goodwin, L., E. Low and L. Darling-Hammond (2017), *Empowered Educators in Singapore: How High-Performing Systems Shape Teaching Quality*, Jossey-Bass, San Francisco.

Griffin, P. and E. Care (2015), *Assessment and Teaching of 21st Century Skills*, Springer Dordrecht, New York.

Hanushek, E. and L. Woessmann (2015a), *The Knowledge Capital of Nations*, MIT Press, Cambridge, MA.

Hanushek, E. and L. Woessmann (2015b), *Universal Basic Skills: What Countries Stand to Gain*, OECD Publishing, Paris, http://dx.doi.org/10.1787/9789264234833-en.

Hanushek, E., M. Piopiunik and S. Wiederhold (2014), *The Value of Smarter Teachers*, National Bureau of Economic Research, Cambridge, MA.

Harari, Y.N. (2016), *Homo Deus: A Brief History of Tomorrow*, Harville Secker, London.

Hargreaves, A. and D. Shirley (2012), *The Global Fourth Way: The Quest for Educational Excellence*, Corwin Press, Thousand Oaks, CA.

Hung, D., S.C. Tan and T.S. Koh (2006), "From Traditional to Constructivist Epistemologies: A Proposed Theoretical Framework Based on Activity Theory for Learning Communities", *Journal of Interactive Learning Research*, Vol 17/1, pp. 37-55. 17(1), 37-55.

Husen, T. (Ed.) (1967), *International Study of Achievement in Mathematics: A Comparison of Twelve Countries*, Vols.1 and 2, Almqvist and Wiksell, Stockholm.

Leadbeater, C. (2016), *The Problem Solvers: The teachers, the students and the radically disruptive nuns who are leading a global learning movement*, Pearson, London.

Martin, M. and I. Mullis (2013), *TIMSS 2011 International Results in Mathematics*, TIMSS and PIRLS International Study Center, Boston College, Chestnut Hill, MA.

McInerney, D. and S. Van Etten (2004), *Big Theories Revisited*, Information Age Publishing, Greenwich, CT.

Nathan, M., A. Pratt and A. Rincon-Aznar (2015), *Creative Economy Employment in the European Union and the United Kingdom: A Comparative Analysis*, Nesta, London.

OECD (2005), *Teachers Matter: Attracting, Developing and Retaining Effective Teachers*, OECD Publishing, Paris, http://dx.doi.org/10.1787/9789264018044-en.

OECD (2009), *Creating Effective Teaching and Learning Environments: First Results from TALIS 2008*, OECD Publishing, Paris, http://dx.doi.org/10.1787/9789264068780-en.

OECD (2010a), *Making Reform Happen: Lessons from OECD Countries*, 11th ed., OECD Publishing, http://dx.doi.org/10.1787/9789264086296-en.

OECD (2010b), *PISA 2009 Results: What Makes a School Successful? Resources, Policies and Practices*, OECD Publishing, Paris, http://dx.doi.org/10.1787/9789264091559-en.

OECD (2011a), *Quality Time for Students: Learning In and Out of School*, OECD Publishing, Paris, http://dx.doi.org/10.1787/9789264087057-en.

OECD (2011b), *Strong Performers and Successful Reformers in Education: Lessons from PISA for the United States*, OECD Publishing, Paris, http://dx.doi.org/10.1787/9789264096660-en.

OECD (2011c), *Education at a Glance 2011: OECD Indicators*, OECD Publishing, Paris, http://dx.doi.org/10.1787/eag-2011-en.

OECD (2012a), *Grade Expectations: How Marks and Education Policies Shape Students' Ambitions*, OECD Publishing, Paris, http://dx.doi.org/10.1787/9789264187528-en.

OECD (2012b), *Public and Private Schools: How Management and Funding Relate to their Socio-economic Profile*, OECD Publishing, Paris, http://dx.doi.org/10.1787/9789264175006-en.

OECD (2013a), *OECD Skills Outlook: First Results from the Survey Of Adult Skills*, OECD Publishing, Paris, http://dx.doi.org/10.1787/9789264204256-en.

OECD (2013b), *PISA 2012 Results: What Makes Schools Successful (Volume IV): Resources, Policies and Practices*, OECD Publishing, Paris, http://dx.doi.org/10.1787/9789264201156-en.

OECD (2013c), *Synergies for Better Learning: An International Perspective on Evaluation and*

Assessment, OECD Publishing, Paris, http://dx.doi.org/10.1787/9789264190658-en.

OECD (2013d), *PISA 2012 Results: Excellence through Equity (Volume II): Giving Every Student the Chance to Succeed*, OECD Publishing, Paris, http://dx.doi.org/10.1787/9789264201132-en.

OECD (2013e), *Teachers for the 21st Century: Using Evaluation to Improve Teaching*, OECD Publishing, Paris, http://dx.doi.org/10.1787/9789264193864-en.

OECD (2014a), *Measuring Innovation in Education: A New Perspective*, OECD Publishing, Paris, http://dx.doi.org/10.1787/9789264215696-en.

OECD (2014b), *PISA 2012 Results: Students and Money (Volume VI): Financial Literacy Skills for the 21st Century*, OECD Publishing, Paris, http://dx.doi.org/10.1787/9789264208094-en.

OECD (2014c), *TALIS 2013 Results: An International Perspective on Teaching and Learning*, OECD Publishing, Paris, http://dx.doi.org/10.1787/9789264196261-en.

OECD (2014d), *PISA 2012 Results: What Students Know and Can Do (Volume I): Student Performance in Mathematics, Reading and Science*, Revised edition, OECD Publishing, Paris, http://dx.doi. org/10.1787/9789264208780-en.

OECD (2015a), *Education Policy Outlook 2015: Making Reforms Happen*, OECD Publishing, Paris, http://dx.doi.org/10.1787/9789264225442-en.

OECD (2015b), *Improving Schools in Sweden: An OECD Perspective*, Available at: http://www.oecd. org/edu/school/Improving-Schools-in-Sweden.pdf [Accessed 26 August 2017].

OECD (2015c), *Skills for Social Progress: The Power of Social and Emotional Skills*, OECD Publishing, Paris, http://dx.doi.org/10.1787/9789264226159-en.

OECD (2015d), *Students, Computers and Learning: Making the Connection*, OECD Publishing, Paris, http://dx.doi.org/10.1787/9789264239555-en.

OECD (2015e), *The ABC of Gender Equality in Education: Aptitude, Behaviour, Confidence*, OECD Publishing, Paris, http://dx.doi.org/10.1787/9789264229945-en.

OECD (2015f), *Schooling Redesigned: Towards Innovative Learning Systems*, OECD Publishing, Paris, http://dx.doi.org/10.1787/9789264245914-en.

OECD (2015g), *Immigrant Students at School: Easing the Journey towards Integration*, OECD Publishing, Paris, http://dx.doi.org/10.1787/9789264249509-en.

OECD (2016a), *PISA 2015 Results (Volume I): Excellence and Equity in Education*, OECD Publishing, Paris, http://dx.doi.org/10.1787/9789264266490-en.

OECD (2016b), *PISA 2015 Results (Volume II): Policies and Practices for Successful Schools*, OECD Publishing, Paris, http://dx.doi.org/10.1787/9789264267510-en.

OECD (2016c), *Low-Performing Students: Why They Fall Behind and How to Help Them Succeed*, OECD Publishing, Paris, http://dx.doi.org/10.1787/9789264250246-en.

OECD (2016d), *Netherlands 2016: Foundations for the Future, Reviews of National Policies for Education*, OECD Publishing, Paris, http://dx.doi.org/10.1787/9789264257658-en.

OECD (2016e), *Skills Matter: Further Results from the Survey of Adult Skills*, OECD Publishing, Paris, http://dx.doi.org/10.1787/9789264258051-en.

OECD (2017a), *Education at a Glance 2017: OECD Indicators*, OECD Publishing, Paris, http://dx.doi.org/10.1787/eag-2017-en.

OECD (2017b), *The Funding of School Education: Connecting Resources and Learning*, OECD Publishing, Paris, http://dx.doi.org/10.1787/9789264276147-en.

OECD (2017c), *OECD Skills Outlook 2017: Skills and Global Value Chains*, OECD Publishing, Paris, http://dx.doi.org/10.1787/9789264273351-en.

OECD (2017d), *PISA 4 U*, available at https://www.pisa4u.org/.

OECD (2017e), PISA 2015 Results (Volume IV): Students' Financial Literacy, OECD Publishing, Paris, http://dx.doi.org/10.1787/9789264270282-en.

OECD (2017f), *PISA 2015 Results (Volume III): Students' Well-Being*, OECD Publishing, Paris, http://dx.doi.org/10.1787/9789264273856-en.

OECD (2017g), *The OECD Handbook for Innovative Learning Environments*, OECD Publishing, Paris, http://dx.doi.org/10.1787/9789264277274-en.

OECD (2017h), *PISA 2015 Results (Volume V): Collaborative Problem Solving*, OECD Publishing, Paris, http://dx.doi.org/10.1787/9789264285521-en.

OECD (2017i), "Is too much testing bad for student performance and well-being?", *PISA in Focus*, No.79, OECD Publishing, Paris, http://dx.doi.org/10.1787/22260919.

OECD (2017j), *Starting Strong V: Transitions from Early Childhood Education and Care to Primary Education*, OECD Publishing, Paris, http://dx.doi.org/10.1787/9789264276253-en.

OECD (2017k), *Computers and the Future of Skill Demand*, Educational Research and Innovation, OECD Publishing, Paris, http://dx.doi.org/10.1787/9789264284395-en.

Paccagnella, M. (2015), "Skills and Wage Inequality: Evidence from PIAAC", *OECD Education Working Papers*, No. 114, OECD Publishing, Paris, http://dx.doi.org/10.1787/5js4xfgl4ks0-en.

Pont, B., D. Nusche and H. Moorman (2008), *Improving School Leadership (Volume 1): Policy and Practice*, OECD Publishing, Paris, http://dx.doi.org/10.1787/9789264044715-en.

Putnam, R.D. (2007), *Bowling Alone*, Simon and Schuster, New York.

Presnky, M. (2016), *Education to Better Their World: Unleashing the Power of 21st-Century Kids*, Teachers College Press, New York.

Rambøll (2011), *Country Background Report for Denmark, prepared for the OECD Review on Evaluation and Assessment Frameworks for Improving School Outcomes*, Aarhus, available from http://www.oecd.org/edu/evaluationpolicy.

Schleicher, A. (2014), "Poverty and the Perception of Poverty: How Both Matter for Schooling Outcomes", Available at: http://oecdeducationtoday.blogspot.fr/2014/07/poverty-and-perception-of-poverty-how.html [Accessed 26 Aug. 2017].

Schleicher, A. (2017), *Teaching Excellence through Professional Learning and Policy Reform: Lessons from Around the World*, OECD publishing, Paris http://dx.doi.org/10.1787/9789264252059-en.

Schleicher, A. (2017), "What teachers know and how that compares with college graduates around the world", Available at: http://oecdeducationtoday.blogspot.fr/2013/11/what-teachers-know-and-how-that.html [Accessed 26 Aug. 2017].

Seldon, A. (2007), *Blair's Britain*, Cambridge University Press, Cambridge.

Slavin, R. (1987), *Grouping for Instruction*, Center for Research on Elementary and Middle Schools, Johns Hopkins University, Baltimore.

Tan, O. et al. (2017), *Educational Psychology: An Asia Edition*, Cengage Learning Asia Ltd., Singapore.

Weiner, B. (2004), "Attribution Theory Revisited: Transforming Cultural Plurality into Theoretical Unity", in D. McInerney and S. Van Etten, eds., *Big Theories Revisited: Research on Socio-Cultural Influences on Motivation and Learning*, Information Age Publishing, Greenwich, CT.

ABOUT THE AUTHOR

Andreas Schleicher is Director for Education and Skills at the Organisation for Economic Co-operation and Development (OECD). He initiated and oversees the Programme for International Student Assessment (PISA) and other international instruments that have created a global platform for policy makers, researchers and educators across nations and cultures to innovate and transform education policies and practices. He has worked for over 20 years with ministers and education leaders around the world to improve quality and equity in education. Former US Secretary of Education Arne Duncan said that Schleicher "…understands the global issues and challenges as well as or better than anyone I've met, and he tells me the truth" (*The Atlantic*, July 2011). Former UK Secretary of State for Education Michael Gove called Schleicher "the most important man in English education" – even though he is German and lives in France. Schleicher is the recipient of numerous honours and awards, including the Theodor Heuss prize, awarded for "exemplary democratic engagement" in the name of the first president of the Federal Republic of Germany. He holds an honorary professorship at the University of Heidelberg.